Beyond Western Economics

How did we reach the point of accepting western economics as central to our understanding of human nature, history, culture and social policy formation? Answering this question systematically exposes the fallacy of economism and releases many social economic alternatives now eclipsed by market fundamentalism.

This fascinating book remembers the "other west" as rooted in common sense and love of community, and shows how it became buried underneath modern idealizations of certainty and wealth creation, revealing that co-operative economies always accompanied, as counter currents, historical tides of capitalism. Combining intellectual history with contemporary events, Trent Schroyer offers a critique of mainstream economic thought and its neo-liberal policy incarnation in global capitalism. The critique operates theoretically, at the level of metaphysics and the philosophy of science, and through case studies of globalization and world events.

Beyond Western Economics surveys sustainable alternatives that regenerate ecological assets, provide models for community and regional capacity building, innovate ways to deepen local economies, protect public assets to secure the poor and organize grass-roots-up financial autonomy. The end of market fundamentalism means taking seriously the many existing and viable alternatives; this is a beginning for other human futures. The book focuses on alternative economic cultures as sources for empowerment, an imperative after the implosion of neo-liberal economics in 2008.

Cutting across a wide variety of disciplines, the book is likely to appeal to researchers and students in Environmental Studies, Cultural Studies, Postcolonial Studies, Sustainability Studies, Comparative Development, Ecological Economics and Religious Studies.

Trent Schroyer is currently Professor of Sociology-Philosophy in the School of Social Science and Human Services at Ramapo College in New Jersey, USA.

Beyond Western Economics

Remembering other economic cultures

Trent Schroyer

Routledge
Taylor & Francis Group
LONDON AND NEW YORK

First published 2009
by Routledge
2 Park Square, Milton Park, Abingdon, Oxon, OX14 4RN

Simultaneously published in the USA and Canada
by Routledge
270 Madison Avenue, New York, NY 10016

Routledge is an imprint of the Taylor & Francis Group, an informa business

Typeset in Times New Roman by Swales & Willis Ltd
Printed and bound in Great Britain by CPI Antony Rowe Ltd,
Chippenham, Wiltshire

British Library Cataloguing in Publication Data
A catalogue record for this book is available from the British Library

Library of Congress Cataloging in Publication Data
A catalog record for this book has been requested

ISBN10: 0–415–77696–1 (hbk)
ISBN10: 0–415–77697–X (pbk)
ISBN10: 0–415–87870–1 (ebk)

ISBN13: 978–0–415–77696–7 (hbk)
ISBN13: 978–0–415–77697–4 (pbk)
ISBN13: 978–0–203–87870–5 (ebk)

Contents

Introduction

Western certitudes about freedom and economics

The fallacy of economism

Western economics emerged as the necessary means to eradicate poverty. In the pivotal debate about the poor laws in nineteenth-century Britain it was deemed necessary that society be guided by the market. Only more economic growth could create the freedom from natural scarcity and ameliorate poverty.[1] Today the same logic is used to justify economic globalization.

Have almost two centuries of market experiments done the job? Is poverty being eliminated by economic growth?

The World Bank reports claims it is doing the job.

The World Bank has just corrected its 2005 assessments of the world's poor upward to 25 percent of the world's population, admitting that it had underestimated the cost of living in poor countries.[2] But corrected numbers reveal yearly declines of poverty are increasing. The trend from 1981 to 2005 shows that globalization has decreased world poverty by half. The conclusion: economic growth is winning the war against poverty.

Can this report can be trusted or its methodology defended? Sanjay G. Reddy, professor of economics at Columbia University, suggests that the Bank is building castles in the sand and that its poverty statistics are unfit for use.[3] The whole method of estimating an 'international' poverty line is an exercise in obfuscation; no one can live on $1.25 per day in western countries and if China is excluded from the data the poverty realities in the rest of the world are much dimmer. China has reduced its poverty, but India and others countries have increased theirs. Averaging purchasing power equivalents fails to deal with differences of what has to be purchased to survive in particular places. Choice of the base-year for trends makes major differences and this is a statistical decision. Economic statistical abstractions mislead, or rather lead to where the interests lie.[4] In addition, poverty measures now fall short because the oil price-spike and bio-fuels speculation have raised the price of food everywhere.

After many trips to villages in the south of India I question the World Bank's optimism. While there are more middle class Indians, there are also more undernourished Indians who are above the official poverty line.[5] Economic poverty definitions that do not recognize high rates of anemic children and women, especially in the socially stigmatized castes and tribal groups, are misleading. Basing social policy on economistic measures in a world where there are clearly social barriers to getting out of poverty makes India an excellent counter situation.

In the last 10 years approximately 100,000 farmers have committed suicide in India leaving behind destitute families that inherit their debt and their shame.[6] Why has this happened?

The underlying reason, when all factors are considered, is the forced dis-embedding of agrarian life from the sharing of village life, and local stocks of knowledge, to a more privatized and much more risky entrepreneurial craft.[7] Co-ordinating green revolution seeds, chemical inputs, irrigations, banking and market timing leads to a pressured lifestyle that is increasingly losing its appeal in rural India. Add to these the increased risks of access to resources by different castes and the terminal choice of many farmers is clearer.

Economistic measures cannot recognize the situations of people who have to live in modern and traditional worlds at the same time. They also know that if they cannot cope they will end up homeless or survive on handouts. For them the loss of the holistic world and the anomie experienced in the new is poverty too. Poverty is not just an economic condition, it is also loss of social bonds and protections of social reciprocity. Measuring economic incomes is too simple a scale for diagnosing poverty. Poverty can neither be defined nor understood using economic indicators.

Or does economics have its prescriptive instrumental idealizations[8] built into its theory? Could it be that an economic theory, grounded in the abstractions of 'self-regulating markets', 'free trade' and an anthropology of human nature as an infinitely-needy utility-maximizer, are all misleading cognitive idealizations for diagnosing social and culturally nuanced contexts?

Is 'economism' a major cognitive fallacy of our time?

Economism can be defined along four dimensions:

1. Economism is a reduction of all human motivations to economic, or material, interests, negating other cultural ends;
2. Economism reads the economic logic of modern forms of economizing into all of history, distorting historical and socio-cultural differences;
3. Economism perceives the human condition as rooted in scarcity and only the expansions of economic growth can overcome this condition;
4. Finally, economism overestimates the contributions of economics to appropriate social policy formation.

Economic exchanges are always embedded in legal, political, social and cultural relations narrowing policy formations to 'the economy' is an economistic abstraction. More precisely 'the economy' is always an 'instituted' process in diverse ways in different contexts as Karl Polanyi has shown.[9]

Economistic idealizations create partial constructions of human interactions and relations to nature. Moreover it assumes that the benefits of the economy accrue to the well-being of separated individuals. Many cultural groups prefer collective benefits which we have largely disvalued in the western world. Economistic projections that more free markets will enable us to achieve liberation from poverty and solve environmental problems obscure social and ecological actualities.[10]

The consequences of this fallacy have undermined political and social freedoms and disvalued different economic cultures. Deregulated 'free markets' distort political governance, and in the extreme devolve into the current U.S. farce of corporate blocking of any significant policy and the wrecking of governance capacities in the publicly unquestioned assumption that 'free markets' always work to guide society and international development.[11]

Combining these points I will argue that the fallacy of economism has ideologically narrowed human options and endangered human survival on the earth. A transforming pluralistic world no longer fits the modern economically designed global institutions, or strategies for development for all societies. Other economic cultures combining social, political and spiritual elements in unique ways have existed, do exist and are being fused in resistance to economic globalization. One economic culture does not fit all. While this is not understood by the 'super class' in the West and the elites in the third world,[12] it is increasingly resisted, and replaced by societies and networked solidarities around the world.

A good example of economistic cultural lag is the exasperated western lamentations and threats about the collapse of the Doha World Trade Organization (WTO) negotiations on July 30, 2008. A worldwide blame game started as to why it failed; the U.S. blamed India and China, Europe blamed the U.S. But both the U.S. and Europe assumed they had a right to access import markets, while sustaining their subsidies that make their export prices artificially low, which undermines third world workers. Presumptions that this is acceptable – because the aggregate economic numbers come out higher – are now rejected. This double standard was resisted at the ministerial meetings in Seattle in 1999, in Cancun in 2003, in Hong Kong in 2005 and perhaps terminally in Doha in 2008.

In 2008 in Doha the negotiations were presented as helping the development of the third world; but informed observers contended the real agenda of the rich countries (most of the negotiations were conducted by seven countries) was market-access to national markets in ways that could have continued to have unmonitored devastating impacts.[13]

Western media did not report that over 100 countries also agreed with the disputed issues; the sticking point was livelihood and food security and how agricultural import surges will affect the poor and subsistence farmers. While India is blamed for not wanting to "offend small farmers in the run up to the next election," realities of farmer suicides, and other security issues, were not relevant to free trade deciders.[14]

The U.S. media promotes the mantra that 'free markets and trade create more wealth' and that seems to be the only message that gets out. Any other path is stigmatized as 'protectionism'. Critical reports of the down sides of economic globalization by human rights groups, environmental groups, labor groups, are neither taken seriously nor investigated. Destruction of local economies, degradation of local and global ecology, destruction of labor rights, corporate control of resources, creating greater global inequality, narrowing political discourse to team competitions for growing the economy, undermining democracies, forcing social rearrangements without compassion, etc.; these are secondary to the primary goal of more wealth.

Western and third world elites either don't understand, or don't care, that the West's current neo-liberal economics has lost its credibility, even if the momentum of the institutional procedures carries it on. Many parts of the world are moving beyond these current economic institutions and culture. On the same day the WTO collapsed, the Indian newspaper *The Hindu* reported that:

> India will give a major push to deepening trade ties among South Asian Association for Regional Cooperation (SAARC) nations at the coming summit in Colombo, according to highly-placed sources.

A result of Doha's gridlock will be more bilateral or regionally-oriented trade and banking arrangements. The increased price of oil will make these regional deals more attractive too.

The hierarchical internal process of WTO meetings and the West's blaming of India and China for the Doha failure show that there is one rule for the West, another for the rest. This is the colonial mentality that motivated western elites when they revised the global governance institutions of World Bank (WB) and International Monetary Fund (IMF) and, especially the free trade regulations culminating in the 1995 WTO. Unfortunately, the vast majority of citizens simply did not get access to the complex details of the WTO procedures – Bill Clinton took care of that when he rammed through the WTO in 1994–5 with as little debate as he could manage. Not even the senators understood what they approved, as Ralph Nader's $10,000 challenge to them to answer 10 questions about the huge document they had just passed proves. Only one senator took him up on that and he voted against the bill.[15]

The official western world view is – there is no alternative (TINA) – to expansion of economic growth as the essential goal and means. There seems no way critical views can get the attention of minds, or into the rooms, where economic decisions are made. For example, media reporting about the turning point in Seattle (1999) was reduced to violence in the street and the complexities evaded.[16]

How did we get to the point where abstract economic theory steers the world that many social movements in the world would reject if the issues were democratically confronted? These topics are evaded and denied in the U.S where a new synthesis of 'economic freedom' combines economic, scientific and secular certitudes and is packaged and sold for world promotion.

Fallacies of western economistic world view

Soon after ascending to power in 1980, Ronald Reagan stated his belief in the magic of the market place. Twenty years later G. W. Bush proclaimed that 'God wants all people to be free' and announced that a trend toward more 'free trade democracies' is happening around the world.

These political and 'prophetic' imperatives now have an objective measuring instrument that can be used to foster excellence recognition and competition. Of course, there are two competing indices of economic freedom.

The Heritage Foundation and the *Wall Street Journal* created an Index of Economic Freedom in 1995, based on the idealization that protecting the liberty of individuals to pursue their own economic interests results in greater prosperity for the larger 'society':

> The highest form of economic freedom provides an absolute right of property ownership, fully realized freedoms of movement for labor, capital, and goods, and an absolute absence of coercion or constraint of economic liberty beyond the extent necessary for citizens to protect and maintain liberty itself.[17]

I take these imperatives to be the central idealizations of the dominant neo-liberal economic culture: they define the western economistic world view.

In a second way of measuring economic freedom the Cato Institute worked out, with the help of Chicago economist Milton Friedman, another version, and its application reports the good news:

> Economic freedom remains on the rise. . . . 90 countries recorded improvements in their economic freedom score, and just nine saw a decline. In this year's (2007) index, Hong Kong retains the highest rating for economic freedom, 8.9 out of 10, followed by Singapore, New Zealand, Switzerland, Canada, the United Kingdom, and the United States.[18]

Economists, such as Jeffrey Sachs, have identified the fallacy of assuming that economic 'freedom' necessarily leads to better growth. Sachs points out that countries with good ratings such as Switzerland and Uruguay had sluggish economic performances, and others, like China, with poorer score had very strong economic growth.[19] James K. Galbraith views it as merely the 'freedom to shop' in a sphere separated from the state control. It is a freedom only for corporations that have the power, resources, and capacities to trade internationally.[20]

But perhaps the most relevant criticism of the new economic freedom comes from capitalists themselves who are warning the world about the unacceptable risks of an unregulated financial globalization.

George Soros says that the belief that markets correct themselves, and the assumption about market equilibriums, is a kind of 'market fundamentalism". Specifically, the current financial speculation undermines healthy investments.[21] He argues that the current system of financial speculation undermines healthy economies in many underdeveloped countries.

Raymond Baker is deeply concerned that capitalism has become obsessed with maximizing and too little concerned with justice and correcting the corruption unleashed by a deregulated financial system.[22]

John Bogle quips in *The Battle for the Soul of Capitalism* that capitalism is now a 'rent-a-stock' rather than an own-a-stock economy; it is no longer an owners' capitalism but a 'managers' capitalism.[23]

From the perspective of those concerned about the sustainability of the earth, 'economic freedom' is a deeply fallacious idealization. Globalizing economic freedom rapidly expands throughput of more and more energy and natural materials that cannot be limited. Consequently the wasting of ecological assets then feeds back and undermines the possibilities for sustainability of the earth and communities. Partha Dasgupta, economist at Cambridge, argues that without subtracting the degraded natural assets from economic measures the results are highly misleading; the inclusive wealth of countries goes down as their GNPS go up.[24] Degradation of fresh water, soil, forests, estuaries, rivers, and the atmosphere, reduces the value of existing wealth. Of course these are also conceived economistically as 'services of nature', or 'natural capital', even by some of the founders of ecological economics that is concerned with bringing economics back down to earth as a subsystem of a finite planetary order. That the earth may have intrinsic values that do not show up on the economistic measuring screens is hard to state in terms of economistic rationalities.

Principles of economic freedom have been applied in aggressive and coercive ways by the financial system to 'develop' other nations. Counter interpretations of contemporary international economic history suggest a different and more complex narrative about what has, and is, happening.[25]

In the 1980s, transitions from a Keynesianism policy framework to neo-liberal monetarism permitted a different international financial system to emerge. International financial expansions before this period operated within the restraints of the fixed exchange rate, or the agreement that the U.S. dollar was the standard currency to which all other currencies could be equated. However, over extension of the U.S. military expenditures forced Nixon to back out of the Bretton Woods monetary agreement in 1972. Initially the Bretton Woods institutions (WB, IMF) were oriented to working with governments. But in the 1980s, new policy procedures required structural adjustment programs that used a creditor leverage to impose privatizations that dismantled and sold off public enterprises and social infrastructures to many private corporations. Many economies became much more indebted and foreign ownership expanded more than anyone could have imagined in the 1970s. From the 1980s onwards, many countries were forced to give up control over their fiscal and financial policy and permit foreign investors to appropriate public assets at lower than fair market prices. The result has been debt servitude for many countries and their peoples, as well as loss of education and health services.

In this history, what Milton Friedman called "economic freedom" turns out to include very little political freedom after economic restructurings. Economic freedom measures the extent of commodifications of all factors of production, and selective dismantling of government controls over the economy. This saddles indebted countries with financial managers in banking institutions determining many of their economic policies. This means loss of control over land, labor and money and decreased political capacity to help people trapped in supposed 'obsolete' economic sectors such as discarded government workers, teachers, small farmers, indigenous peoples, craft workers, small business people, *et al.*

Without concerns for social freedoms and justice, economic freedom becomes corporate and entrepreneurial freedom and in the end a gauge of the extent of corporate financial penetrations into economies and households.

If we contrast 'economic freedom' to what Franklin D. Roosevelt, in his 1941 'Four Freedoms' speech offered – freedom of speech, freedom of religion, freedom from want, and freedom from fear – the difference is like night and day. Indeed, this is a new day and the corporations have stolen it. What people really want from their political and economic systems is equality of opportunity for youth and for others, jobs for those who can work, security for those who need it, the ending of special privilege for the few, the preservation of civil liberties for all and the enjoyment of the fruits of scientific progress. 'Economic freedoms' in comparison to these basic freedoms are ideological justifications for corporate domination of the world.[26]

The same financial engineering that has made the financial sector rule over national political institutions is now being focused on the broader working class within developed countries. In the U.S, sub-prime mortgages, credit cards and student loans, and consumer credit systems create a new form of consumer debt servitude. These financial 'services' are designed to maximize profits first; real 'service' is forfeited as a secondary and not a relevant issue and it is up to the 'individual' to deal with. When President Bush signed the 'Bankruptcy Abuse Prevention and Consumer Protection Act of 2005' it was widely ignored, but it helped seal in the numbers of people who have lost their homes to sub-prime mortgage foreclosures and the indenturing of young people who did not read the fine print of interest costs of credit cards or college loans.

Paths beyond western individualism

Cultural reasons why the West cannot see the growing rejection of western economic rationales are assumptions about 'individualism', community and the importance of religious traditions.

The monadic self-oriented entrepreneur of neo-liberal economic theory is the high water mark of this economistic idea of individualism. Culturally the western ideal of the economic 'individual' is an abstraction everywhere; only in the West, where it originated and became central to law and economics, is it taken for granted. Only in the West has the 'individual' become a value in itself and is then used to explain universal 'equivalence exchange'. Understanding where this strange prometheism of the 'individual' came from and what it means is a fascinating anthropological inquiry.[27]

An American example illustrates this. Ayn Rand's virtue of selfishness continues to help define American individualism; a 1991 survey indicated that her *Atlas Shrugged* was the second most popular book after the Bible . By 2007 her books had sold 25 million copies and are still selling.[28] Allen Greenspan, ex-head of the Federal Reserve, was her devotee; and many economics classes continue to assign her books. American conservatism, while obsessed with personal liberty is indifferent to inequality and social justice.[29]

But these forms of individualism are growing thin and even in the West it is being transcended. There are several overlapping paths beyond western individualism that have to be considered:

- one is a European sociological interpretation of post-materialist individualization with an interesting new approach to religious participation;
- second is an American view of the emergence of cultural creatives that advocates a 'great turning' back to earth communities;
- third is an Indian view of post-secular critical traditionalism.

All of these paths are discussed in the chapters of this book, as are other relational concepts from other economic cultures.

A European view of the 'institutionalization of individualism' describes an individualization process that results in an altruistic and co-operative "individualism" as part of a search for a 'freedom culture'. Ulrich and Elizabeth Beck-Gernsheim have proposed that "human mutuality and community no longer rest on solidly established traditions but, rather on a paradoxical collectivity of reciprocal individualizations."[30] This refers to a 'second modernity' in contemporary societies where risks can no longer be 'managed' and personal awareness of this changes people's orientation to institutions. Whereas this may apply to the elites of non-western societies, it is an empirical question as to how many people are experiencing this greater anxiety. That Professor A. R. Vasavi uses this to describe the experience of Indian farmer suicides is evidence that it may also apply to those struggling to survive in development situations.

Individualization means that persons are now living in post-national constellations where political capacities are undermined by adjustments to financial markets and where confidence in government is declining. State's capacities to provide social welfare and foster democratically legitimate social and political policy formations are shrinking.[31] The low esteem that American voters hold for the Congress is an indicator of the failure of the governance process to deal with growing crises resulting from Bush's wars and the failures of the financialization of the economy. Markets are replacing, or deeply limiting, socially protective political policy in many spheres. Taking over, or intentionally wrecking, the regulatory capacities once maintained by consensual political and social norms correlates, in the U.S. especially, with grid locked political responses to global warming, public health, environmental protection, energy, etc.

But there are some positive cultural consequences of individualization. As normative orders change, social persons are released from past conventions and experience new horizons making possible a renewal of self-understanding and options. Wider interactions in networks of commercial, technological and civil society associations help restructure personal identities and cultural outlooks. More persons are able to open their horizons to others beyond shared traditions and include other views about freedom and practice into their life-worlds. Such personal re-integrations involve liberation from prejudicial orientations toward multiculturalism and an expanded cosmopolitan outlook.[32]

A second path beyond western individualism is David Korten's parallel reflections using the image of 'The Great Turning'.[33] Korten speaks about a cultural awakening as emerging from the widened experiences of travel and greater awareness of living in the webs of life in 'earth community'. He cites research that claims 24 percent of the U.S. population are 'cultural creatives' who are open to new inclusive and spiritual practices. These are the participants and leaders in the many movements that are opposing the corporate culture of violence and elevation of material wealth as real wealth. He sees this cultural turning as culminating in a worldwide civil society that can express a world public opinion as powerful as the power of the U.S. He mentions his solidarity with Tom Berry's eco-spirituality, Joanna Macy's Buddhist vision of the 'Great Turning', and Riane Eisler's partnership models of organization.

Ashis Nandy, an Indian political psychologist, has reflected on the impacts of British colonialism on Indian life and culture. For Nandy globalization is a "second edition of colonialism". But 'global' is not universal in that it cannot transcend indigenous institutions altogether.[34] Nandy does not make the assumption that the way forward is to force secular enlightenment. Instead he suggests religious traditions should develop a critical account of colonial domination in their own categories and at the same time be critical of the oppressions of their traditions too. Nandy identifies this form of reflexivity as 'critical traditionalism', in contrast to 'critical modernists', like Jürgen Habermas, a leading European critical theorist, who is concerned with the unfinished normative order of modernity.

Nandy is careful to point out that he is a non-secularist because his accommodative version of eastern secularism is different from the western one, which is also a force in India. Whereas western secularization treats religions as a counter ideology that cannot be allowed into the public sphere, Nandy claims that the original eastern view was equal respect for all religions in ways that can include them in public sphere discourse.[35] In this way each religion is also constantly revising its internal understanding of the others; and that promotes a deeper and more informed public dialogue too. He claims that ultimately resistance to structures of oppression come from one's own internal moral self, from what Robert Bellah has called 'reasons of the heart'. Nandy states,

> We are now moving towards a post-secular world. That does not mean that we are all going to turn into believers. It means that the sacred might come to occupy an important place in our public life. The peace movement might succeed in re-sacralizing human life to some extent, exactly as the environmental movement is already trying to re-sacralize nature. The Sandinistas, inspired as they were by liberation theology, understood this. Even when it looks as if democracy and secularism must go together . . . you cannot in the long run stop people from bringing their entire self into politics.[36]

In the post 9/11 context, Jürgen Habermas has surprised the left and come around to a position parallel to Nandy's in that he too suggests that religious citizens may express and justify their convictions by resorting to religious language:

> . . . secular citizens or citizens of a different faith may be able to . . . discern in the normative truth content of a religious expression intuitions of their own that have possibly been repressed or obscured. The force of religious traditions to articulate moral intuitions with regard to social forms of a dignified human life makes religious presentations on relevant political issues a serious candidate for possible truth contents that can then be translated from the vocabulary of a specific religious community into a generally accessible language. The liberal state has an interest of its own in unleashing religious voices in the political public sphere, for it cannot know whether secular society would not otherwise cut itself off from key resources for the creation of meaning and identity.[37]

In dialogue with Joseph Ratzinger (Pope Benedict XVI) Habermas arrives at some unique reconciliation with the post 9/11 world and proposes a 'post-secular' responsibility for both religious and secular citizens. But the religious discourse can enter into political discourse only in the deliberations and not in the official decision making which must be equally accessible to all citizens whatever their religious views. A post-secular public discourse puts greater expectations upon all. A secularism that presumes that science is the only form of knowledge discredits all religions and has to be transcended. Likewise religious participants must find ways of translating their intuitive views so that it can be understood by all.

The U.S. has its own critical traditionalists that are not given the public attention they deserve. For example, current distortions of Christian metaphors into 'end time' justifications of violence have received a withering critique by Chris Hedges' *American Fascists: the Christian Right and the War on America* who exposes the sinister maneuvers of evangelical Christian 'politics'.[38] In addition, Hedges' *I Don't Believe in Atheists* is also a critique of scientistic secularism.[39] Or Walter Wink's reconstruction of the meaning of Christ's non-cooperation with everything that is humanly humiliating in *Engaging the Powers* challenges all who use Christianity to justify violence.[40] This is a critical traditionalist understanding of the domination of 'the Powers' which progressives should appropriate to challenge Christian fundamentalism.

In the interests of understanding other freedoms and religious foundations of other economic cultures it is necessary to understand criticisms of the unrecognized losses of secularization. A contemporary example is Charles Taylor and his views on secularization as an instrumental rationality fostering 'excarnation' and an exaltation of disengaged reason.[41] A simplistic anthropological definition of 'excarnation' says it plainly: losing the flesh and only retaining the bones (as in ancient burial practices).[42] Taylor's philosophical reflection sees 'excarnation' as literally a disembedding of the significance of spiritual meaning in human culture and its replacements with head-oriented living and interacting. Taylor describes this as a great disembedding of the individual from the web of social relations that defines the original 'social person', as well as a disembedding from the cosmic sacred. Taylor agrees with Ivan Illich that a displacement of the web of love that constitutes a religious community, or what Illich calls a vernacular domain, predominates in transitions to economic modernity.

Felt bodily performances and their symbols are replaced by theory-oriented objectifications. Metaphoric language of analogical vision of poetry and spiritual perception are transposed into secular prose or worse the 'plastic words' of scientific explanations that only experts can interpret.[43] Resistances to this loss of poetic and participatory understanding is taken up by many voices that perceive the cultural losses of instrumental reason. Remembering T. S. Eliot's anti-economic insight may be useful here:

> ". . . the Hollow Men, who, knowing the price of everything and the value of nothing, have lost the ability to feel or think deeply about anything." ('Hollow Men' refers to a 1925 poem by T. S. Eliot. "Knowing the price . . . value of nothing" is Oscar Wilde's definition of a cynic.)[44]

In Chapter 4, on Ivan Illich, secularization is interpreted as forgetting and erasing the poetic, performative qualities of the world in field after field; a world of fitting proportion and appropriateness is replaced by a mechanical world where integrations of common sense are replaced by value assessments of risks and cost-benefits. While local festival and pageantry continue everywhere the actual integration of these into a self-understanding of the modern individual is harder to do or reduced to a moment of the fun culture.

But the loss is a fading of community too. The renewed quest for 'community' in modern life continues this recognition of the importance of bonded solidarity as another source of human reasoning, as described by Gadamer, Nisbet, Oakshott, etc. (see Chapter 6).

Multiple economic cultures – survey of contents

How did we get to the point of accepting western economism as truth? Was it the overwhelming power of western institutions and capital?

Milan Kundera, a French writer of Czech origin, says that "man's struggle against power is the struggle of memory against forgetfulness".[45] The liberating power of memory retrieves the sources of social imagination and empowerment, and in linking with what was opens paths to what can be. Memory reconciles the past and the present futures.

The chapters of this book are remembrances of the origins of economism and other economic cultures in the interest of better socio-economic futures.

Chapter 1 will retell the story of how western modernity began with a new theory of markets and an ethics of mutual benevolence. A new frame for human existence was disclosed when the ideal of market order gradually replaced older forms of political order. The exchange of goods and services became a new sacred sphere in that a mechanism of providence was revealed. But re-imaged economic powers also sanctified the productive worker too and yielded new leverage against unproductive monarchies and aristocracies.

The market order justifies itself as a new civilized culture for calming the passions with economic self-interest and enabling harmonious exchanges between trading nations. Nineteenth-century conflicts between advocates of free markets versus political interventions emerge and get repeated in twentieth-century struggles between liberals and socialists, libertarians and Keynesians.

In Chapter 2, reconstruction of Karl Polanyi's views will explain how the modern market mentality emerged and how 'economism' was founded, showing that free markets and free trade are not 'self-regulating', but increasingly require greater administrative arrangements.

Polanyi describes different forms of social integration as supporting different economies. Universal concepts of economics do not represent socio-economic practices from worlds where loyalty, fraternity, familism, communalism (understood in secular or sacred ways) are norms assumed by the associations shaping economic practices. As economism is institutionalized, and its shadow spreads, other social and cultural practices are marginalized, or buried, under displacements of 'essential' techno-economic progress. Of course, resistant enclaves continue such as the trust-based Indian family entrepreneurial groups who continue to dominate the Indian economy despite opposition from professionally managed corporations.[46]

Chapter 3 reconstructs some of the abstractive idealizations of dominant economism and raises questions about their adequacy and counter-productive consequences. The dominant economic order is rationalized by the scientific certitudes of economic individualism, financial liberation, the possibility of sound science and risk management, and economic development.

These economic idealizations are not universal; they are historically unique theoretical constructions. Indirectly they are legitimated by manipulations of the electronic media as a new form and force of production. Image-information services are disproportionately consumed and controlled by the powerful corporations and states. People's political-economic views are increasingly shaped by these technologies in ways that include increased disinformation and propaganda to distort actuality. For example, the deceptive techniques used by the tobacco corporations for decades have now been applied by the oil corporations to evade global warming and to continue their domination of the Republican Party and energy policy.

People living in modern media-intensive virtual realities are more vulnerable to manipulations idealizing economic freedom achieved by free markets and free trade. The icon of the self-regulating markets is used to explain everything despite the massive administrative apparatus needed to maintain it. Sudden crisis management in 2008 of the mortgage and credit mess in the United States suddenly made visible some of the institutional apparatus essential for 'free markets'.

I am concerned with another approach to economics. A comparative and interdisciplinary analysis of economies; one that includes embedded cultural norms, forms of association, geography, ecology, etc.

Chapters 4 and 5 document two critical traditionalist visions that go far beyond critiques of economism and define the human condition very differently. They define limits of 'development' that differ substantially from the dominant economic logics for the westernization of the world. These chapters survey the religious practices and insights of two outstanding religious leaders – Ivan Illich and

Mahatma Gandhi. Focusing on each of them in their specific worlds reveals 'other' paths for economic cultures.

Illich interprets the corruption of western Christian institutions and demonstrates how western institutions were centralized and professionalized in ways that colonized vernacular communities. At the same time Illich's genealogy discloses other forms of social and convivial life that remain models for social life today.

Mahatma Gandhi is interpreted within the horizons of modern Indian history, and his ideas of the harmonization of life pursuits, self-rule, self-reliance and trusteeship are tested in terms of their relevance for subsequent Indian transformations.

Coverage of Illich and Gandhi on key socio-economic views is significant for thinking about alternative economies. Both enable us to understand other cultural sources for reform, regeneration and socio-economic transformation in contemporary societies. A research program for alternative economic cultures can be shaped by Polanyi and these cultural visions.[47]

Chapter 6 uncovers the 'other west', rooted in common sense and love of community that got buried over by modern methods for certain knowledge. The forms of reciprocity and gift giving that characterize both secular and spiritual quests for community are accompanied by a more reflexive individualization which is actually a way back to related personhood in a new sense. The debate about the gift traces the curve of this learning. Ironically, it is the discovery of social sharing and commons-based peer production that also leads us back to a world of social economy. It is from this perspective that we survey forms of co-operative economies that have always accompanied, as counter currents, the historical tides of commercialism.

In Chapter 7 the poverty of economic indicators for ecological equity is corrected in a survey of new indicators and a discussion of groups that are restoring and regenerating their ecological assets. Interpreting the meaning of the commons, the agrarian crisis and agrarian economic cultures, and other models for community and regional capacity building follow.

In Chapter 8 different approaches to social learning for people's economies in regions and communities are presented. The methodology of the Grameen Bank is used to describe how social learning for a new economic culture emerges. A survey of innovative ways to create local economies, protect public assets to secure the poor and different grass roots up models for financial autonomy is also done. Description of solidarity economics, and fair trade practice, is continued by a discussion of the importance of Henry George.

In all these ways of organizing alternative economies, I am concerned with how to sustain existing forms of security, within mixed economies, rather than risk their solidarity, community, family, region in an all out growth strategy.

Origins of this inquiry

I have been privileged, as the program coordinator and then Chair of the U.S international non-profit organization 'The Other Economic Summit' (TOES), to have heard many voices relate their stories about how they respond to modernizing development as promoted by the Giant 8 countries. Encountering views from all over the world reporting critiques and horrendous stories of western economic impacts has made me seek a deeper understanding of the role of the West in earthly affairs.

TOES events were encounters of thinkers and doers from many places and vocations and remained unique as an effort to bring together counter views to the official G-7 world views. These gatherings were a precursor to the World Social Forums (WSF) that began later. Many global NGO conferences and events are planned with the participatory intention of bringing together people who further empower each other by finding common ground with others, as well as opportunities for future interlocking of their ongoing projects. Coming out of the world social forum process is a global movement for Solidarity Economics which can become an ongoing canopy for achieving this end.[48]

Ivan Illich confronted me with a very different world as I participated in the networks that he called an 'invisible college'. I struggled for many years to understand the profound meaning of his riddle-like pearls of wisdom and I have been deeply changed by this effort. The gift of his friendship remains with me.

Related cultural and philosophical interests also led me to participate in the networks formed by the Montreal Intercultural Institute. One consequence of these associations was 10 trips to India documenting many exceptional cultural alternatives to development and innovative social innovations. I am deeply indebted to Siddhartha and the Fireflies Intercultural Center that he founded. The rich social justice discourse and actions that he and his network of friends are doing in India is a major source for this book and have changed my world view.

I have also learned from many western scholars whose similar turning around to question western categories has been a major event in their biographies, in ways that predated and paralleled my own. For example David Korten, Stephen Marglin, Frederique Appfel-Marglin, Hazel Henderson, Ward Morehouse, Carolyn Oppenheim, Michael Shuman, Fred Dallmayr, Lee Swenson, Bill Batt, Joel Kovel, Martha Herbert, Romesh Diwan, James Morley, David Lewit, Walter Wink, Ruth Caplan, Robert Engler, Joan Gussow, Alanna Hartzok, Tula Tsalis, Bob Wallace, Douglas Lummis, Lawrence Martin, Gene Bazan, Jeff Boyer, Tom Golodik, Susan Hunt, Jeffery J. Smith, Winifred Armstrong, and Ron Brady.

Friends encountered from other cultures remain with me in memory and in this book such as Majid Rahnema, L.C. Jain, Ashis Nandy, A.R. Vasavi, Manu Chakravarthy, Chandan Gowda, John Clammer, Kalpana Das, Jean Letschert, Wolfgang Sachs, David Cayley, David Barkin, Rajni Bakshi, Njoki Njoroge Njehu, and Shiv Viswanathan.

I owe special thanks to my wife Tula Tsalis who has helped me throughout the process of working on this book, and has also read and edited every chapter several times.

My thanks also to Aravind Govind and Maria Bareli, who have helped with the technical aspects of getting the book together.

The following is an attempt to systematize what I have learned from many sources and aligned reflections. In this way these reflections chart a transformation of understanding and self-understanding.

Part I

Critical histories of western economics

1 Origins of idealization of the self-regulating market

The emergence of the economic culture of commercial market society

How did the idea of market self-regulation as the source of societal wealth, which creates a new economic culture, emerge in English history? Up to the end of the eighteenth century the civic culture of classical republicanism had been the dominant political philosophy in England. This changed in the first three decades of the nineteenth century when the victory of the economic liberals ushered in the classical liberal economic world view which has returned as neo-liberalism of the 1980s. We will pick up that story in Chapter 2.

Historian J. G. A. Pocock argues that the ideology of the market system emerged within a debate between the civic humanists' defense of 'virtue' and the moneyed interests' justification of the civilizing mission of empire.[1] Pocock claims that the debate between virtue and empire has continued since the seventeenth century; while the constellations change, the central issue of dialogue continues. It is clear that American empire building has been surging despite denials from Donald Rumsfeld that the U.S. never acts as an imperial power.

But many strong dissenters charge the loss of American integrity and virtue. For example, Andrew Bacevich's *The Limits of Power: The End of American Exceptionalism*[2] is a sharp indictment of the corruption of virtue in America. U.S. leadership has refused to face the problem of oil dependency which has led to an imperial presidency who conducts wars to secure the 'American way of life'. The American people are deeply enmeshed in this corruption, as is the Congress which has given up defining the common good. Empire versus virtue goes on.

Pocock's researches into the history of classical republicanism from Aristotle to seventeenth-century England provide access to civic humanism that remains an important source for political discourse, especially in the United States.[3] Critical constitutional theory seeks to restore the civic humanist dimension of U.S. political history and re-image the socio-cultural conditions under which constitutional self-government is possible. This classical republican renewal restores a vocabulary that has always been central to western normative discourse – such as 'virtue', 'the public' and 'common good', and finally 'corruption'. For example Richard Fallow's commentary in the Harvard Law Review asserts, behind republican revivals, "lies a set of assumptions about human nature, the nature of the good for individuals and society and the means by which the good can be identified".[4] These classical norms of political civic culture have been consistently denied, or co-opted, in order to justify expansions of free market capitalism. Nonetheless, civic culture remains relevant for the critique of the corruption of today's neo-liberal empire.

'Corruption' means the destruction of the preconditions that make political participation possible. In civic humanism it indicated an undermining of civic virtue resulting from the loss of freehold land, the victory of moveable property (capital), and the moral-ethical consequences of commercial specialization and division of labor. This critique of commercial capitalism was developed as a civic humanist critique of corruption as early as 1698. Republican civic humanism could reconcile 'liberty' with equality only insofar as equals had nothing to fear from political action or opinion. In the English context, this meant independent freehold of land and the right to defend this with arms. The republican paradigm of civic virtue resisted the growth of trade and credit as the emergence of a momentous corruption that would spread fear for security from one level of society to all. They also believed that the 'moneyed interest', whose increasing power rested on the new 'moveable' forms of property, also corrupted government to act in its exclusive interest. As a reaction to the dynamic of commercial capitalism, the country Whig party, opposed to the Tories, or the 'Court Party', ironically and defensively radicalized a political culture that normatively established a notion of the common good.

The historical watershed for corruption was the Glorious Revolution of 1688, when transition to William and Mary also meant the foundation of a major war effort that required an explosive development of the credit and banking system of the realm. This escalation of corruption was irreversible, since land increasingly became valued as 'moveable property' and the extension of public credit and financing military-economic expansions through a natural debt expanded, from 1697–1715.

The actors, issues and forms of discourse of that era cannot be adequately understood in the concepts provided by Hobbes and Locke, or Marx, but have to be related to the evolution of the Whig ideology through several phases that cannot be simply represented as the 'Whig interpretation of history'. A culturally sensitive account of the emergence of the market ideology can be gained by following the ways in which civic humanism, oriented to limiting economic empire, was discredited and 'scientifically' displaced by historical theories of evolution and political economy. In this way it is possible to see how the market system comes into place geared to the stabilization of authority and stated in juristic terms, because that justified cutting back expectations of political participations that could limit empire.

The watershed of the Scottish Enlightenment

Historically, the systematic evasion of civic humanism and emergence of 'juridical humanism' of Adam Smith occurred as the Scottish Enlightenment's response to the union of Scotland and England, in 1707, into the United Kingdom. Scotland lost its sovereignty and, in the terms of civic humanism, its civic virtue too. But as it was re-colonized, a new view emerged in the Scottish civic public that justified it 'scientifically'. Other development paths were discussed – such as Andrew Fletcher, who had advocated a federalism more consistent with Scottish autonomy and the independence of its militia.[5] But oppositions to Fletcher, after the uniting of the United Kingdom, expressed the interest in joining economic progress that had been increasingly rapid since the financial revolution. These rebuttals of Fletcher had to overcome claims of the loss of civic virtue for Scotland, and at the same time advocating commercial civil society, rather than political civil society. This required a new principle for defining 'virtue'. The principle of 'politeness' had been innovated as part of the latitudinarian tolerance of opinion or conduct campaign during the Restoration to replace prophetic with sociable religiosity, and political enthusiasm with a morality of manners and taste.[6]

The Scottish historical school of David Hume, Adam Smith, William Robertson, Adam Ferguson and John Millar thus provided the theory of history which explained how classical republicanism was superceded in the history of civilization through a progressive movement from barbaric to feudal to polite commercial society. But this effort followed the lead of the cultural principle of politeness which began with the seventeenth-century politics of culture diffused by Shaftsbury and Addison, who had attempted to transform the prophetic Christian into a polite and civil subject.

After the financial revolution, the 'old and true Whiggism' was transformed into a 'polite Whiggism' that used the aura of civility and enlightenment to justify the consolidation of a Whig oligarchy, circa 1714–19. Achieved through the Septennial Act of 1716, the polite Whig aristocracy effectively shrank local influence in the borough electorates and achieved 'political stability'. Thus the United Kingdom's turn to commercial civil society was part of the fusion of an oligarchic ideology where claims to 'enlightenment' culminated a century-long politics of culture oriented to suppressing the passions of the Puritan and the radical republican in the name of peace and manners.

This was the turning point in the emergence of modern economic culture; the evolution of political theory and political economics has since constituted a foundational discourse that swings from constitutionalism, to utilitarianism, to contractarianism. In all of these the legalistic emphasis has been used to justify capitalism and has always involved the strategic goal of wealth creation and the institutional arrangements that Smith calls the system of 'natural liberty'.

Idealizations of self-preservation versus dedication

William Hennis argues that the great internal conflict of 'bourgeois society' is between the concepts of self-preservation and 'dedication' as a religious identity. Although the term 'bourgeois society' is not entirely descriptive of the United Kingdom in the eighteenth century, the opposition Hennis identifies is central to the transitions of skeptical and scientific Whiggism in the Scottish Enlightenment. The normative ends of human society were changed from political participation to self-preservation and the meaning of virtue changed from the pursuit of internal goods of traditional practices to the appropriate ordering of our self-interested passions. Classical religious discourse on how to reconcile privatization of God's dominion with sustaining the needs of the poor and property-less found a new resolution in the Scottish historical identification of national wealth as the means of reconciliation of individual and collective rationality.

'Juridical Humanism',[7] synthesized from sixteenth-century Spanish and Dutch origins, originated in international law and the problems that derived from the administration, possession and distribution of 'things'. This new beginning of 'natural law', which comes from Hugo Grotius' juridical construction of justice, was limited to rights of appropriation.[8] This was to be achieved by the means of respecting the rights of others; but here 'rights' were essentially proprietary rights of holding what is not yet owned by another.

In the 'original state of nature' there were 'commons' only in the sense that no one owned them – as yet. In this way exclusive right is the basis of property and the basis of civil society – which law and government must preserve. This denies the practice of English common law, or relies upon a proclaimed ideology of restoring it, while actually transforming it into national law.[9] The Scottish Enlightenment forms a new vision of human civilization as constituted by individual proprietary rights and promotes a view of the social order as securing peace by arranging the institutions in a ways that secure individual rights.

A second step was the addition of a skeptical twist; namely, that human nature is not restrained by reason but actually constituted by affections and passions. In this formulation, moral philosophy replaces traditional virtues with a 'universal' theory of human nature which would explain the grounds of morality and justice. The new orientation is stated by Hutcheson who saw moral philosophy as "the art of regulating the whole of life" and who defined 'moral sense' as that inbuilt practical disposition to virtue; a universal determination to benevolence within human nature itself. This is a naturalistic formulation of the 'moral sense' and it provided the basis for a new universalistic account of morality.

David Hume's subsequent analysis of humanity as creatures of instincts and passions ends by seeing moral standards as devices to meet human needs. In Hume's 'new science of man' the hope of realizing the civic humanist notion of virtue as the fulfillment of an innate power of the human soul is dismissed and an abandonment of all teleological traditions as political community is accomplished. Hume's essay 'Of Commerce' asserts that sovereigns must take mankind as they find them and not attempt to infuse them with 'a passion for the public good'.

Idealization of civilizing mission of wealth creating market society

Hume's analysis of the human passions defined the interest in gain and commerce as one which could override the love of pleasure. With gain in their eye men will acquire a passion for the increase of their fortune – hence commerce and industry must have freedom to prosper in order to facilitate the virtues of frugality and "make the love of gain prevail over the love of pleasure". By institutionally narrowing the drives of individuals and by curing one vice by another, i.e. the self-interested love of gain, a commercial society, and indeed a world of such societies linked by free trade, could secure peace and order. In such a 'world-society' the major public goal would be the providing of military force for self-defense and the administration and enforcement of laws that protect private property and economic transactions. Therefore government does not exist to realize a higher form of self, or a positive community, but only for the instrumental goal of securing what Adam Smith called the 'natural system of liberty'.

Commerce was, for Adam Smith, a substitute for virtue because it liberates man's natural instinct of self-preservation. Such liberation is also a liberation from the reign of traditional and political virtue. For Adam Smith virtue was the practice of 'propriety' or the judging of what is appropriate in the empathic understanding of another's passions in a particular situation. Smith's own moral propriety was in judging that it would be appropriate for the inferior ranks of people to be instilled with thrift and good management through the societal operations of the law of supply and demand.

Subjected to the price mechanism of the free market, people would control their desire to consume grain and would thus learn the propriety of prudence. In such terms Smith justified the elimination of the Corn Laws and therefore the traditional commons norm of 'food security'.[10] Although Smith admits, as Mandeville claimed, that men pursue riches in order to live better than their fellow men, i.e. for vanity, and commercial society is prone to be corrupted by such a vice, it is nonetheless better to liberate the instinct for self-preservation because this also increases the opportunity for political freedom and greater national wealth.

What is new in the emergence of juridical humanism from Grotius to Smith was an instrumental theory of law and government where the rules of justice aim primarily to secure the material interests of households and the nation. A law-governed society does not aim to enable persons to realize higher forms of civic virtue but to provide security of property, and to facilitate its pursuit. In this sense government and civil society is rooted in 'necessity', 'natural inclination', and 'habit', not in classical civic humanism's idealism of the fulfillment of human autonomy through political participation and discourse.

This 'necessity' is intrinsic in the nature of human nature, which unlike animals who find their needs meet in nature, which is always finding that no object is sufficient and that there is 'always need for improvement'. This restless need to improve upon the materials essential to meet human needs results in the new arts and divisions of labor. In the age of merchants it is therefore a necessity to maintain the motivation to keep what results from economic improvement, otherwise there is no reason for economic improvement after the 'crude' needs of agrarian life are met. It is also necessary to dismantle the apprenticeship model of public learning, because, as mentioned earlier, it was inefficient and analogous to caste structures in India, where a free labor market is necessary.[11] This action is a model case of the removal of a cultural institution in the interest of competitive commerce.

Internationally the logic of economic improvement also operates through these institutional arrangements to polish crude and barbarous dispositions by overcoming the resistances of the various pre-market passions through the disciplines of commerce, which cultivates the virtues of industriousness, frugality, punctuality and probity. Men are attached to each other in commercial civil society through mutual utility and are transformed into becoming supple, bending and serviceable. As a 1704 book on commerce states:

> Sensing the necessity to be wise and honest in order to succeed (men) flee vice, or at least his demeanor exhibits decency and seriousness so as not to arouse any adverse judgment . . . he would not dare make a spectacle of himself for fear of damaging his credit standing. [12]

Formation of national and international markets was the mechanism that brought about a new social order where the unequal distribution of materials and talents fused together in one great law-like circulation of wealth. This national–international system of commerce was justified as rooted in economic necessity and assimilated both the ideas of divine providence and the notion of causal laws of physiology in an analogy of the circulation of blood and wealth – according to François Quesnay, a French Physiocratic economist and physician. Internal to this economic 'law of nations' the 'particles', i.e. economic individuals, operated optimally by fulfilling their passions for gain and luxury and were also simultaneously constrained to civility. Defining the nature of human nature as a desire for more creates a world of scarcity since both human beings and nations are constrained by the necessities of limited resources and talents as well as the causal operations of the circulation of wealth.

The original theory of the capitalist revolution emerged as the discovery of the means to transcend the necessity of scarcity; through the mechanism of work and wealth creation both scarcity and the civilizing mission of humanity is fulfilled. This meta-narrative of modernity assimilates the Christian fall into the curse of labor and the Newtonian idea of law-like order of Nature into a myth of economic scarcity and the saving mission of commercial civilization. But its actual consequences are far broader and now require rethinking. There is another way to see this grounding of modernity in the need to transcend scarcity which we will turn to in Chapter 2.[13]

Evolutionary empiricism: economic culture as spontaneous coordination

Skip to the twentieth century when theorists were trying to reground the classical liberal order of market organization on updated scientific foundations. Systematizing how the merchant class is successfully consolidating its economic practices against the heavy handed interventions of crown and aristocracy is one project, but renewing this when a new form of socialist authoritarianism emerges in the twentieth century is another. Frederick von Hayek takes on the task in the context of a fading Austrian Hapsburg monarchy and against surrounding enthusiasm for Soviet socialism.

Whereas Hayek was, to his credit, skeptical about every issue throughout his intellectual life the one thing that he never retreats from is the mission of finding a refutation of socialism. This was his lifelong mission.

Hayek's justification of market capitalism relies upon recognition of a superior cultural evolution provided by spontaneous self-organization. A spontaneously emerging economic order is an 'anti-rational rationalism'[14] that denies there is any design that can improve upon the aggregate of individuals who follow their own interests in responding to changing circumstances. The collective result, for Hayek, is a self-correcting, self-organizing process that utilizes all kinds of dispersed knowledge in evaluating the scarcity and value of resources as well as maximizing wealth creation. The presumption is that it is not coercive.

However, the market functions not only to bring about mutual interests but it can also form highly contested conflicts of interest, as the contemporary global discourse about 'free trade' shows. Nonetheless, Hayek assumes that the outcomes will be optimal in so far as they are occurring in a set of liberal market institutions. Only groups guided by impartial, and non-individualistic, interests will decline; which means those not primarily oriented to competitive markets.[15] This overly optimistic assessment of the absence of internal social conflicts, fails to see that fraud, deception and market failures can also emerge, and which do not represent economic gains. Hayek's argument converges with Social Darwinism in that what emerges is superior; asserting evolutionary wisdom as always providing liberty becomes especially thin for pre-liberal and post-liberal fascist societies.[16]

Whereas the point Hayek wants to argue is that the presumption of conscious control over social life will not work, the result is a lack of clarity about what does and does not provide for more liberty. The liberal order is supposed to enable increased instrumental capability to efficiently coordinate the information required to form ever more highly specialized divisions of labor capable of creating greater wealth.

Whereas Adam Smith actually used the metaphor of the invisible hand very few times in his writings and did so for poetic persuasive purposes, he did not glorify unconscious patterns but was concerned with intentions and consciousness. The gap between Smith and later theorists for self-regulating market has lead David Korten to argue that Smith's theory of a market society can be positively affirmed today in contrast to Hayek's theory which justifies coercive capitalist society.[17]

Hayek really believes that spontaneously ordered structures are superior to conscious thought, where 'social' means patterns not conscious to the individuals.[18] For Hayek:

> The market is not a set of pipes channeling capital though roundabout channels, but rather an information processor, organizing and conveying the appropriate information to the relevant actors, by an instrumentality that could not be fully comprehended or manipulated by any central planner.[19]

He asserts that the mind could not come to an adequate understanding of its own operations and that 'Reason' could not, on its own devices, fully comprehend why markets are the superior format of social organization.

Evolutionary rules of just conduct are universal emergent practices and not necessarily characterized by their comprehensibility. They are forms of tacit knowledge that are not systematically conscious and are essentially negative and abstract – such as the rules of private property, contract and tort. Thus Hayek links individual rationality and collective integration as occurring in a way which eliminates need for any social reflexivity; no cultivation of reflective judgment is required to maintain the spontaneous social order. It is the very 'aggregation' of these tacit conformative behaviors that preserve social wisdom and maximize knowledge utilization. Ultimately a harmony of interests is operating that posits a cybernetic feedback equilibrium that does not admit the rational transformative role of ongoing public discourse.[20]

Hayek's systematization rests on the notion of maximum utilization and self-organization of knowledge, an optimal use of knowledge in a non-coercive and open market exchange process. Evolutionary emergent economic rationality is the fulfillment of human ontogenetic evolution as well as justifying a superior cultural evolution. The ultimate realization of human potential is the modern entrepreneur; the market and minimal state i.e. contract law and police security, are final forms of societal evolution. The idea of spontaneous self-organization's mediation of millions of market interactions shows that it is a theory of the external coordination of human interactions and is not mediated by culture, but by the logics of calculating economic value. Cultural evolution is justified as resulting in this strategic 'culture' of economic rationality.

But can a strategically justified social order actually function without a moral and cultural legitimation in the form of public norms that can be contested, given new problems? Without reflexive interventions massive anomic rebellions, as well as tyrannical crisis stabilizations, can emerge and block needed social transformations. There is no clear way that emergent problems of authoritarianism can be dealt with in Hayek's theory and it becomes a strategic rational account of social order that can only be marginally transformed by political reflections. John Grey admits that this approach cannot hold on to normative frames that can be swept aside by post-liberal constellations of power such as corporatism or fascism.[21]

Jürgen Habermas has repeatedly demonstrated that only when people accept mutually binding norms can they agree about how to change them or reform them in a procedurally legitimate way.[22] This implies that ontogenetic evolution does not stop with the modern entrepreneurial decision maker but goes on to more reflexive forms of self-correcting action that is not exhausted by market competences.

But contemporary evolutionary empiricism goes on. Peter Berger, in his book *Capitalist Revolution: Fifty Propositions about Prosperity, Equality, and Liberty*, tries to justify capitalist culture by referring to the massive nature-like facticity of "well-being" which supplies an equivalent to legitimation.[23] According to Berger it is a "fact" that modern capitalism has an incapacity to provide an over arching justification of work and living; people accept materialism as reality. Indeed there is a truth to that, but the massive aid of planned disinformation also helps, as does the wrecking of national political institutions in order to allow an oligarchy of corporations to rule.

Internal colonization of spontaneous orders and the problem of social freedom

Hayek's spontaneous self-organization is not a socially integrated order but a strategic meta-order which cannot be transformed by social and politically reflexive persons. Indeed the distinction between technical and socially mediated rationality is not relevant for Hayek.

Both Jürgen Habermas and André Gorz describe all modern societies as involved in the balancing of two types of societal integration which Habermas has called system and social integration. Gorz calls self-regulation a 'hetero-determined' order and a socially regulated order as co-coordinated by co-operative interactions. Both define how extensions of the first can potentially override and colonize co-operative practices. Gorz's thinking is more accessible than Habermas' and can make the point more simply.

Gorz sees self-regulating orders as defining procedures, as well as personal relations in administrative systems. This differs from interactive forms of communicative co-operation where groups are socially self-regulated. But self-regulating practices, as they are instrumentally extended, are not conducive to enabling personal meaning and this creates a split between the ordering of work and life.[24] However, Gorz claims there are two types of self-regulation: one which is spontaneous and technical (SR-1) and another that is external and power driven (SR-2).

Spontaneous SR-1 is the integration that emerges from unique configurations of freely associating buyers and sellers in a market, or from the ever changing constellations of drivers in a traffic situation. This is not an integration of persons based on norms, but an external technical integration that has no meaning to individuals. This is not 'self-regulation' but an emergent external form of ordering.

Programmed SR-2 is an integration of individuals by administration of industrial functions guided by technical rules essential to achieve goals, such as offering workers money, security, prestige, or power attached to hierarchical gradations. Gorz claims that both incentive and prescriptive regulations force individuals on pain of penalties to adopt forms of functionally required behavior.

Classical liberalism, in the Hayekian version, claims that it is the spontaneous self-regulating market that creates greater wealth, information, innovations, etc., and denies that the external power driven regulations create internal colonization whose overall impact undermines personal autonomy.

A socialist interpretation assumes it is possible to reconcile work and life by replacing the spontaneous SR-1 of the market with the programmed regulations of the socialist society SR-2 that has personal meaning. Here the public and private are unified by socialist consciousness as a professional ethic, or calling, which idealizes dedication to party and the socialist order. Understanding one's self activity as an instrument of historical justice and equality provides a life with heroic meaning. However, the utopia of functionally instrumental work arrangements becoming unified with personal meaning is an identity that has been challenged by many critics as illusionary and not real autonomy.

Hayek's self-regulation analysis is challenged by this view. Both financial capitalism and state socialism will progressively undermine socially constructed integrations by excluding the formation of reciprocal relations based on co-operation, group membership and solidarity.

The way modern societies have so far reconciled the split between functionally regulated society and socially-regulated community is the so called 'Fordist compromise' where the market system must create enough wealth to offer workers compensations for instrumentalism in work. This proceeds by conditioning people to accept consumerism and the commercial advertising of luxury fantasies as possible consumer realities. This promotes withdrawal into the private sphere, the disintegration of social solidarity and mutual assistance, and promotes excessive individualism uninterested in community participations. The Fordist compromise has been breached by economic globalization; supposedly workers are now competing on a global scale and the workers' share of the economic pie has been rapidly declining and rewards are no longer supportive of consumer satisfaction.

So is it possible to realize a socially free modern world? Do we have to accept that market institutions are the embodiment of historical wisdom and resist distortion of their operations as cotemporary libertarians do? The answer begins with a different approach to economism and economic cultures.

2 Substantive economics and the abstractions of economism

Disembedding of the market and the utopian liberal creed

Karl Polanyi's *The Great Transformation*, published in 1944, stands as an alternative history of the modern economy that many on the political left and right now accept.[1] His understanding of the 'always embedded market' is not consistent with the dominant economic viewpoint.[2] The following reconstructs Polanyi's text as a seminal text worthy of careful interpretation.

Contrary to von Hayek, the first market-guided society in history was not a spontaneous evolution: "The road to the free market was opened and kept open by an enormous increase in continuous, centrally organized and controlled interventionism."[3]

In three major interventions, the British economic liberal state created a competitive labor market (the Poor Law Amendment Act of 1834), the automatic gold standard (Peel's Bank Act of 1844), and opened international free trade (Anti-Corn Law bill of 1846). These political interventions 'disembedded' labor, money and land from the social protections that stabilized politically-guided mercantilism in Britain.

'Disembed' means to annul customary and legal frames used in traditional protections of land, labor and money and to replace them with formal rules that facilitate their economic exchanging. Since land, labor and money are not literally produced for sale on markets, and that is why Polanyi calls them 'fictitious commodities', treating them as if they are commodities transforms the human social world in ways that now seem normal. But in retrospect this has had momentous consequences that we need to remember.

The debate about the poor laws, circa 1780–1830, was the pivotal discourse that led to the implementation of the first market-guided society and the economic liberal culture in the United Kingdom. Overriding traditional 'right to life' norms, e.g. customary and legal access to food, shelter, security, was unthinkable in a Christian Commonwealth, but that was the final outcome of the great debate about why the masses of poor were increasing. In the end the views of Townsend, Malthus and Ricardo led to a new understanding of human society as situated in nature and subject to its law-like equilibriums. Society was no longer 'political society'; it was now seen as part of the law-like patterns of nature, and the self-regulating market as a naturalization of society.

This debate is analogous to the contemporary world economy debate about the need to not worry about the lost jobs from corporate outsourcing to cheaper wage labor areas; overall economic growth will eventually lift all beyond the natural scarcity that produces poverty, and new economic opportunities will emerge.

The self-regulating market, and the naturalization of society, explained away the historical reality of the poor displaced by successive enclosure movements and the formation of a national economy. The unintended consequences of this abrupt elimination of customary right to life were not recognized by economic liberals in the 1830s, or today in financially 'forced' globalization projects. Expanded wealth creation and greater labor productivity was the new focus for state policy and industry. The new science of political economics justified adjusting policy to the 'laws' of self-regulating markets. Market equilibriums now replace moral and political rationales for forming policy; the domain of economic life is conceptualized devoid of normative ideals and beyond the scope of political interventions. This naturalistic conceptualization was a cognitive re-ordering that colonized all past meanings of personhood, social and political status, and social justice, and so Polanyi comments: "What induced orthodox economics to seek its foundation in naturalism was the otherwise inexplicable misery of the great mass of producers which we know today, could never be deduced from the laws of the market."[4]

Freedom from misery would be ameliorated by the growing power of science, technology and industry over nature. But this belief in technical and scientific progress had unexpected consequences soon after the original economic liberal experiment.

Almost immediately after political interventions created the first market-guided societal process, counter political interventions emerged to protect the now vulnerable and economically exposed fictitious commodity spheres. Legislations emerged to protect workers' health and security, the right to tax for ecological reasons, and the protection of the national currency. In reaction, economic liberals claimed an anti-liberal conspiracy. But A.V. Dicey, a leading British jurist, conducted a classic public opinion study and discovered that the entire political spectrum supported the legislative acts that would protect health, safety, land, etc.[5] This was no conspiracy. Polanyi's summary of this entire transformation was ironic: "the road to laissez faire markets was planned, but planning was not."

Such historical reconstructions were the basis for Polanyi's conclusion that economic liberalism did not emerge as a natural evolution, it was a utopian construction. Rooted in pessimistic naturalistic metaphors, Townsend, Malthus and Ricardo imaged natural necessity requiring self-regulating economic growth.

Polanyi's socio-cultural account of the source of human misery

Grounding classical economics on a naturalist foundation has turned out to have fateful consequences. Karl Polanyi is clear in the tenth chapter of *The Great Transformation* that the conceptual grounding of classical economics on naturalistic foundations contributed to a new perspective that saw poverty as 'nature surviving in society'.

In one concept, that also absorbs Max Weber, Polanyi signals his framework for the analysis of the impacts of market formation and the source of human misery: "... disintegration of the cultural environment of the victim is the cause of degradation, not economic exploitation."[6]

Polanyi uses this principle in his analysis of how the new social technologies of classical economics were applied in the U.K. and in non-modern worlds, to aggressively destroy subsistence worlds in order to create 'nature-driven' motivations to adopt wage labor situations and habits. It was also a critique of Marx, who rightly sees the exploitation present, but fails to recognize the role of cultural institutions. It is ultimately the destruction of these social and cultural protections that enough desperation, 'the whip of hunger', forces people to become wage workers. Imposing 'hut' or 'head' taxes, or destroying subsistence sources of food, were tactics used as means to force labor into the free market creation. Forcibly ending traditional status and subsistence institutions is effectively the systematic creation of natural scarcity, e.g. lack of food, and social scarcity, i.e. loss of community bonds. Scarcity then becomes the manufactured condition that justifies the disvaluing of all traditional social forms as insufficiently oriented to power over nature. Economic creation of more national wealth then becomes the solution for poverty. Today the creation of scarcity can be done with financial arrangements – remember the Indian farmers. A reflection on the philosophical foundations of market society in scarcity concludes this chapter.

One case can illustrate this issue. In *The Great Transformation* Polanyi comments that the famines in India, in the last part of the nineteenth century, occurred because the village community had been demolished.[7] This was brought about by the underselling of hand woven cloth that was dumped on India by British machine made cloth and called 'free trade'. At the same time the forced disruption of traditional security stockpiles of food and the free marketing of grain was pushed in a context where local incomes had failed. Mike Davis' analysis of this in *Late Victorian Holocausts* takes off from Polanyi's insight and shows that commodification of agriculture eliminated village reciprocities that traditionally provided welfare to the poor during crises.[8] Here, as in many cases of imposed market formations, the use of force to achieve the market system creates scarcity and requires violence. Mike Davis' thesis is that before the forcibly imposed free trade and free market upon India the 'development gap' did not exist; the 'third world' was created in these economic freedom interventions while strong traditional forms of protection against famine were dismantled.[9]

Polanyi argues that poverty is not solved by economic means alone since it is ultimately a social problem. He congratulates Robert Owen as the man who saw this clearly in nineteenth-century Britain and who saw sustaining community as an equal goal for economic progress.[10] However, the economistic viewpoint on poverty was shared by all who accepted the naturalistic foundations of economics and the labor theory of value. The labor theory of value, which has become the foundation of most resistance to the oppression of labor in Marxism, is none the less only part of the story, and focusing on it to the exclusion of institutions and culture just continues the same dynamic of dispossession of wealth and creation of social scarcity.

Convergence on the labor theory principle in the nineteenth-century British classical economics determined the economic view of how to eradicate poverty. When poverty is viewed as nature remaining in society the omnipresent imperative is to create greater productivity of labor to create more wealth and eliminate poverty. As a result, measuring labor inputs resulted in new principles and administrative procedures that colonized work processes and relations, as described by André Gorz (see Chapter 1).

Exploitive interactions between bearers of labor power and capitalists were now justified as consistent with maximizing production. The new guiding norm was economic equilibrium, or 'equal exchange', that Karl Marx's 'immanent critique' of capitalist development aspired to expose as ideology. But Marx never comprehends that the critique of this cognitive abstraction is ultimately a fateful continuation of the naturalization of social relations that his entire 'critique of capitalist accumulation' aspires to transcend.[11]

Karl Polanyi argues that discovery of the 'labor theory of value' from Locke, Smith, Ricardo and Marx has been

> . . . a mistaken theorem of tremendous scope; he [viz. Ricardo] invested labor with the sole capacity of constituting value, thereby reducing all conceivable transactions in economic society to the principle of equal exchange in a society of free men.[12]

The consequences of this labor theory transformed into policy forced the creation of a labor market that was "an act of vivisection on the body of society". This radical policy was justified, and policy makers steeled to this task, by an assurance that only 'science' could provide.

Polanyi continues:

> [T]he smashing up of social structures in order to extract the element of labor from them was and remains the main purpose of economic development in the nineteenth century (and still in the twenty-first century). In order to achieve 'freedom of contract' all organic forms such as kinship, neighborhood, profession, and creed have to be liquidated if they claim the allegiance of the economic individual.[13]

Consequentially a naturalistic economism was embraced by both historical ideologies focusing on liberation through greater productivism – Liberals and Marxists. Both promoted increased labor productivity as the motor to greater economic growth and human betterment and differed about equality and just distribution. But there have always been counter movements, such as economic co-operatives, to the formal economic break up of organic community practices as will be expanded below.

What was initiated in the U.K. in the 1830s and 1940s, returned in an upgraded and elaborated form, as neo-liberalism, in the 1980s. Then and now it is an overt strategy for restructuring societies to become market 'guided' in ways which serve a class of investors, increases aggregate economic quantities, and proposes that trickle down will create jobs and eradicate poverty. Naomi Klein, who was influenced by Mike Davis who was influenced by Polanyi, has documented the expanded violence of this strategy in *The Shock Doctrine*. She shows precisely how crisis situations are used to justify major privatizations, and deregulations that are not comprehended by affected people. Development of this shock treatment was the key to continuing the neo-liberal take over of Chile and Uruguay (1973), Argentina (1976), etc.[14]

The original economism has deepened into an ideology of historical production that sees increased labor productivity as a major motor to greater economic growth and sets aside socio-political policy for full employment, which was affirmed by Keynesian economics and overtly by Gandhian economics in a different way, as will be explicated in Chapter 5.

Wage labor, over and against work intrinsic to community-based subsistence or craft livelihoods, or municipal configured economies, becomes normative for the formal liberal economy. This systematically marginalizes every other kind of work association and defines a new understanding of human productive value-creating activity that changes the concept of human personhood and basic human associations. In opposition, Polanyi postulates that the social nature of human personhood is expressed in the reciprocities of self-limiting social communities.

> As long as a man had a status to hold on to, a pattern set by his kin or fellows, he could fight for it and regain his soul. But in the case of the laborer this could happen only one way; by his constituting himself the member of a new class.[15]

Labor union movements emerge to resist and socially protect the exclusion of workers from their fair share of productive work, just as movements have emerged to socially protect land and ecology and national money systems. Hence Polanyi asserts that history in the era of market society is the result of a 'double movement' of expansion of markets for genuine commodities and the social protection of fictitious commodities. Today this pattern can still be used to describe the economic globalization and its counter movements to protect land, labor and money.

Polanyi's historical thesis of 'the double movement' retains the logic of a 'dialectical relation', or reciprocal causalities that cannot be analytically separated, but must be analyzed as a holistic interrelation. In this idea Polanyi retains the Hegelian–Marxist insight into ethical resistance to the imposition of a quasi-natural causality, or commodifications, upon social arrangements that maintain a human world and a productive nature. But Polanyi's post-Marxist understanding of this holistic interrelation is a historical hypothesis, not a revolutionary strategy. Actions always emerge to socially protect those spheres of human society that are not real commodities. Polanyi's substantive economics approach is oriented toward pragmatic solutions, not the effort to guide human emancipation with theoretically constructed universal imperatives.

Polanyi's concept of 'the double movement' was formed as a historical description of the dynamics of the emergence, and consequent social and political responses, to the rise of market society. But it is also a historically based hypothesis that can be used to guide research into the changing forms of economies and societal arrangements. Theory formation is very different here; the object domain is comparative economies not the formal economy. For example, it can help explicate how commodity forms are used to objectify new 'factors of production' such as information and knowledge that now release new counter-actions to protect against 'biopiracy' or enclosure of commons knowledge.[16]

Economism versus substantive social economics

Idealization of the market system as a self-regulating frame appropriate for all societies is an economistic ideology, where economism means projecting market logics, such as efficiency, into all human interactions. For Polanyi the abstract separation of economics and politics does not form a 'neutral instrumental sphere', or a system, because regulatory frames, national and international, provide metanorms, or principles for their operation in all cases. The economy is always embedded – in one way or another.

Polanyi's critique of the fallacy of economism is central to all his work along four dimensions:

First, it reduces all human motivations to economic or material interests. Second, there is no separate part of society that could be named 'the economy' since it is always embedded in legal, political, social and cultural relations. More precisely 'the economy' is always an 'instituted' process in diverse ways in diverse contexts.[17] Third, reading the economic logic of one form of economizing into all of history is a historical fallacy. Fourth, it defines the human condition as rooted in scarcity and the expansion of the economy as its solution.

Polanyi's critique sees the 'economistic form of human understanding' as a technical utopia that sees human history as a process of overcoming natural necessity as economic liberation from poverty. This transforms political freedom, which requires public discourse and institutions to secure, into an economic struggle to overcome the limits of natural scarcity.

This liberal creed becomes a vocation for those who internalize this emancipatory message, analogous to the dedicated socialist who sees the development of production as ultimately liberating all of humanity. Any perusal of the libertarian literature on the web reveals a passion and commitment that intends to inspire at the level of a political religion – just like Marxist socialism.

Polanyi's contrast between formal and substantive economics can help renew a substantive sense of socio-economic options and break with the pseudo-necessities of theoretical constructs.

There are two different senses of the word 'economic'. One is defined by the methodological criteria of formal economic concept formation and the other departs from actual historical and institutional contexts and focuses on the technical-institutional problems of socio-economic life. Formal economics derives from the systematic objectifications of measurable scarcity, and construction of logics of economizing action. Substantive economics focuses on the historical processes of material-provisioning that depart from particular contexts. Where formal economics develops 'universal', quantifiable concepts, substantive economics must always proceed immanently and historically since the ways that people provision themselves and socially institutionalize these provisioning processes differ.

Polanyi claims he took this distinction from Carl Menger's second edition of the *Grundsatze der Volkwirtschaftlehre*. Menger claims that there are two equally fundamental directions of the human economy. One toward the economizing of insufficient means, scarcity; the other toward the technical requirements of production, independent of scarcity. Whereas they can coincide, and are interdependent, they also emerge from separate problem sources. Given an insufficiency of means, how a choice is made involves a dimension that presupposes normative ends that are not defined by scarcity of means. Socio-cultural interests intervene in the perception of "economic" ends. When we relate ends to means we do so according to a range of normative ideas from truth and beauty to right and just.

Whereas formal economizing logics refer wise use of insufficient means to a hierarchy of preferences, material-substantive economic action is oriented to the livelihood ends defined by custom, tradition or chosen norms. Scarcity determines economic action only where insufficiency of means defines the ends themselves; otherwise the allocations of means occur in ways defined relevant by contextual normative ends.

The end of sustainability is an interesting case where the two can be inter-linked; whereas efficiency analysis is required, so too are unique local solutions for agriculture, forestry, water harvesting, etc. For example, the use of techniques peculiar to special ecological areas for alternatives to water-intensive rice cultivation, such as the Indian use of Jeevamritam, a concoction of cow dung, urine, pulses and jaggery.[18]

Substantive economics is oriented to understanding concrete forms of socio-economic life; formal economic analysis is applicable in so far as these economic practices are adjusting to the national-international market system. Even market systems have changing institutional frames and motivational ends that can be analyzed in terms of its substantive contexts and its resulting technical problems of means. Substantive economics' object domain includes how human provisioning occurs in particular contexts, how organization and distribution of goods and services actually operate, how financial and governance procedures aid, or retard, economic well-being and how customs, institutions and ideologies likewise aid or retard well-being.

Polanyi did not use the word 'development' in his thinking; he was very skeptical about seeing people's development lined up on a evolutionary hierarchy and saw the inner worth of all persons. But the theoretical reason for Polanyi's skepticism toward developmentalism is to see Max Weber and Karl Mannheim's distinction of substantive and formal rationality as convergent with the meaning of substantive economics. They take seriously the epistemological claim that material and ideal interests are inseparable within established 'orders of life'. In so far as the actual forms of material provisioning vary, so the substantive rationality of specific orders of life differ. The ideal and material are always unified in so far as people meet their needs within a specific environmental context and to which they are oriented by their culturally acquired competences and stocks of knowledge, and are part of a human group that has a shared concept of the good life. Meeting their substantively defined 'needs' requires solutions of specific technical problems of means, not problems defined exclusively in terms of price or the maximizing of economic goals.

An example of the differences between substantive and formal economic discourse is illustrated by the opposed sets of rationales about the collapse of the Doha WTO negotiations in July 2008. Free traders see the end of the negotiations as a tragedy that will worsen the food crisis and allow trade to regress 30 years. A substantive view sees the fact that small and poor farmers world wide cannot compete with imports of subsidized agribusiness corporations from the U.S. and Europe; they would like to get access to their own regional and national markets. Moreover, the WTO rules against stock piling food, a crucial aspect of food security. For the substantivist, agriculture should never have been in the WTO agreements. The outrageous number of farmer suicides in India has been traced to the stress of trying to become a competitor on the world market. In the context of the oil price hikes, countries can now try to develop their own capacities to provide food and they can make their own reciprocal trade deals.

Application of formal economizing principles to non-market oriented life-orders is economistic in that it produces knowledge that is coercive to indigenous practices in so far as it disvalues and displaces social solidarities and embedded knowledge. An optimal situation would be the reversal of colonization by having formal economics serve substantive ends. For example, the Rodale institute brought its agronomists and economic experts to serve the practices of organic farmers.

There have always been ongoing debates in economics between formalists who want to build an economic science and substantivists, or institutionalists, who are not regarded by the formalists as producing real predictive or explanatory knowledge. Without getting diverted into these methodological issues there are good reasons to continue to do substantivist economic analyses because they contribute directly to public discourse about the technical, material, ecological and socio-cultural means and the consequences of existing economic practice and policy. Indeed it is essential to represent the substantive ends and practices of specific communities and regions to regional and national planning policies before they are forcefully imposed. What many people have been calling a 'new economics' is basically substantive economics and it can contribute directly to restructuring assumptions and practices about participation in socio-economic associations and policy formation.

Polanyi's program for substantive economics represents a post-Marxist synthesis whose relevance is its potential as a theoretical frame for substantive and critical social economics. Polanyi's appropriation of Marx is regulated by Weberian precepts which, unlike most Marxist and Neo-Marxist perspectives such as Jürgen Habermas', jettisons evolutionary 'developmental logics'. Polanyi remains more historical and descriptive and less guided by theoretical 'real abstractions'.

Polanyi has absorbed Weber and the German historical school and does not try to read the path of western development as a dialectical ladder that is oriented to an evolutionary transcendence of the market system. Polanyi's substantive economic analysis does not get caught in the circle, or 'bad infinity', of 'how is working class consciousness possible?' Comprehensive theorizing does not assure 'objective possibility', only contextually appropriate judgment goes beyond the present.

Substantive economics and western market industrial formations

Substantive economics begins by dissenting from Adam Smith's theory of market formation that has become prescriptive for techno-economic 'development' policy. Put briefly, market exchange will develop because natural differences in resource distribution create scarcities that compel specialization and institutions of exchange. The technical advances of an increased specialization of labor supposedly lower the production costs and increase market demand and growth.

Karl Polanyi's critique refuses to reduce market formation to formal techno-economic determinants. Polanyi suggests that in the socio-political reordering of long distance and local trade by political interventions formed a national economy. It was changing modes of regulation that explained the historically particular formation of the self-regulating English market system.

Techno-economic explanations were reinforced by Henry Ford's success in extending the principles of mass production. These were widely copied, even if Ford's radical capitalist goal of producing cheaper products, was replaced by luxury goods production. A substantive economic history must account for why the model of mass production and the neo-classical efficiency logic became dominant while more socio-economic craft forms were ignored.

An alternative perspective sees small firms as the real job creators in the contemporary economy, as they had been in many industrial districts throughout the nineteenth and twentieth century. Contrary to the Smithian–Marxian convergence on the logic of industrial-technical development, there have always been thriving craft-production sectors and regions in western industrialization processes. Flexible craft artisans used ingenious innovations to extend the range of human skill rather than expedite its decomposition.[19] A substantive history sees these industrial districts as highly innovative because of their informal combinations of co-operative family firms, and city and regional institutional forms. Community economics has been more important than the generalizations justifying extensive economics of scale and mass production recognizes.

Today investments in intensive labor-based approaches to infrastructure building could generate much needed employment, especially as alternative energy systems in wind and solar are expanded. Greater reliance on local resources can also create employment and stimulate local economies. A labor-intensive approach can be applied to energy, agriculture, forestry, manufacturing, environment protection, and local services.

Stephen Marglin, in a classic essay 'What Bosses Do'[20] showed that the choice of technology within the industrializing shop was, in many cases, for purposes of hierarchical control and legitimating the authority of the boss rather than for efficiency. Justification of the division of labor within the particular shop is not, as Karl

Marx following Adam Smith assumed, a matter of technical efficiency. Successful disvaluing of craft workers' autonomy in the conceiving and executing of work ultimately depended upon the cultural justification of a system of political economic knowledge that became central to the transition from mercantilism to capitalism. Classical political economics imaged an efficiency-producing self-regulating market in ways that justified eliminating all social norms and forms of knowledge that secure workers' control over their work situation.

Cultural alternatives have, in the past and today, been fused around situations where craft production or other micro-industry combinations can be supported by socio-political arrangements that facilitate the optimal integrations of local-regional, national and even wider markets.[21] It was within the technical competences of weavers, craftsmen, farmers to competitively conceive and execute their tasks in ways that are – in many socio-political circumstances – not transcended by production necessities of technical learning. The movement to the industrial system cannot be conceived as an automatic technical learning process; other socio-cultural mediating factors are involved.

These innovative social economic alternatives were continually reinvented in old and newer forms and aided by new technologies. For example, Pierre Joseph Proudhon and Terence Powderly, leader of the American Knights of Labor, promoted systems of co-operatives supported by co-operative banks. The progressive views of both Marx and the classical economists rejected these schemes because they were tied to the particularities of specific crafts, trade fraternities and mutual-aid societies in municipal centers. Economic historians have named these as 'proto-industrial districts', where livelihoods, remained tied to craft traditions and facilitated by communities and/or municipalities. Resisting wider market dislocations of their livelihoods they worked out embedded co-operative solutions to changing economic circumstances and created municipal social economies, enabled by municipal institutions.

Craft production theorists, or social economists, argued that competition and productive association were complementary and that flexible machinery could extend human skills. Sabel and Piore show that the socio-political arrangements of the Lyonese silk industry, the Saint-Etienne ribbon, hardware and bicycle industries and the Solingen cutlery and Remscheid edge-tool industries, do not line up with the classical economic model of mass production, but rather demonstrate the ongoing relevance of craft production. Piore and Sable argue in *The Second Industrial Divide* that the craft model of 'flexible specialization' should be seriously imitated and adopted today.

United States industrial development had the greatest affinity for extensive mass production systems, while the French and Italian regional developments were much more rooted in intensive flexible technologies and organizational institutions, aided by legal and informal social protections that made decentralizations possible. Again, the mechanisms that permitted this diversity were not economic but socio-political and, above all, legal.

It was specifically the spread of mass production models through war and military preparations that forced the subordination of flexible industry and blocked the will to this variety of experimentation. National economic planning, such as in post World War II France, coercively undermined the autonomy of many of the independent industrial districts. On this account the major determinant for the submersion of the other paths of techno-economic 'development' are the legal actions of centralized political states and their legitimation by the efficiency model.

Efficiency logics continue to be derived from the militarization of industrial systems. As early as the nineteenth century, U.S. manufacturing innovation had been shaped by the military quest for interchangeable parts in the federal armories. In contrast to European methods, which depended more on skilled workers, the American mass production system, derived from military standardization, used automatic systems that cost much more and depended upon military financial support.[22] Although specifics of David Noble's analysis have been questioned, his general thesis is that technological design follows the 'Boss's' interest in maintaining control and not in maximizing the flexible specializations of skilled craftsmen.

Economic cultures beyond developmentalism

Karl Polanyi saw modern capitalism as not totally replacing substantive economics with formal economics. For that reason he did not theorize about economic development and was concerned with different types of social integrations that supported mixed forms of economic exchange. Old and new economic cultures are possible as well as new combinations of substantive economic practices. Many existing communities, municipalities, and city-regions may be the forms of political and economic culture that have not yet consolidated into global movements. Chapters 6 to 8 explore some of these.

The study of economic culture includes, as Karl Polanyi recognized, the effort to understand and evaluate practical economic rationalities, such as the formal rationalities of economic liberalism.[23] The study of economic cultures is not to justify evolutionary economic progress; this ignores the multiple normative frames behind different types of economies. For example what Peter Berger celebrated as the second *Asian Capitalist Revolution* has been interpreted as a unique culturally mediated form of state guided mercantilism which was constitutive of their regional success, not self-regulating market mechanisms.[24]

The fate of humanity in the epoch of capitalism was the central question that guided Max Weber's passionate study of economic cultures. Weber's analysis of the economic ethics of world-religions and of the 'spirit of capitalism' derived from his concern for an integral conduct of life which he believed to be retained in modernity only in the form of vocations, such as science or politics, that go beyond the immediate satisfactions of the passion for gain. Likewise Weber's interest in the *Protestant Ethic and the Spirit of Capitalism* was its uniqueness as an innerworldly calling that had the everyday necessity of a vocation and the indirect consequence of building strategic institutions for capitalism.

Weber's inquiry into the 'spirit' of capitalism departed from the defining question of the potentiality for the ethical interpretation of the world; do modern social orders of life cultivate ethical personalities with obligations to others? Or is the world of traditional dedication being irreversibly replaced by the new self-interested economic individual? This study continues this inquiry.

But Weber's research program has been 'reconstructed' by both apologists for capitalism and by its critics too; they have incorporated it into frames forecasting western cultural and societal rationalization.[25] A minority interpretation claims Weber's analysis of 'rationalization' was not to develop a theory of western modernity but to judge the immediate consequences of rationalizations upon the life conduct of involved humanity.[26]

Rethinking Weber in this way sees him as more concerned with culture and spiritual traditions and makes his skepticism about the historical inevitability, or evolutionary universality, of liberalism more concrete: "Whoever wishes to be the weathervane of a developmental tendency should abandon these old fashioned ideas as quickly as possible. The historical origins of modern freedom had specific and unrepeatable constellations as its precondition."[27]

In contrast the entire post-World War II period has been an avoidance of this historical insight, and today's theoretical idealization of economic freedom re-creates the same separation of economic and political institutions that formed the first phase of western market society. The haste to create evolutionary accounts rejects discontinuities and multiple paths. An old Buddhist aphorism seems relevant here: 'repetition is another name for suffering.'

The ultimate interest of the study of economic culture goes beyond economistic developmentalism and characterizes and evaluates what communities, municipalities and city regions are doing to achieve economic autonomy and unfold their capacities today.

On scarcity: the charter myth of modernity

The modern western progress theory of economic freedom begins with a claim of the human condition as rooted in scarcity. Thomas Hobbes originally conceived this as resulting from the endless comparison of riches, power, and possessions between people in ways that make all things potentially scarce, given human beings unlimited desire for recognition. From this crucible of envy and desire, imitations of lifestyles of the privileged classes become models for one's own ambitions. The world is transformed into competition for limited resources, driven by unlimited desires.

When John Locke confronted Hobbes's problem of scarcity, he called it 'the state of War', and ultimately proposed an economic growth solution which has won over the grim Hobbesian 'war of all against all', or the Leviathan gambit of a social contract with a strong state. In justifying the emerging modern social order, John Locke considered it a divine right that allowed men to appropriate only as long as "there is enough, and good left in common for others". But according to Locke we have transcended the limits of the commons. Locke's conclusion was that an emerging system of appropriation based on money changes the original human condition. A money economy enables everyone the opportunity to achieve greater individual autonomy due to the transcendence of the conditions of 'natural scarcity' with new forms of wealth creation.

John Locke's solution to the Hobbesian 'State of War' became the charter myth of modernity. His identification of economic growth as the means to overcome scarcity and avoid social envy was the road taken by western modernity. Expanding into the 'new world' by improving the land would create enough wealth to maintain England and the masses of people who migrate there. The myth of economic wealth creation as the solution begins with the devaluation of unimproved nature and the legitimation of labor as the basis for the system of individual property appropriation. If nature could be subdued surely wealth and prosperity will follow all through modern life. Human labor is the key to wealth creation. This led, especially after Adam Smith's *Wealth of Nations*, to the belief that the state should stay out of the economic sphere and limit itself to being an impartial umpire in the wealth creation process.

Thus growth without limits is the mythical condition under which the modern western way of life was formed and is now being globalized. But the rush to wealth creation "is precipitated by fear of scarcity, and the destruction of nature would only be accelerated as the world's rich would continue to raise their own consumption. The search for limits must start with a recognition of this fear."[28]

Focusing on fear and terror-driven panic for 'getting yours' hits all too close to home for Americans. Reinforcement of this myth has been made by Bush Senior's message to the Earth summit in 1992 that 'the American way of life is not up for negotiation' and Bush Junior's message to Americans after 9/11 that they should go out and consume!

Ironically, the thesis that we must all economically and technically transcend scarcity establishes scarcity as the human condition in a more central way, as Ivan Illich's alternative research program 'the history of scarcity' demonstrates in Chapter 4.

3 Idealizations of utopian capitalism

Idealizations of utopian capitalism and the contemporary world

Given Polanyi's account of the nineteenth-century origins of economic liberalism, we have historically come full circle. On an expanded scale, we are back to nineteenth-century economic liberal idealizations of free markets, free trade, free labor, and private property. These are now brought together by the ideology of 'Economic Freedom'.

"Belief in unlimited economic wealth creation is utopian", John Gray, a social conservative political philosopher, concludes in *False Dawn*: "a global democratic capitalism is as unrealizable a condition as worldwide communism."[1] Jürgen Habermas claims that globalizing markets are stable only if international political regulators exist to restrain the consequences of limitless expansions. Polanyi's 1944 projection that an unregulated global market system would eat up the earth and human community now appears prophetic.

The following points to the fundamental idealizations that make up the unrealizable imperatives of neo-liberal economics, such as a deficient notion of 'human nature', the idealization of deregulation, the concept of scientific certitude, the applied ideal of 'development' and the civilizing consequences of contemporary capitalism.

Idealization of maximizing rationality and entrepreneurial freedom

Margaret Thatcher asserted that there is no such thing as 'society'; what has been called 'society' is the aggregate of private individuals. People are not viewed as having a mutual interest in each other and interpersonal associations do not take precedence over commercial associations. What is important is the 'individual's' access to economic opportunity. Political 'freedom' is reduced to maintaining a minimal state that does not block price determinations. 'Justice' is securing the decisions made on a procedural model of contracts about the exchange of equivalents under conditions of free competition. Politically, people do, and permit, what they will; this is the private meaning of liberty[2] which neo-liberals erroneously take to be the same as freedom.

Neo-liberalism images human well-being as resulting from liberating individual entrepreneurial liberty and skills. But reflecting on the social content of this ideal of excellence reveals that the meaning of 'personhood' has been redefined in a very specialized way; it is not the social person but the rational maximizing manager whose decisions are separate from any obligations of morality, or citizenship. Superior rationality of corporate managers is required for fiduciary responsibility to the stockholders; other consequences of management's instrumental decisions are secondary. Bush's imaging of individualized social security would be the ultimate training ethos for socializing this idealized character; endless worrying about retirement accumulations would be the final solution for eliminating any active civic culture.

Neo-liberal imaging of human development is inspired by Frederick von Hayek, von Mises and Milton Friedman; they all idealize an individual utility maximizer. Of course von Hayek would assert that these competences have to be formed in the context of spontaneously formed market institutions, from charter schools to fraternities and corporate hierarchies.

Corporate managers in the U.S. are paid enormous sums to make the best maximizing decisions for the stockholders and theoretically they do this because they have the highest incentives to do this for themselves. In 2007 the average income of American CEOs was $10.5 million, while the top 50 managers of private investment firms made $579 million.[3] This is many times higher than CEOs' compensation in other countries. The gap is justified as caused by the expansion of value in top American corporations since 1980, and because of the greater risk and engaged leadership of the American CEO. Spotlighting these super compensations also dramatizes the 'freedom' of the U.S. entrepreneurial spirit and promotes the corporate culture of American business governance.[4]

Too much concern about social solidarities conflicts with individual liberty and is therefore considered politically problematic. Political autonomy is not a major issue. People as citizens are not viewed as co-authors as well as those addressed by law. The purpose of law is to protect property and the private sphere. Fostering institutional frameworks that secure property rights is the first requirement for increasing capacities to conduct 'free markets' and 'free trade'. Equally important is securing legal frames oriented to contract law and cost-benefit evaluations that enable the expansions of markets for land, water, health care, environmental pollution, services, etc. Bush has demonstrated that war-making can be a commercial opportunity from food service to security systems to 'nation building'.

Focusing on social justice as a social or personal end is not desirable. Neo-liberal political culture is a mixture of toleration, mutual indifference and cynicism. The market responds to prices, not norms. A culture of entrepreneurial innovation and liberty must be promoted. Comprehensive regulations are to be resisted since the market is 'nature' unleashed. All regimes or regulations are 'command and control' systems and must be replaced by voluntary compliance. This includes corporate responsibility. Temporary contracts and individualized arrangements replace institutions in professional, emotional, and cultural spheres as well as international relations and the work place.

In order to create competitive markets, the positive role of the state is to facilitate the integrity of money and maintain the military and police as essential for security. Too much concern for health care must be 'managed' in the interests of commercial life. Thus the U.S. can say all its SWAT teams are up to par, but 47 million Americans have no health insurance.

But can human social cooperation be maintained if these arrangements are really institutionalized? Massive anomie, as normless behavior, and alienation, as a despair about blockages of meaning and opportunity, can emerge.

Media critics seriously suggest that media superheroes, such as Batman and the Hulk, are popular because many Americans are socially isolated and image themselves as self-made individuals who have to endure all against the odds. Media consumption of these cartoon superheroes is massive and expresses the underlying sentiments that Americans carry. When people have a chance to express these feelings, loneliness is the most often reported malady of American social life.

As mentioned in the introduction, Ayn Rand's virtue of selfishness has helped define American individualism.

Idealization of financial deregulation

Deregulations have been idealized as the means to increase economic growth. General studies have indicated that the real consequence of deregulation and privatization in Britain, Brazil and Bolivia, is the movement from publicly justified prices to a situation where secrecy prevails. Hence the link between cost and price is no longer accountable. With this secrecy there is no possibility that the 'free market' can operate. For example, privatization of some 'public' utilities is kept secret despite appointed consumer committees that monitor price settings. The irony is that the United States had one of the most democratic public service systems in the world; Americans paid very little for their public services. The Enron Corporation's gaming of California electrical utilities was the most extreme case of taking advantage of deregulation and began the trend to democratize re-regulation.[5]

Given the current economic situation in the U.S. it is relevant to focus on deregulations of financial markets. In 1984, James Tobin, winner of the Nobel Prize in economics, gave a famous talk about the inefficiency of the financial system:

> . . . we are throwing more and more of our resources . . . into financial activities remote from the production of goods and services, into activities that generate high private rewards disproportionate to their social productivity. I suspect that the immense power of the computer is being harnessed to this 'paper economy,' not to do the same transactions more economically but to balloon the quantity and variety of financial exchanges . . . I suspect that Keynes was right to suggest that we should provide greater deterrents to transient holdings of financial instruments and larger rewards for long-term investors.[6]

But the trend has been increasingly oriented toward speculative investments, rather than long term investments in the productive economy. The U.S. is the center of this kind of radical financialization but in a world of offshore unregulated banks the risk becomes global. The contribution of the financial sector to the U.S. GDP was estimated to be 20–21 percent in 2003 while the contribution of the manufacturing sector was only 12 percent.

Thus, American investments are less concerned with the productive side of business and more concerned with leveraging money for short-term profits. Financial markets were aided by both private and public institutions to fulfill their 'fiduciary responsibility' to stockholders with less concern about employees or consequences. Great efforts were made to create more deregulations that permitted more leverages of debt to make higher rates of return. This trend was not stopped by the Enron scandal reforms; deregulations have since permitted more expansion of pyramided debt. The final omnibus bill was passed in the dim days of 2000 when the country was awaiting a decision on the Gore/Bush election. No one noticed, except the speculators pyramiding more debt, that the addition of deregulated 'swaps' turned the game into uncharted waters.[7]

The 'Enron loophole' exempted most energy trades and trading on electronic energy commodity markets from government regulation. The 'loophole' was drafted by Enron Corporation lobbyists working with U.S. Senator Phil Gramm to create a deregulated market for their experimental 'Enron Online' initiative. The legislation was signed by President Bill Clinton in December 2000 to allow for the creation, for U.S. exchanges, of a new kind of derivative security, the single-stock future.[8]

On June 22, 2008, U.S. Senator Barack Obama proposed the repeal of the "Enron loophole" as a means to curb speculation on skyrocketing oil prices. Financialization had increased expectations for greater profits and this new practice pushed non-financial business too, as the recent interconnected crisis in housing, cars, and energy sectors demonstrate.

William Tabb describes the dangers of deregulation of financial capitalism:

> Rather than monetary authorities controlling an expanding and contracting money supply in counter-cyclical fashion, speculation creates liquidity in a pro-cyclical fashion. In expansion, borrowing is easy and at low cost. In contraction, credit crunches deprive the system of loan capital, inhibiting recovery. In the current cycle, as financialization and securitizations spread from mortgages and student loans and risk is passed on to whoever buys these securities and to those who buy them in secondary markets globally, it is not at all clear who is exposed to how much risk. Because no one knows who holds how much of the questionably valued securities, fear and uncertainty prompt widespread panic, which becomes harder for regulators to contain, given the global scope of contemporary financial markets and the growth of unregulated off-shore non-bank financial firms.[9]

In case the game fails the Federal Reserve will permit the tax payers to carry the burden and create more dollars which contributes to inflation. Profits are privileged while risks are socialized. Hence Bear-Sterns being forced, by the Federal Reserve

Bank, to accept JP Morgan Chase's bid of $2 for what was $70 value in one week is a prime case of corporate socialism. Bush's Secretary of the Treasury, Hank Paulson who had called for more deregulation rather than allow the Justice Department to enforce laws put in place during the Enron scandal, is – in the middle of July 2008 – back paddling furiously and beginning to act like a radical Keynesian. Likewise the follow up of Fanny Mae and Freddy Mac bailout in July and August 2008 has suddenly changed the federal focus to more regulatory overview, or more accurately bringing the resources of the government to help out the financial class. This was considered essential to secure the entire shadow banking system that had emerged around sub-prime mortgages and the perfect storm created by high oil prices, and failing auto industry. But counter to 'free market' ideology, the depth of the problem is unknown since transparency – essential for the right price – was not present during the debt accumulations and is still buried under massive efforts to save the financial mixing of commercial and investment banking, which until recently was separated by regulations. This crisis is the fruit of deregulation.

No matter what is done it will not change the exploding hedge fund market – the major innovator of this gaming form of financialization. The top 100 hedge funds, having two-thirds of hedge fund assets of about a trillion dollars, used new instruments of investment and securitization of risk.[10] Hedge funds are a new form of 'invisible hand' in the sense of being very secretive while increasing their market share very rapidly. In 2007 hedge funds managed $1.5 trillion worth of assets worldwide.[11] Their expansion in Europe is very rapid; they hold as much as 25 percent of Germany's largest corporations and now replace banks in maintaining fiscal 'discipline'.[12]

One of the unrecognized aspects of these extensions of financial capitalism is the breaking of the link between productivity and wages. Many productive firms taken over by financial mergers find that the new owners do not consider themselves as employers but as serving their stockholders. Cutting workforce is just another lever for profit-taking even when the productive units are profitable and productivity is increasing. Such delinking has broken the assumptions of workers and unions since the end of World War II; any reversal of this trend will require state help to renew unions since the U.S. workforce is now only 7 percent unionized.

It all pivots on the results of the 2008 elections since it is unlikely that a McCain presidency will allow unions to be renewed. But the corporate 'soup lines' will continue as corporate welfare is alive and growing.

Idealization of scientific certitudes and risk assessments as the basis of economic decisions

Main stream economics is no longer just neo-classical analysis but systems theory, game theory, decision theory, etc.; all are now part of the strategic engineering, or maximizing, that supposedly is the 'science of economics'. How economics splintered into multiple methodological approaches and still retained the role of the knowledge system most seriously involved in societal guidance is a question for political and sociological knowledge inquiry. Economism takes new forms.

All these strategic techniques went into the construction of the 18 sets of agreements that formed the basis for the procedures of the World Trade Organization (WTO) validated by the U.S. in 1995. A central emphasis in the WTO 'free trade' agreements is eliminating 'unnecessary technical barriers to trade'; where 'necessary' is defined in terms of a 'sound science or a scientific consensus' by the experts assembled by the WTO. Trade dispute procedures are internal to the WTO network and although position papers from outside experts are sought, the "world science court" is controlled from inside. However, the "openness" of sound science is questionable.

Sound science decisions are constructed as the results of 'risk assessment and consistency in risk assessments'. These criteria cover the field – assigning risk and making decisions about the consistency of different aggregated risk spheres – and are entirely technical tasks. There is no recognition of political judgments of acceptable risks to health, safety or the environment; everything is in terms of technical necessities! Political compromises between different assessments and the relevance of public discourse as a medium for assigning acceptable risk, or designing risk management, is eclipsed by precise measuring procedures. All uncertainties have been assimilated to risk assessments, and technical decisions define the process of the 'management of risks' too.

The certitudes of econometric cost-benefit risk assessments are given precedence over political judgments in free trade policy. This puts the burden on governments, if they have higher standards, to demonstrate that internationally harmonized standards – as ceilings – are wrong. This forces all judgments to be converted into the cost-benefit logic of the trading system and eliminates public debate about acceptable risks.

Uncertainties can result from either the intrinsic complexity of the phenomenon, or the extrinsic difficulties of getting precise measurement, or both. Under conditions of uncertainty it may be impossible to get adequate assessments of risk and the efforts to do so with probability assessments is confusing and misleading. 'Sound science' is not, in the context of uncertainties, sufficient to make prudent judgments and for that reason many political systems have adopted the 'precautionary principle' to avoid dire consequences.[13] This precautionary principle is not accepted by the WTO or the United States.

Sound science is the global neo-liberal order in microcosm; governance is forcibly reduced to economic necessity. When citizens realize that the WTO harmonization process does not recognize, or evades in an anti-democratic way, the principles of public discourse, national sovereignty and the social commons, they may wonder how free is 'free trade' policy. Trade policy had to be disembedded to be beyond the reach of most democratic procedures. Today's break down in the efforts to reform the WTO is evidence that this has now been recognized as unfair. Citizens have, at least in the third world, come to understand that trade dispute resolutions isolate the trading system from any democratic policy-formation processes. This puts countries in the position where they face trade wars and/or payments of compensation to other traders for loss of markets if they have politically assigned higher health, environmental and safety standards. Which means compliance is usually the cheaper path.

Stephen Marglin argues that the creation of a continuum between uncertainty and risk was a move that effectively denies their difference by constructing a spectrum along which experts can organize probability assessments. As such this creates a systemic distortion by making it appear as if experts can create more certain knowledge in situations where uncertainty prevails. As Marglin puts it:

> The existence of mixed cases and fuzzy lines become the pretext for abolishing the distinction altogether. If one is disposed in that direction, it is an easy intellectual step from the fuzziness at the edges of the distinction to the ideal that all probabilities are personal or subjective in nature, and this is the dominant view in economic theory today. As with utility maximization, it does not matter for the theory whether individuals consciously calculate the subjective probability distributions required by the theory. 'As If' behavior will do just fine.[14]

On the basis of such assumptions, game theory and decision theory began to systematize and model behavior as strategic interactions. In mathematical theorizing a conviction grew that it was possible to make optimal decisions that followed the probability distributions in the valuation of different outcomes. The ambiguity of uncertainty in situations disappears under the theorizing of decision-making options. In opposition, critics, such as Keynes, have argued that the ambiguity of uncertainty cannot be eliminated by probability as relative frequency of outcomes, and that subjective belief changes any structuring that decision theory supposedly provides. What the theory of subjective probability does, however, is put all human activity into the context of a maximizing paradigm, and expert knowledge systems are validated. Thus Marglin concludes that:

> Coping with uncertainty, which ought to be regarded as a distinct form of action based on a distinct system of knowledge, is reduced to a logic of calculation and maximization in order to maintain the purity of the economic conception of knowledge and behavior.[15]

In such situations Keynes suggested that macromanagers fall back on conventional insights, or 'animal instincts'. Marglin argues that all cultures are combinations of formal knowledge and embedded knowledge and, like many of the critics mentioned earlier argues that the West has elevated this preference for formal knowledge to an ideology. At this point Marglin's agreement with Hayek becomes clear. Efforts to arrive at a thoroughly scientific basis, what Marglin calls algorithmic knowledge, for economics and business practice are bogus.[16] Knowledge is always a combination of algorithmic knowledge and embedded practical knowledge.

Commenting on the social consequences of supposedly algorithmic knowledge systems, Ulrich Beck claims that the logic of production and greater wealth creation is in conflict with the logics of greater risks and the distribution of insecurity.[17] Trends forming a global risk society collectively define a new situation of uncertainty despite the ways in which scientific knowledge becomes even more central.

Thus one side of the current post-industrial discourse idealizes the assessment of risk and remains tied to the industrial model of knowledge production. But a continual questioning emerges from the everyday impacts of new interventions of science, technology and economic development, and constantly expands the range of issues and overall uncertainty surrounding policy formation.

Advocacy for 'sound science' based policy, essential for greater prosperity, is in conflict with those insisting upon more comprehensive democratic debate about acceptable risks and this defines the future stage for discourse about the appropriate medium for national or global governance. The ongoing failure to conclude the WTO agreements opens the door for these new directions.[18]

Counter movements against this growing criticism of inflations of sound science, or algorithmic knowledge systems, strive to defend the scientific reliability of risk assessments and the logic of wealth production. For example, the anti-environmental movement, and its early statement as a 'third wave' in environmentalism, demanded more adequate knowledge for environmental policy formation. This movement was sharply disputed but always the debate goes on.[19]

Quests for certainty are constantly opposed by demands for social protection, for more consultation and interventions essential for pollution prevention, human health, safety and ecological sustainability. Ultimately the debate about certainty and wealth creation becomes a struggle for the primacy of techno-economic system steering, versus the participation and autonomy of the social solidarities that would take over more of the discourse guiding societal change. Whereas the first would like to make the process of human progress more 'self-regulating' as a 'nature-like' evolution of scientific and economic innovations, the latter would insist upon more discourse and co-operative forms of governance that link the global and local in many more locally mediated ways.

Idealization of economic development as means of poverty eradication

'Development' was an applied use of economic theory for the supposed purpose of eradicating poverty. However, the actual origin and end of this development crusade is debated.

Ever since President Truman announced his four point program in January 1949, poorer countries have been defined as 'underdeveloped' and in need of catching up with the 'free world'. The timing and the strategy of this speech was to counter the communist world revolution that became critical after the take over of Eastern Europe by Soviet puppet governments in 1947. As a counter-communist ideology the promise of 'development' became identified as the path for the third world to participate in the 'free world'.

Culturally the term 'development' immediately had the consequence of transforming all poor people into deficient 'needy' and 'underdeveloped' people.[20] Prospects of 'development' transformed traditional social practices and knowledge into defective lacks. Liberation from subsistence, upgraded technologies, access to consumer lifestyles – all emerge as a set of progress expectations that went beyond present socio-economic arrangements.

Thus begun the age of development. However, decade after decade resulted in failed development goals and led to restatements of development with refined targets.[21] At first, still guided by Keynesian policy, massive development loans were arranged by the World Bank, and regional Development Banks with the aim, in the 1970s, of creating a New International Economic Order (NIEO). But after the switch to neo-liberal monetarism and the Mexican debt crisis of 1982, a new international framework emerged. International Monetary Fund (IMF) loans imposed financial austerity and privatization of public enterprises that enabled global financial managers to create massive debt while selling off infrastructure and resources to global investors for the enhancement of export capacities. But all of this debt had to be paid in dollars, empowering the financial managers to guide policy in ways that blocked national economic strategies. What happened then was a turning of third world economies into *rentier* economies yielding interest and rent to financial interests.[22] The debt crises of the 1980s, and after, were served, and deepened, by the IMF.[23]

William Easterly has commented that no one has really documented the incredible misery that the global debt has bestowed on peoples all over the earth. Easterly's *The Elusive Quest for Growth* reconstructs the numerous flawed theoretical frames that guided the massive investments made by the World Bank and other international investors for decades. In the end he labels it "capitalist fundamentalism" sharing the judgment of Joseph Stiglitz about the reign of free market fundamentalism.[24] Economism was the name of the development game.

The Chicago school of neo-liberal economics had became a template that was imposed in draconian ways that went way beyond normal procedures of the global money lenders. An anti-communist drama was created for ideological and empire-building ends. In Latin America, major 'show' cases forced executions and revolutions of 'free market' societies in Chile and Uruguay (1973), Argentina (1976) Bolivia (1985), which depended upon real or simulated crisis, as Naomi Klein has documented in *The Shock Doctrine: The Rise of Disaster Capitalism*.[25] Hundreds of Latin American graduate students were supported to get PhDs from the University of Chicago in the1960s while the Ford Foundation and USAID picked up the tab. After the staged 'revolutions', the ground was prepared for the design of neo-liberal economies. The basic formula for the reform and re-construction of the economy and society at any cost was essentially the same: the creation of debt and hyper-inflation, forced deregulations, selected privatizations of public wealth, and drastic cutbacks of public services and jobs. A completely unfettered 'free market' was the crown jewel sought. Similar results happened when countries are sucked in by economic hit men to take major development loans.[26] Structural adjustment conditions for loans required that jobs be stripped away, unions broken and government budgets slashed. At every point democracy was discouraged as not being economically wise. Democracy was also limited in order to create the free trade lock, which excluded sectors that could not be helped by national political process. In Latin America the reality of 'economic freedom' was terror, violence, and 'planned misery'.

Mike Davis' eye opening *Planet of Slums* documents the consequences of neoliberal globalization. One-third of the world's population has been marginalized by development dynamics, which were accelerated by the structural adjustment programs of the late 1970s and 1980s.[27] Capital investments in countrysides, coupled with the de-industrialized over-urbanization in the 'cities', further multiplies the invisible poor. A rare facing up to this actuality was the admission that the U.N.'s Millennium Development Goals for Africa, projected to be achieved by 2015, would not be realized for generations.[28] Rescue of those forced to enter into ever widening patterns of 'resettlement' is less and less likely, despite images of the great opportunity for entrepreneurial heroism at the bottom.

Let's get real! There is no way that free markets and free trade in this corrupt development game will create enough wage labor jobs to eliminate the world's 'poor', although it has a proven record in creating more of the super rich. The exploding number of slum dwellers and expanding migrations from degraded agrarian communities fall through the cracks of state and international 'development' strategies and out-of-date accounting systems. Given the 2008 oil price spike, the cost of food makes measuring poverty at so many dollars per day a lost cause. These grim realities do not get recorded because policies focuses on aggregate economic measures and do not develop context-specific ways of accounting for the misery of those beneath the screens.

Remembering Polanyi's hypothesis that the causes of poverty are social, not economic, searching for alternative social learning innovations is implied. Imposing another green revolution is not green enough to help. But thinking about alternative social and ecological arrangements is not part of the investment focus unless it is required by local citizens or political institutions. Starting from the ground up is another way to think about these issues.

Ivan Illich admonished development economists in Sri Lanka in 1979 to recognize the blind spot of development mentality. That is, to see beyond the increasingly visible externalities of development, such as pollution, which economists are learning to measure. Focusing on the invisible 'counter-productivities' of development, for which there are no forms of measurement, is the real alternative.

Counter-productivities are those counter-intuitive 'negative internalities' of modernizing institutions that no longer serve as tools for human autonomy but have become 'radical monopolies' that define human needs and simultaneously atrophy learning competences of captive clients. Such capacity losses in agriculture, medical, or transportation systems are not perceptible to the development mentality because they rely upon a prescriptive understanding of necessary modern institutions that only the formal economy can provide. What are involved are the actual competences of people, in interaction with local institutions and ecology, to deal with their own problems. For example, the capacities of family farms or peasant villages to provide sufficient regional food rather then export cash crops and import food stuffs (see Chapter 7).

Expectations of westernized development impose controls that disvalue local solutions as part of a wider expectation for technical improvement in production processes. Separating of local consumption from production in scarcity-creating ways is the illusion of economic freedom. A simpler life and a simpler economy works if people build it with their own local competences and overcome the forces of colonization that come with economic development.

Illich's assessments of counter-productivities focus attention on the regimentation, dependence, exploitation and impotence that these negative internalities of development enforce. His interest is to enlarge each person's competence, control and initiative in a strategy of convivial reconstruction (see Chapter 4).

Illich proposed that contemporary societies are shaped as the result of ongoing choices along three dimensions:

1 choices of property relations, social hierarchies, resource allocations, etc.;
2 choices between high or soft technologies in spheres such as energy, goods, etc.;
3 a generally unrecognized choice between the extremes of having, as in consumerism, or doing, as in vernacular self-defined and implemented work.

This latter dimension is systematically excluded when economic investment and technical productivity is presumed to be the necessary, and only acceptable path to prosperity. Foreshortening social and political visioning to technical means–goals logics only, results in the evasion of the political discussion about social goals and means.

Illich claims that in addition to 'who gets what' there are two areas of choice that have always been and are now non-expert, or 'lay', issues that can make a huge difference:

- local judgment about appropriate means for production (e.g. traditional agriculture not imposed chemical agriculture);
- and local judgments about the selection of forms of community or regional intermediary structures that foster common sense forms of self-reliance.[29]

For example, the participatory budgeting process in Brazil increases local participation in political decision making in ways that have made a great deal of difference in the poorest neighborhoods of Brazilian cities and beyond. Or community support for agriculture (CSAs) in the U.S. supports many of the remaining small farmers that are now essential in the light of high cost of energy. These options for local food production and financial planning will greatly widen as is discussed in Chapters 7 and 8.

Such public choices are now being facilitated by local governance for substantive use of common environments which also protect local livelihoods and foster public debates about trade-offs between growth and freedom. For example, the communities of western Pennsylvania came together to exclude agribusiness overuse of water and soil resources that would disrupt local small farming.[30]

Local economic policy formations are not viewed as 'productive' for efficiency or aggregate growth by external financial elites. However, many local groups and municipalities are now in situations of growing economic crisis and have to become imaginative and make context-specific choices. These 'alternatives' invert necessities of 'development' and replace consumer goods by personal action, or industrial tools by convivial tools. For example the steep up-hill struggle of traditional and organic agriculture against chemical agribusiness which higher transportation costs have now given a boost.

Idealization of globalizing capitalism as civilizing and 'peace-keeping'

Globalizing military peace-keeping entails endless preparation for war. This logic of power had an affinity with the ever expanding world economy and its allied militarization. A systematic deception of power politics persists in the promise of greater peace with more economic expansion. This has inverted the original cultural meaning of peace of the land into techno-economic justifications for its techno-economic opposite.

In traditional usage the word 'peace' always implied the possibility for each culture to flower in its own incomparable way. In contrast the export of peace by Rome, by Constantine, by Charlemagne and by contemporary 'economic peace' has always been an imposed peace that creates wars as it attempts to force commerce as the leading goal.[31]

In a multi-cultural perspective peace begins with sustaining social communities, but its modern linkage with economic development is a subversion of this basic cultural meaning. On this account the pax economica exalts wealth production while actually destroying popular peace – which is the ability to subsist as part of an inclusive 'we'. Universalizing economic improvements destroys a cultured commons essential for peaceful human habitation.

Bernard Neitzschman calls the 120 ongoing regional wars since World War II a 'third world war' and locates the dynamic in the imposition of development imperatives upon traditional 'nations', trapped in newly formed nation-states.[32] These 'nations' collectively constitute a third of the world's population and are misnamed 'ethnic' groups, in state system terms, but are actually seeking territorial or political autonomy – for example the Kurds, Basques, Flemish, etc. These regional conflicts, derived from economic development planning, require forcing these peoples into the nation-state. These nations are invisible because they are not on the maps and get stigmatized as terrorists, communists, bandits for trying to assert their identities. Conflicts derive usually from externally imposed structural violence and the predominance of a war mentality internal to developing countries. An example is the suppression of the Sunnis after the American victory in Iraq.

The neo-liberal economic growth strategy has step by step become a war system that now sends signals of preemptive armed violence as the method to avoid war. War preparations and politics become one: fear becomes the new social glue and the passage of Patriot Act I and II expresses the 'necessity' of national secrecy policies. The metaphor of 'war' is increasingly used to image the necessity to mobilize all social forces and suspend and limit normal political discourse: the cold war, war on drugs, and now the 'war on terrorism'.

Neo-liberal regimes expand the security state, as well as the militarization of police system, to maintain 'law and order'. Artificial stimulations of a security-oriented daily life, such as the terror warning systems, were used as constant (fear) reminders of the necessity for national security rationalizations. The war system sees itself as a permanent state of affairs that requires manipulations of nationalism and patriotism. Peace-keeping as a culture of violence transforms our view of the human condition – war is the actual human condition.

An era that forces economic globalization of humanity has no clear vision of how to sustain peace beyond the endless preparation for war. The U.S. in the context of war on terrorism, presents itself as representing all of humanity and must act beyond international law which necessitates torture and rendition. War is now the regulative order and no longer subordinated to international law. War becomes regulative of post-national configurations; it imposes its own frames and creates its own laws and jurisdictions on all human experience. It makes the world safe for economism and rules out any other social ordering.

Naomi Klein connects shock therapy, as used in forced regressions in mentally ill patients, as applied to the 'science' of torture techniques. Described as the science of fear, this analogy is used to indicate how neo-liberalism wanted to shock societies back into a clear slate so that they could be started again as pure free market and free trade economies. In both cases violence is justified by 'scientific' certitudes.

Klein's gruesome accounts document the incredible callousness and collusions with violence that accompanied the impositions of free market systems around the world, it was the certitudes that accompanied these 'scientific' interventions that is astounding – to quote Frank Knight, one of the founders of the Chicago school of economics, who claimed that each economic theory is "a sacred feature of the system not a debatable hypothesis".[33]

Professional economics is supposedly as hard a science as physics and chemistry and the free market is a perfect scientific system. However, application of this 'science' to human society in Chile, Brazil, Argentina, Indonesia, Poland, Russia, South Africa and others, is a story of unbelievable brutality in the interest of 'free market' capitalism. The certitudes of the belief system behind such market fundamentalism suggest it is actually a quasi-religious system whether held by neo-conservatives or libertarians. Willingness to force this cognitive system upon people in the name of 'science' fails to justify its violence.

Emmanuel Levinas, sometimes called France's most famous philosopher, reflects on the contradictions of western cognitive totalities and actual human experience:

> Violence does not consist so much in injuring and annihilating persons as in interrupting their continuity, making them play roles in which they no longer recognize themselves, making them betray not only commitments but their own substance, making them carry out actions that will destroy every possibility of action. Not only modern war but every war employs arms that turn against those who yield them. It establishes an order from which no one can

> keep their distance; nothing henceforth is exterior. War . . . destroys the identity of the same.[34]

The idealizations of free markets and free trade are ideologies that present themselves as essential for prosperity and peace. But as totalized concepts of human prospects, each moment is scarified to economic futures that will supposedly bring forth prosperity for all. All life becomes centered by economism. This economistic idealization of capitalism has become a secular vocation, or quasi-religion, that releases violence.

Violence is like an infection – it is contagious. The more injustice occurs the more revenge and discord releases a cycle of reciprocal violence. In modernity confidence that the enforced rule of law has broken the cycle of revenge and reciprocal blood feud, and has been replaced by juridical processes, seems today too optimistic. It seems that the structurally induced violence of economic development has returned as terrorism and the get tough 'Rambo mentality' haunting American popular culture. The inability of the U.S. to combat drug violence, which is related to the boomerang of the world debt, was only the beginning. Now the privatization of security such as the Blackwater private security corporation, and a police system that is highly militarized, together with the continual expansion of prison capacity in the U.S., all point toward a contagion phase of the cycle of violence. With the reactive 'war on terrorism', and the grotesque acts of torture and rendition to expose 'terrorism', the cycle of violence has begun.

Personal choices are reduced to identifying with the aggressor and getting 'tough', or being psychically numbed into withdrawals; or exiting through an 'inner migration', as the Germans trying to escape from Hitler's terror put it. Alternatively Norman Geras, who tried to understand why Germans did not want to see the Jews being marched to cattle cars, arrived at the notion of a 'contract of mutual indifference' in order to continue everyday life.[35] Do these explanations account for why the masses of Americans are passive about these realities?

By presuming that custom is replaced by law, and substantive practices by formal economics, the passion for theoretical knowledge blinds those dependent upon theory to the ongoing relevance of customary commons and the regenerative possibilities of reconciling solidarities through spiritual compassion.

Under the light of totalizing reason harmony and peace are imaged as incompatible with remembrance of the tragic disorder and events of violence. Thus Plato turns out the poets from his utopia in the hope that excluding the representations of tragic violence would also eliminate the appeals of violence, and in so doing has created a model for the rule of law which has many repressive consequences.[36]

As Levinas suggests, "the peace of empires issued from war rests on war". A more fundamental relation to 'the other' is essential, not just the promise of peace through economic globalization.

Part II

Critical traditionalist cultural visions

4 Illich's genealogy of modern certitudes

Who was Ivan Illich?

An account of the life and thinking of Ivan Illich is offered here as a prime example of how other insights into human origins and ends can model living a sustainable and healthy life on earth. While Illich has always perplexed modern persons, his insights into the institutional and cultural origins of western civilization are unique.

Recognized in his early Church work as a radical priest who opposed the imperialism of American missionary efforts in Latin America, Ivan Illich has always perturbed conventional thinkers. His counter-intuitive positions were riddles to theory-oriented rationalists. Every one of his genealogies of modern certainties are an 'in your face' critique of what is taken for granted as modern institutional certitudes, e.g. schooling, development, energy, etc. Yet each 'critique', is actually a 'genealogy', as I will explicate further, and departs from a remembrance of concrete past practices corrupted by modern systems.

Anyone who reads Illich's *Deschooling Society*, *Tools for Conviviality*, *Gender*, etc. is not fully informed by the texts themselves about Illich's intentions. He wrote, not affirmatively about God, but to indicate how the social relations described in these books were not consistent with an ecclesiological ideal community. All his books from 1971 till 2002 were written to enable people to understand the pathologies of modernity so that they might acquire the inner dispositions to live more in conscious relations within community and have a decent life on this earth.

Until his last posthumous book, *Rivers North of the Future*, only those close to Illich understood that all of Illich's writing after 1971, when he stopped functioning publicly as a Catholic priest, till this last book, were exercises in Apophatic negative theology.[1] Even though I was a sometime member of what he called the 'invisible college' I did not know this – he never talked about theology.

Domenico Farias, a long time friend of Illich, asserts that Illich went beyond Apophatic theology and actually aspired to an Apophatic anthropology too. While masking his continued vocation, Illich was also radically open to other traditional practices. Apophatic anthropology is the rigor of not talking about God, but actually loving as Christ enfleshed has done. It is the practice, not the theology, that matters.

Ivan Illich's regenerative methodologies

Illich's early theological interest was ecclesiology, or the study of the mystery of faith and the mystical body of Christ. In secular terms, what the Church conceived as the ideal community. His genealogies use early Christian ecclesiology as an actual evolving historical practice to show how choices made by the later Roman Church and modernity lose these practices. As Illich notes ecclesiology is twenty times older than modern social science, and as a critical hermeneutics may have more depth.

Results of his genealogy were an understanding of how the Church's gradual substitution of power for faithful free choice resulted in more and more comprehensive regulations for Christian life. Each of these attempts to further stabilize and institutionalize grace, over time became perversions that led to loss of the freedom that Christ brought into the world. Specific losses include the criminalization of sin, the perversion of hospitality into service, the rise of value orientations that undermines contextual judgments of the Good, and the creation of the needy and isolated modern individual. The western Roman Church distorted its relation to local vernacular domains[2] when it took over educational functions that empowered professionals to dominate the cure of souls and standardize pastoral services that had hitherto been worked out locally. The church's pastoral care model weakened the autonomy of self-limiting vernacular domains. These genealogies are examined further below.

Illich's 'regenerative methodology' is also stated as continuous with classical methods going back to Ancient Greece. But tantalizingly he also implies that the wisdom of the Eastern Orthodox Church retains many elements held by the pre-scholastic western Church and then lost by western perversions.

Illich, at some places, presents his historical researches as an Ancient Greek Epimethean quest for prophetic reappropriations of the past. The term 'Epimetheus' in classical Greek meant 'hindsight', and Illich seeks to uncover the truth of the past in his historical reconstructions in order to respond to the present. One could also read his radical doubt of the certainties that are central to modernizing institutions – such as schooling, 'resources', 'development', 'need', 'life', 'communication' from this 'Epimethean' perspective.

His interest was to deflate these conceptual certitudes in order to liberate the imagination and open the reader to surprise and new discoveries in everyday life. But also to illustrate how it has been done and can be done in vernacular realms of ordinary community behavior. Simultaneously it is to recover the spontaneity and unpredictability of human existence and form a resistance to the technical terms that would distort this quality of living.

This method might be seen as a traditionalist parallel to the Hegelian–Marxist 'immanent critique', or the critical analysis of the existing social relations in terms of their intrinsic norms. However, the institutional certitudes that Illich deconstructs are not just pseudo-necessities of false ideological consciousness that yield new action potentials; exposed are the technical abstractions that empower experts who have come to be masters of specific social technologies and spheres of human interaction. Illich's interest is not to dissolve false causality but to show how they shrink the competences and learning capabilities of passive bodies or consumers. It is not the deeper understanding of the objective situation which is the point, but rather releasing the motivations of persons to use their imagination and insight to find solutions. Ultimately it is the trust in human resourcefulness, hope, and creativity of nature that guides Illich's 'critiques' not reflections on class war or psychic struggle. It is insight, not reflective knowledge.

Thus Illich's critical methodology differs from modern social science efforts to keep social order in step with progress, as in positivism, or critique the socially unnecessary forms of domination with an emancipatory intention, as in critical theory. His intention is to be regenerative in the interests of recovery of greater capacity for practical judgments of the good and right proportion in common sense living in convivial worlds. Or to participate in Christian Freedom in the sense expanded below.

But one has to venture behind the epistemological breaks that emerged from the thirteenth to the seventeenth century in the West to understand that Illich's seemingly secular frames of critique also derives from an intent to recover the sacred in everyday life. However, he does not profess theological frames nor idealizes religious traditions. Instead he focuses on the historical turns that distort the self-regulation of convivial communities – or Christian Freedom.

He shows, he does not say.

Ecclesiology as critical regeneration theory

Illich shares the research interest of Gerhard Ladner in giving a historical account of what Christ brought into the world. Ladner, in *The Idea of Reform*,[3] documents that man's reformation toward his original image-likeness to God was of central importance to early Christianity. In the first six centuries after Christ the idea of 'reform' was a guide for monastic practices where transformation of self in penitential rituals was an expression of inner 'reform'.

The possibility of reform was seen as part of the original liberty of man and his liberation from external domination. Christian freedom stands above legal necessity as a precondition for striving towards liberation from social and moral pressures.

The Good Samaritan answers the question, 'Who is my neighbor?' by expanding the boundaries of community as his freely made loving choice. The parable is not about an obligatory 'ought', which would be a legalization of conscience; it's meaning is free choice of inclusion. Ultimately the choice expresses the spiritual telos of humanity; it is not a normative imperative as in Kantian ethics.

Illich's works presuppose this radical notion of Christian reform as a departure point in seeking to help people find a way back to the renunciations that are essential to rise above the pathologies of modernity. To represent the contemporary meaning of the idea of reform, one must describe what is necessary to step outside of the existing world and have confidence in forgiveness, mercy and love. Ultimately this comes down to living with the least contamination of flesh, eyes and language.

What it takes to renew the Church and community today, in an age of systems, is the capacity to renounce the illusions of power and recognize the gift of Christ and gift of 'radical contingency' (discussed below). Jesus brought a new idea of friendship into the world, one that differs from civic culture in the classical sense. Illich's gambit, since faith in God has been obscured, is the hope for a new society is spread by the vocation of friendship. We are led to discover God in each other; the coldness of turning away was revealed by Christ as sin, as betrayal of love.

Ivan Illich often called himself a historian but in actuality he reads history as a traditionalist in special ways. Accurately viewed as a negative, Apophatic, theologian-philosopher he researches history in order to critique existing social orders by showing that 'this is not it'; i.e. a fulfillment of the Christian escathon in this world. His early theological focus was upon ecclesiology, or the study of what the Church has conceived as the ideal community since the fourth century.

The application of ecclesiological thinking involves critical reflections into the mission and internal liturgical rituals and practice of the Church and how it is situated within the surrounding community. These reflections resulted in monastic movements as indicted by periodic reforms – such as the Benedictine reform, the Alcuin reform, the Clunic reform and finally the Gregorian reform, which Illich sees as the watershed that finally spawned modernity.

As Gerhard Ladner has shown, the idea of 'reform' that emerged from the history of Christian monasticism begins with the meaning of transformation of self in crucial penitential rituals – as public expressions of inner 'reform'. In the Gregorian reform the Roman Church finally takes over this penitential territory from the communities and monasteries and empowers the priest to officiate in the confessional – breaking with the Eastern Church who refused to benefit from the new theological mapping of purgatory and its escape options.

Origins of modernity in perversions of Roman Church 'reforms'

Illich shows how the western Roman Church distorted its relation to vernacular domains when it began to take over educational functions that empowered its spiritual 'professionals' to dominate the cure of souls and the pastoral services, which were heretofore defined within the vernacular world itself. The church's pastoral care model weakened the autonomy of self-limiting vernacular domains – especially that of vernacular gender.

This genealogy is further developed in an essay on 'The War against Subsistence' where Illich shows that the fundamental ideologies of the industrial age are derived from the monastic reforms from the ninth to the thirteenth century, where the personal pastoral services of the professional priests were more and more asserted to be essential for salvation. He says:

> The idea that there is not salvation without personal service provided by professionals in the name of an institutional mother church is one of the formally unnoticed developments without which, again, our own age would be unthinkable. True, it took 500 years of medieval theology to elaborate on this concept.

> Only by the end of the Middle Ages would the pastoral self-image of the church be fully rounded. And only in the Council of Trent (1545) would this self-image of the Church milked by clerical hierarchies become formally defined. Then in the Constitution of the second Vatican Council (1964) the Catholic Church, which had served in the past as the prime model for the evolution of secular service organizations, aligns itself explicitly in the image of its secular imitations.[4]

In addition to the discovery of Roman Church professional monopoly over the new spiritual territory of 'purgatory', the emergence of the image of the Church as a 'Mother' who has responsibility over the *eductio prolis* – the upbringing of Christians is the key perversion. The Catholic priest, now a curate, was upgraded from a celebration of sacramental liturgical blessings to the administration of the sacraments which had expanded in the eleventh century. So too did the services performed and technical instruments used by the Church expand. Along with professionalization of the priesthood new technological innovations, such as the organ and the Church clock, increased the religious institutions' dominance over the vernacular domain. Again, these were resisted by the Eastern Church.

Other technifications of the cure of the now genderless Catholic soul by the curate included new manuals and language for the confessional. Compulsory confessional, once a year presided over by a male professional using written rules for the cure of souls and the creation of a schooled conscience, overshadowed the gender-specific vernacular practices that had balanced the vernacular domain in the early Church communities. All these professionalizations prepared the 'universal' Catholic soul for the rule of written law and universal education. All of these regulations reduced Christian Freedom and its practice. These are also the conditions essential for modern state formation and they change the reciprocity of monastic practices and surrounding communities in ways which excluded vernacular traditions and wisdom about learning that they contained.

In the past, inclusion of regional vernacular traditions into monastic practices was on the basis of how monastic and church-centered villages influenced mutually stabilizing influences upon the aristocratic warrior cultures and slave-owning empires. But that changed as the Church consolidated its power and simultaneously the power of the state.

From Mother Church to Mother State

The Papal Revolution of 1075 created a professionalization that separated the regular priests from the secular clergy who were organic to the communities and not connected to the emergent corporate entity of the professional priesthood. This professionalization, emergent from the Clunic reform, turned the 'spiritual ones' (in opposition to the laity) into the first translocal, transfeudal, transnational class in Europe to achieve political and legal unity. One could say that this was the first international corporation.

The Papal Revolution rapidly sponsored the first Crusade (1096–1099), the second (1147) and the third (1189). These increased the power and authority of the papacy, but also turned the Mediterranean Sea into a route for Western expansion. This correlates with the explosion of the resettlements of towns and cities, massive immigrations to new parts of Europe and commercial trade expansions. The first universities emerged that subjected theology, jurisprudence and philosophy to systematization, and Latin now constituted the scholarly language.

The Church in disembedding itself from vernacular society, formed a new system of law to execute its hierarchical administrative functions and showed the way to the creation of new social institutions. Most significant was a disembedding of law from the customs of communities that legitimated strong central authorities – both sacred and secular. The Church's new organizing principles differed from those of previous centuries. It established arrangements that are being repeated in many places around the world today – as traditional communities are pulled into modernizing and globalizing dynamics.

As the Roman Church becomes a centralized 'Mother Church', in the Middle Ages it represented itself as an all-caring authoritarian teacher and sovereign order. The internal debate about the dual authority, Pope or King, raged throughout medieval Christendom, swinging from those who justified papal supremacy, e.g. Gregory the VII, Becket, John of Salisbury, to state supremacy, e.g. Dante, William of Ockham, Thomas Aquinas. Illich claimed that the actual institutionalization of the modern state was modeled on the Papal State.

A historian of law, Morris Berman also interprets the Papal Revolution of 1075–1122 as establishing the first legal state – which thereafter became the model for state formation throughout Europe. This revolution had many complex consequences – to state just a few of them that are assumed in Illich's analysis:

> 'Freedom of the Church' became a cry that meant not only wresting power from the kings to appoint bishops but also freedom from the laity too – it represents a disembedding of the Church from other institutional orders that had mercantile consequences and broke the Benedictine monopoly over religious life . . . the collective clergy became a unified corporation for the first time – the first model of a transnational corporation; . . . the codification of Church Canon law, essential to justify the papal revolution, was systematized in ways that could be integrated with secular laws.[5]

The revolutionary character of this 'reform' gave out a new sense of the possibility of effecting change in this world and this new found glory was embodied in Gothic Cathedrals with soaring spires and vaulted arches. This revolution also represented the irreversible separation between the Western and Eastern Church as well as contributing to the formation of modern individualism, discussed ahead.

Cultural colonization of vernacular speech

A significant case of utilizing the new state power was Queen Isabelle of Spain who tried to create an administrative state, by calling in the Office of the Inquisition to get rid of useless nobles and replace them with lawyers and technicians. She was confronted with two enormous projects in the same year of 1492: Columbus's quest for Cathay and Nebrija's proposal for the "marriage of empire and language".[6] She wanted to govern, not simply rule in the traditional sense, with the usual tolerance for vernacular diversity in Spain.

Consequently Spain became the first European state to develop a formal grammar – or a taught mother tongue. With Nebrija's new systematization of Castilian Spanish all verbal expressions of Spaniards would have the stamp of the state in their linguistic practice. This new precise Spanish required formal teaching of the mother tongue. A new form of state control over the wild untaught vernacular diversity was beginning. Moving from artificial Castilian to Latin would then be an easier step. In retrospect it may be that Nebrija's project provided more unity to the state than new world wealth; the printing press and bureaucratic control were reigned in and the wild expression of many vernacular hybrids and multilingual styles put in their place.

What Illich is documenting is the formalizing of language as a commons that turns it into a "need that cannot be met by vernacular life". Dependence on formal teaching of the mother tongue is the paradigm for all other dependencies created in an age of commodity-defined existence. The general framework implied here is that every attempt to substitute a universal commodity for a vernacular activity "has led, not to equality, but to a hierarchical modernization of poverty".[7]

What Marx was struggling to understand in his reflection on the fetishism of commodities is given a more general and deeper cultural interpretation here. Step by step the war against subsistence has defined as commodities what was essential for living communities, and in each case has resulted in new hierarchies and new forms of domination.

Perversions of the contingency axiom that 'reformed' the Church

Illich's last book *Rivers North of the Future* begins with reflections on the crucial Christian notion of 'contingency' which expresses the ontic state of a world, which has been created from nothing, is destined to disappear, and is upheld in its experience through divine will. This point involves the theological philosophical debates that led to modern instrumental reason – I have put a very brief account of this debate into appendix 1.

The final point of this analysis is that contingency did not have to devolve to where nature's laws became independent of God's will and nature lose its living qualities. Consequent theological elaborations of the axiom of contingency led to imagining a set of 'intermediaries' viewed necessary for heavenly movements (e.g. angels) as well as operational instrumentalities deemed necessary for reforming Church practices. In the context of an emergent, denied and yet latent dualism, the radical contingency meaning of these 'intermediaries' faded from memory and they became a sub-category of Aristotle's *causa efficiens* and then effectively, tools for human self-assertion. A human regime of will and human self-assertion replaces a cosmos of gratuity, or gift.

Illich notes that 'intermediaries' present in the cosmological writings of Aquinas were screened out in translations by contemporary theologians who knew these notions would not be acceptable to a scientific ethos.[8] When macro-micro intermediaries became viewed as instruments, it put the world into human hands and led to replacing the spirit of contingency with a spirit of tools and technology. This opened the age of technology which Illich claims lasted for 700 years until the age of systems emerged about 1980.

Intermediaries, as reforms of Church administration, changed the social and spiritual relations of Church and community in multifold ways. For Illich these instrumental reforms were consolidations of the Church powers in this world and erased felt senses of appropriateness unique to localities, replacing them with universal rules for the faithful. Blessings were expanded to seven sacraments that only certified churchmen could use as divine instruments. Legal oath taking, forbidden by the New Testament (Matthew 5), became legal foundations for all levels of a feudal hierarchy – family, city and macro political orders. For Illich these reforms brought the legal mentality back into the heart of love, and sin, as a turning away from the Holy Spirit, was turned into a regulated legal crime. What for the Good Samaritan was a gut-driven act of love is turned into an obligatory norm of conscience, losing the quality of Christian freedom.

New fears and new psycho-spiritual pathologies

Illich relates these perversions of the reformed Church order to new pathologies of sensibility and psyche of the 'organized' faithful. Fears created by the newly defined inner forum of conscience, subject to juridical review by self, priest and state, carves out a more vulnerable and internally fearful form of selfhood.

A Christian responds, in the light of the incarnation, to a face, a person or an icon, that brings with it a sense of awe about seeing the infinitely good. But after a formalized criminalization of sin, a confusion arises in non-public, privatized forgiveness, we enter into a new psychic topography. The inner forum, the new sphere of conscience, and individuated responsibility to a confessional priest as magistrate, opens up a non-communal inward experience of fear, dread, aloneness, abandonment and despair. Rather than being supported in an ethos where the 'I' is always surrounded and supported by the 'we', the believer now is more fearful of temptation by hidden cosmic powers. Fear of demons, witches and magic are the results of new experiences in institutions that would regulate grace.

While fear of losing the bond with God or being excluded from loving is a reality of human life, the fear that is released after the criminalization of sin is compatible with the rise of the docile believer who is manipulated by the new juridical order and 'fatherland' and therefore easy to mobilize for crusades, both then and now. As Charles Taylor remarks in the foreword to *Rivers North of the Future* the new polite civilized order is 'the Christian order'. The 'polite', 'civilized' moral orders of Protestant England, Holland, and later the American colonies, lost much of their 'transcendental' content in being domesticated to accept state legitimacy.

Transformations of Church liturgical procedures were central to changing relations between the Church and local communities. Some of these changes created conditions leading to the Church's domination of vernacular life and the emergence of a spiritual, legal, political and economic individual.

Illich interprets the socio-genesis of western individualism as beginning in transformations of perception and disembodiment of our senses in the practice of liturgical reading. Reading sacred texts was originally a speaking event where the reader pronounces the undivided line aloud in order to recreate a pilgrimage through the text. Reading was an oral activity in which the page is a vineyard, where the reader tastes the words that are plucked from the page.[9] The pilgrimage of reading leads toward the light and to contemplation and prayer.

Early in the twelfth century, the lines became divided and sub-headings appeared, as well as an indexed and numbered sequence of paragraphs and subparagraphs. These seemingly minor transformations in mental space ordering actually changed the cultural uses of memory and the practices of relating the eye to the ear, seeing to hearing. What was once a public hearing by voice and action became transformed into a 'writ', an external object outside of sensual experience.

The communitarian public-ness of vowing in marriage, or positioning in land, became a hard copy writ with huge impacts upon lay literacy. The relations of perception and imagination were altered and created a superficial confusion of 'appearing signs' (writs) with reality. This confusion of virtual mappings has continued to expand and we now see charts, graphs and statistical probabilities as actualities. For Illich the productive role of imagination is to form metaphoric images of the invisible and not get misled by taking abstractive theoretical frames as 'real'. We lose the ability to read the 'flesh of the world' and instead orient our attention to virtualities.[10]

Certifications of individual 'identity' became a new social expectation that overwhelmed local customary practices. These new symbolizations of the 'individual' provided a new metaphor of the inner conscience-as-text that could be read by authoritative priests, inquisitors and of course God and the devil. Institutionalization of these expectations into juridical processes empowered the monopolies of the Papal Church, and the emerging City and nation-states, in ways that made the local associations incapable of providing what the new individual needed. The new 'needy individual' empowered these radical monopolies against communal-vernacular associations and fostered perceptions of scarcities that communities cannot provide. The implications of this transformation are multifold.

Formalized credentialized frames became essential for individual orientations to wider political and economic exchanges, local reciprocities were no longer enough. The institutionalizations of 'identity' expectations were the origins of the colonization of local cultures and became preconditions for what Marx later called 'the fetishism of commodities'. From this perspective on colonization we can appreciate why Illich sees the last 500 years as a 'war against subsistence' and presents a research program focused on what he called 'the history of scarcity'.[11] Comprehending the origins of scarcity becomes the counter research program to the Marxist critique of capitalist exploitation.

Disembodiments of modern sensibility

Secularization produces extraordinary disembodiments which lose the phenomenological density that the felt body acquired after Christ. The mystery of the incarnation, of God becoming flesh and man becoming divinized, meant that Christian hope was oriented not only to hearing the gospel but also to the vision of God's face. The gaze of the believer is a homesickness for the beyond, for the grace of the face of God. This results in seeking the face of God in the face of everyone, developing an inner sense that is a source of felt body experience in this world.[12] Faith, for Illich, is rooted in the flesh of the body; our tendency to accept modern abstract virtualities as reality loses touch with this sensuous felt body and its intuitive sensing of the sacred.

For Illich modern sensibility has been profoundly disembodied; the gaze is no longer a willed action subject to our moral decisions. The early Church's images in frescoes and icons were linkages of the visible and invisible; gateways and thresholds to what is in heaven. The inner eye sees the inner image. In later scholasticism the visual cone was inverted with the object radiating an image of itself that is secularized. Seeing is now a passive reception and digestion of images from outside; our eyes are now cameras that receive information. Illich reminds us that many ascetic traditions talk about the guarding and training of the eye, since appropriate seeing is a virtue.

Secularization means that the poetic, performative qualities of the world are erased and forgotten in field after field; a world of fitting proportion and appropriateness is replaced by a mechanical world where integrations of common sense are replaced by value assessments of risks and cost-benefits. While local festival and pageantry continue everywhere the integration of these into a self-understanding of the modern individual is not easy to do. Lost is the aesthetics of liturgy – of bringing beauty, music and dramatized experience of the Holy Spirit together in ritual service.

The unique practical interest of Illich's spiritually grounded method can be shown by contrasting it to Catherine Pickstock's supposed 'Liturgical Critique of Modernity'. Pickstock presents an account of Catholic Liturgy that argues that only within this practice is the ethical and the aesthetic, the private and the public, held together, and human life participates in a meaningful cosmos. Only in the ensemble of music, architecture, and liturgical performance does beauty and transcendence come to create an event of participation in the sacred. She argues that modernity, having broken with liturgical traditions, is only able to construct pseudo-liturgies such as the art-as-life opposition to universalizing commodifications. In this sense she claims that only traditional communities governed by liturgical patterns are likely to be the sources of resistance to capitalism or bureaucratic norms. Specifically she holds that the Catholic hierarchy is a needed expertise to enable these linkages and provide the events that release this insight.

Whereas this reflection is a significant critical traditionalist effort she has not presented a concrete remembrance of the operations and practices of the Church itself and how it relates to this 'transcendence'. So it has no immanent critique of the evolution of the Church or any implications for wider concrete models for socio-economic practice here or around the world.

So too does Illich's celebration of liturgical drama depart from an image of the liturgy of the Church as a womb out of which the mystical community comes into the present. But his reflections on the history of the Church imply that this has been done in a controlling and this-worldly consolidation of power way. When the Church overextended hospitality into corporate service or overstabilized the parish in ways which controlled neighborliness the practices of the Church were not life-affirming. But it is ultimately the change of the nature of promise or bondedness from an early *conspiratio* to legalized oath-taking that turns freedom into law-breaking. These insights focus on the failure of the Church to realize its community ideals in ways that suggest how to reorient Church and community.[13]

For Illich modern evils are best discerned through the eyes of faith because modernity has been 'dis-eviled' by secularizations which override the felt body's sensibility and substitutes abstractions that sacrifice the present to virtual futures – such as 'progress', 'development', 'globalization', etc. Illich sees these future-oriented categories as 'man-eating idols'.

The contaminations of techno-globalization are the increasing power of multimedia and visual imaging that substitute virtual experience for actualities. Most persons today get their signs, symbols and images as consumers of a growing industry of commercial and ideological image producers. Contemporary human 'consumer sensibility' is deepening participation in virtually created 'worlds'.

These image fabrications have specific interests guiding their construction and do not express living and felt social 'worlds'. Image-information services are disproportionately consumed and controlled by the powerful corporations or states and constitute ever new versions of social control, manipulation, and propaganda consumption.

But the logics of the new disinformation systems have evolved in sinister ways:

> In pronouncements by the military in the U.S. and United Kingdom, 'full spectrum information dominance' begins with 'weaponizing of information.' The goal is to put a positive spin on all information in order to degrade any dissent. The 314-page U.S. Army manual on information was issued November, 2003. It begins with the premise that 'information is an element of combat power' which goes beyond propaganda construction and distribution. What is now relevant is 'mastery of the situation' and the goal is to 'have our way and nothing done can make any difference'. What is not seen by the public is development of a systemic capacity to deny, degrade and destroy unfriendly information. This is a partial answer to why President George W. Bush (and corporate interests) continues to deny everything that might cast official policies in a bad light. The concern is not for truth, the concern is that nothing stop the execution of their policies.[14]

Our world is involved in a crisis of truth – exacerbated by the nexus of corporate PR and disinformation; for example, Exon's denial of global warming, the propaganda state, the weaponization of information, etc.

Current economic ideologies – such as 'economic freedom' – are constructed via these virtual techniques and presented by the reigning powers as social 'necessities'. Only in this way is it possible to explain how deeply flawed projects – such as neo-liberal economic development, or the Iraq war, can be sustained against the tide of negative information and experience that constantly feeds back from these inhuman actualities. Only in this way is it possible to understand why the majority of watchers of Fox News continue to believe that Iraq conspired with the 9/11 conspirators. A recent book by Ron Suskind *The Way Of The World: A Story of Truth and Hope in an Age of Extremism* brings this crisis home to the U.S. White House too.

Creating vernacular free spaces

Illich claims that

> today in addition to 'who gets what' two areas of choice have always been and are now become non-expert, or 'lay', issues: the legitimacy of local judgment about the appropriate means for production (e.g. traditional agriculture not imposed chemical agriculture) and the selection of forms of community or regional intermediary structures that foster common sense forms of self-reliance.[15]

For example, the participatory budgeting process in Brazil increases local participation in political decision making in ways that have made a great deal of difference in the poorest neighborhoods of Brazilian cities. Or community support for Agriculture in the U.S. can support the remaining small farmers before all choice for local food production disappears.

Those are public choices oriented to subsistence use of common environments that would protect local livelihoods and foster public debates about trade-offs between growth and freedom. For example, the communities of western Pennsylvania came together to exclude agribusiness overuse of water and soil resources that would disrupt local small farming.

Such choices have been exercised in various political ways since time immemorial. But since 'development' has become the means–end logic of national economic 'planning' local resistances are usually viewed as quaint and not 'productive' for the national aggregate of growth or efficiency. Unless local groups and municipalities get very imaginative about getting their interests protected. Because such choices are always context specific and take a variety of forms that cannot be generalized they are rejected by experts as not productive. Alternatives mean local varieties of the inversion of 'development' in that they would replace consumer goods by personal action, or industrial tools by convivial tools.

This does not mean a return to the past; as Illich says: "I do not oppose growth oriented societies to others in which traditional subsistence is structured by immemorial cultural transmissions of patterns. Such a choice does not exist. Aspirations of this kind would be sentimental and destructive."[16]

No bipolar oppositions are implied, the point is to attempt to secure political or participatory space for forms of governance that enable exceptions to national-international forced development or ideally maximize this option in today's complex national-international systems.

Gandhi, Schumacher, Shuman, Sachs, etc. will be shown ahead to assert that greater options for communities result from promoting self-defined work and creating local community institutions for local economies – in opposition to the totalities of the left and right ideology. In the context of the recognition of globalization as colonization there may be an emerging common ground for some left and right agreements about small scale local self-regulating autonomy. On the other hand critics from both right and left charge that such vernacular arrangements have co-existed with slavery, serfdom and other forms of enforced dependence. But vernacular free spaces are only where it is possible for workers to be owners of their tools and resources in interaction with agreements about the use of the local commons. That would mean today the achievement of arrangements for sustainable communities – a project that many corporations would like to help with in the form of partnerships that guarantee them profits; to continue when it is no longer profitable is the test of 'partnership'.

Behind these reflections is a unique perspective and methodology for recovering what is being lost in modernity, and painfully being recovered every day by groups struggling all over the world. The following is an attempt to understand this methodology – this begins with the central notion of the 'vernacular domain'.

The vernacular domain is the sensibility and rootedness that emerges from shaping one's own space within the commons associations of local-regional reciprocity. It is the way in which local life has been conducted throughout most of history and even today in a significant proportion of subsistence- and communitarian-oriented communities. It is also central to those places and spaces where people are struggling to achieve regeneration and social restorations against the forces of economic globalization. A vernacular way of being, doing and making is historically illustrated by subsistence villages, classical cities as well as self-governing municipalities and city regions during most of history.

Convivial living as post-industrial society practice

In *Tools for Conviviality* Illich extends the anti-development vision that stresses community and subsistence logic into formulations that can be applied to all in post-industrial service societies. These principles are aimed at orienting people to enlarge the range of each person's competence, control and initiative in commodity-intensive consumer societies. Aware persons practicing these principles would be able to select modern technologies that serve politically related individuals rather than hierarchical managers from state or corporations. Illich's vision is that where tools are responsibly limited, a quality of playful gracefulness permeates personal and communal relations – as against the competitive or feigned solidarity of modern capitalist or socialist societies.

Use of collections of social organizations as a form for restoring communities is what Polanyi calls regenerative social restoration and Illich calls convivial reconstructions. In a world dominated by the quasi-religion of economic freedom this perspective should be taken seriously – especially by those who are advocates of sustainability and who have not yet accepted the market as the real decider.

Illich focuses on the scale and structure of 'tools' – which can be machines, institutions, techniques – and presents criteria to guide research into the dis-economies of destructive logics of over determined engineering of the human and natural world. Where tools expand beyond limits they become radical monopolies that transform the free use of natural abilities into dependencies or robot-like repetitions of other defined work.

The following are negative design criteria to guide the sustaining of a multidimensional balance of human relations to tools and to the environment:

> *Over-growth versus biological balance*
>
> Where there is a presumption that humans can be fit into a world conceived as a technological whole, the earth's ecologies become unlivable and the natural scales and energies essential to maintain social reciprocities are disturbed. Illich put this forward in 1973, long before ecological economics said it systematically.
>
> *Over-industrialization versus convivial work*
>
> Dominance of industrial process can make people prisoners of welfare and enforced compulsory consumption – this does not promote a balance between what people can do for themselves and what anonymous institutions can do for them.
>
> *Over-programming for the industrial environment versus sustaining the power of creative imagination to create meaning*
>
> Tools that become too specialized and centralized exclude convivial learning that is derived from the primary involvement of people and balancing the knowledge mix so that independent learning is possible. Mass production models have, since Adam Smith's 'pin factory', stressed productivity rather than innovative creativity. In recent decades flexible specialization has emerged to form an alternative to industrial specializations.
>
> *Economic productivity versus the right to political participation*
>
> Centralization of power and idealization of growth creates imbalances that render people helpless to choose the option of greater happiness at lower levels of affluence. Fevered development strategies emerge to protect local jobs while simultaneously blocking open discourse about alternatives that would create work opportunities from differing production arrangements; for example, Michael Shuman's assertion of the returned relevance of import substitutions – discussed in Chapter 8.

Enforced obsolescence versus the rights to tradition

People lose shared places and memories and established judgments on precedents when unlimited rates of change are forced adjustments. This devalues shared normative pasts that are essential to establish cultural limits in place.

Each of these points defines essential balances to be preserved if people are to cooperatively act to create and protect convivial living. This does not mean abolition of industrial or service productions but a reduction of compulsive learning and a protection for individuals and communities to choose their own styles of life through smaller scale renewals. Otherwise radical monopolies emerge that force the 'materialization of values' by means becoming coercive ends. Therefore they release blind envy as augmentations of self-interested economic 'progress'.

The unique milieu essential to sustain self-defined work, liberty and autonomy in tools and self-governance, presupposes what German phenomenology calls the '*lebenswelt*'. That is a taken for granted sphere that is not permeated by excessive technical idealizations or the authority of professional cognition deriving from centers of power in every institutional sphere. But it is much simpler to call it the 'vernacular domain' which is essential to sustain human liberty and meaning and to critique the forces and hierarchical powers.

Converging with what Habermas calls 'internal colonization' it also objectifies how language and sensibility are forced to be submissive to dominations by technical language justifying coercive force. Habermas sees that the 'economistic' form of understanding undermines cultural meanings, but he does not recognize that ordinary language must be used to resist the destruction of everyday interactions. Only in this way can critical reflections become part of everyone's everyday life and not require an army of professional critical philosophers and sociologists to tell people what is happening to them or how they can seek 'emancipation'.

Loss of vernacular gender as condition for economism

Illich claims that feminist research has uncovered truths that change the way we understand the modern category of 'work' and at the same time revitalize the notion of 'gender'. Illich appropriates these perspectives and adds to them a historical perspective that changes our understanding of the origin of modernity too. In contrast to human beings having a 'sex', Illich was persuaded that gender was always culturally determined because we never see a 'human', non-gendered body, or hear an asexual voice.

Against the sphere of subsistence activity Illich contrasts wage labor – a new form of work that emerges and becomes normative for the formal economy. Citing E. P. Thompson and others, Illich points to how resistant crowds were to the undermining of the traditional food security norms that protected the poor and starving from the intervention of police and goons from crown corporations. When police tried to incarcerate the poor who were not able to pay their bills, the 'moral economy' intrinsic to the subsistence domain resulted in spontaneous crowd refusal of coercion for what was customary practice in situations of hunger. Formalizations of the commodity logic were applied to food security, first by Adam Smith, despite the 'right to live' being protected by subsistence custom, and it took massive restructuring of social life to make this change happen.

How, to use Marx's formulation, did the capacity to create use values turn into the commodity value of exchange values, or in Marx's terms the exchange value of labor power? Marx's analysis of the fetishism of commodities is a formal one of the development from simple reproduction of exchange to expanded exchange sequences – but it does not explain the actual historical transformations that rupture the vernacular domain and usher in the work ethic and wage labor and the genderless economic individual. This is done by Illich in the *Gender* book.

The necessary transformation was turning the economic division of labor into a productive and unproductive kind, and that was first enforced through the domestic enclosure of women. The subsistence domain is a commons maintained by a gendered division of labor – where 'labor' is not the same as work as Hannah Arendt has sharply argued. Loss of vernacular gender and the emergence of genderless sex is the 'universal' precondition for the emergence of the regime of scarcity.

But for this major disruption of the subsistence domain several other cognitive transformations had to come together – such as:

> Gender in the subsistence domain is an asymmetrical duality that takes different shapes in different contexts. Here it is important to distinguish patriarchy, which uses gender to justify male dominance and power from a more balanced regime of gender complementarity.[17]

Imaging of the woman as literally a 'home-body' whose nature was to support wageworkers is what Illich calls 'shadow work'. This confuses the gender specific roles of subsistence domain with the particular bifurcation of work in the nineteenth century when the wageworker and shadow worker emerged together. The point that Illich argues is that wage labor requires more and more supportive shadow work to maintain, and that this is an index to the counter-productivity of the regime of scarcity.

Self-limiting social communities evolved from envy protections that are symbolic ceremonial evasions of violence. Subsistence-oriented institutions, such as cycles of ritual feasts, pageants, dramas, etc. are oriented to the reduction of invidious individualism and envy. These associations can also be distorted by disruptive interventions of empires and hierarchical interventions. But the purpose of these events is to neutralize the dangers that emerge from the unequal accumulations of wealth by economic individuals.[18] Such techniques are forgotten in communities where the display of private accumulations and cultural imitating of consumer lifestyles become the norm.

Truth-seeking presupposes friendship: Illich and Gandhi

Illich demonstrates how truth-seeking presupposes friendship (*philia*), and that creativity is improved in such an ethos, just as in Chapter 5 we will see that

Gandhi's truth-force (*satyagraha*) presupposes spiritual solidarity. Both assert that our institutions of learning have lost this social and moral dimension and have become radical monopolies that control learning rather than facilitate autonomous self-reliant forms of learning.

Illich's own learning style was to set up a minimal form of inclusive monastic life wherever he lived and share this vocation with friends invited to the table, just as Gandhi established seven ashrams that modeled inter-religious solidarity. In this way both Illich and Gandhi's inclusive practices of freedom challenge the failure of all modern academics and politicos to aesthetically unify insight and action. Their acceptance of voluntary poverty, affirmation of powerlessness and spontaneity, as well an insistence on playful graciousness as the best response to purposive control systems tells us that these practices yield a different 'truth'.

In the end they both reveal to us different sacred paths to human enlightenment that, in a secularizing age, converge more than they differ. Both identify those things that are non-secular like friendship and human dignity while acting in a secular world. In doing so they demonstrate that the sacred is present in a secularizing world in new ways.

Their lives were their message

5 Gandhi's truth testing and India today

From Illich to Gandhi

Illich traveled to India and soaked up Eastern philosophy and practise during long interactions with the Indian Hindu and Catholic priest Ramon Panikkar in Benares, along the Ganges river.[1]

Insights from his Indian encounters were expressed at the Sevagram Ashram, where Illich sat in Gandhi's hut and reflected:

> While sitting in Gandhiji's hut I . . . . have come to the conclusion that it is wrong to think of the industrial civilization as a road leading towards development of man. . . . When I ask the planners of the day, why they do not understand [the] simple approach which Gandhiji taught us, they say that Gandhiji's way is very difficult and that the people will not be able to follow it. But the reality of the situation is that since Gandhiji's principles do not tolerate the presence of any middleman or that of a centralized system, the planners and managers and politicians have very little attraction towards it . . . . Their modes of consumption are such that they have been deprived of the power to understand the truth.[2]

Illich's notion of the 'vernacular domain' is where the political and the economic are not disembedded from the cultural. He uses the notion in a generic way to refer to what is lost and colonized by institutional radical monopolies and how convivial reconstructions can restore it to forms appropriate for today.

This notion converges with Gandhi's culture of *Swaraj* – an ancient *Vedic* sacred term that means self-rule in the sense of self-restraint. Self-rule is not independence from restraints, whose absence would impede others' quest for freedom, or justice. But since quests for justice can mean the repression of freedom for others, the rightful duty of *Swaraj* is to learn to balance self-rule with *swadeshi* self-reliance, as independence from alien controls. Ultimately these self-governing and self-reliance limits are tied into the image of political culture of *Rama Rajya*, the sovereignty of people based on moral authority. These concepts are explicated below.

Gandhi, in a parallel to Illich's critique of modernity, saw British civilization and rule in India as promoting ideals of wealth that were based on individual self-centeredness and the loss of bonds of community that are contrary to moral and spiritual common good (*dharma*). Such spiritually-based and seemingly anarchistic social ideals are viewed as very unrealistic, even naïve, by contemporary political thinking. Both Illich and Gandhi are very insistent about a vision of human social fulfillment rooted in a moral-spiritual ethos and expressed by *karma yogi* (see below) or Apophatic practice.

Globalizing 'development' imperatives emphasize means–end logics of economic growth or efficiency planning. Vernacular or self-rule choices are viewed as quaint and not 'productive' in the computation of national aggregate measures. Indeed vernacular choices are always context specific and take forms that cannot be generalized. Where put into practice, they are local inversions of 'development' that replace consumer goods by personal action, or industrial monopolies by convivial tools. For Gandhi the same ends are realized in local *panchayats* that are essential for 'welfare for all', or *sarvodaya*.

Contrary to those who claim that Illich or Gandhi are reactionaries these visions do not mean a return to the past. Reducing Illich, or Gandhi, to bi-polar thinking misses the point – spiritual practice is the focus. Creative forms of intermediary structures and self-rule converge with current alternative strategies of 'going local', and 'cosmopolitan localism'. These practices project how limits are needed to maintain local ecologies, sustain cultural diversities and enable livelihoods. Socio-economic logics of limits are different from the logics of growth-oriented 'sustainable development'. In fact all contemporary anti-globalization movements emphasize non-violent limits of decentralizing and subsidiarity.[3]

However, the legacy of Gandhi in India is hard to assess today when more and faster economic growth are nationalistic goals. Historically understanding this denial of Gandhi begins with insights into the ongoing legacy of British colonization of Indian culture.

Ongoing internal colonization of Indian governance

Insightful analysts claim that ongoing impacts of British colonialism remain a hidden determinant of a non-critical political ethos. Centuries of hierarchical caste oppression was manipulated by British colonialism that reinforced and deepened the feudalization of social life. British colonial breaking of the back of the peasantry with imposed commodities that undermined indigenous craft autonomy, and the empowerment of the *Brahminic* and *Kshatriya* (warrior) caste dominations narrowed the capacities of the original British political integrations.

The same British mechanisms of colonization also shaped anti-colonial forms of resistance. Ashis Nandy argues in *The Intimate Enemy*[4] that anti-colonialism was ironically channeled via a form of identification with the oppressor and led to the reassertion of those elements of Indian traditions that stressed the hyper-masculine, and the hyper-martial.[5] The result was a cultural suppression of a more nuanced, multi-valorized understanding of gender as well as the sidelining of the non-violent, mythopoetic Hindu cosmos. More literal, and more 'rational' forms of social policy and control resulted, which have been uncritically accepted.

Given India's incredible cultural, religious and economic diversity, Nandy argues it is necessary to consider if western state institutions adequately express the multi-dimensional worlds that make up Indian civilization. Critics agree that the modern state remains a radical imposition of top-down modernization, from Nehru's rule onward, that does not culturally fit or express Indian complexity.[6]

The colonial form of administration has a momentum that continues to undermine full democratization. For example, it created the 'collector', an office that continues as the district commissioner, who is the chief representative of the executive government in a district. L. C. Jain laments that this ongoing remnant of colonial government has become the kingpin, not the community, in all development decisions.[7]

While some states, such as Karnataka have modified this, it continues as a systematic block to the autonomous functioning of local governance. Nehru was asked, just before he died, what his biggest regrets were. He replied "failure to reform the administration", and added "that is responsible for the continued poverty in India."[8]

After personally encountering numberless stories of the ongoing corruption in administration one is tempted to say Nehru got that right. The constitution has facilitated democracy at the central and state level, but the result at lower levels is overlapping bureaucracy and ubiquitous corruption. This is the ongoing structural failure of Indian governance, and until the *panchayats* start to function without state and local government blocking that will continue.

Hence it comes down to the need to make the decentralized *panchayat* system work. Naxilites, today's Maoist Marxists, are now dominant in 160 districts out of 608. Where there is trust in the political institutions they do not become dominant. But again the bureaucratic response to allowing local *panchayats* to devolve government functions is resisted in almost all states, and new 'local area' development programs are started that subvert the devolving of administrative tasks.[9]

Aid to impoverished starving groups never gets there because the self-help groups formed are often *zamindars*, money lenders, who are above the poverty line; their servants and laborers and those below the poverty line never get the money.[10]

Ultimately Indian governance fails to integrate the spiderweb-like matrix of cultures and many layers of government. Interventions of western derived 'expert' knowledge discourses are applied in ways that disvalue India's traditional knowledge systems, especially agronomy, forestry, hydrology.[11] Critiques of hyper-professionalization of an expanding consumer culture exist in the West, but in India they diagnose a deeper pathology of imposed western 'monocultures of the mind' that are inappropriate for local stocks of knowledge.[12]

Other expatriate Indian writers aggressively attack the absurdity of modern institutions sitting within 'authentic' traditional Indian cultures and suggest that India has participated in the colonization of itself. V. S. Naipaul's *India: A Wounded Civilization* provides a harsh judgment when he opines:

> India is left alone with the blankness of its decayed civilization. The freedoms that came to independent India with the institutions it gave itself were alien freedoms, better suited to another civilization; in India they remained

> separate from the internal organization of the country, its beliefs and antique restrictions.[13]

Naipaul also charges that Gandhianism has been a disaster for India, leaving India without an ideology: only "magic, the past, the death of the intellect, spirituality annulling the civilization out of which it issues, India swallowing its own tail".[14] Gandhi's *Swaraj* has always been misleading and retreatist and reinforces numberless little tyrants!

After years of visiting huts in villages filled with destitute and helpless and hopeless people, driving down congested divided three-lane highways avoiding cows sauntering in the opposite direction, one is prone to consider the critical views suggested by Naipaul's diagnosis.

Is Indian culture adrift in its own mythological mirrors, culturally affirming its spirituality while politically mimicking and internally extending colonizing governance procedures, with horrendously ignored and uncorrected consequences for the poor and excluded?

Is an internal colonization occurring where hybridizing traditional and modern components become sentiments that operate beneath the cognitive mind and reaffirm unconscious motives for obedience to family, and now the colonizing institutional order? Is this mimicry continuous with the enthusiasm that the Indian middle class has for American nuclear linkages and financial transformations required by economic globalization?

Diverse perspectives on Indian culture

I have learned, or more accurately 'unlearned', most about India from those who are making ongoing reconciliations with both the modern secular world and their own communities and religious traditions – appropriately called 'critical traditionalists'.[15] They are the intellectuals, educated in western enlightenment traditions, who then turn around to more deeply understand India, and its oppressions, in its own traditional terms. Such people were key informants and methodology guides.

Retrievals of critical elements of spiritual traditions is a focus of critical traditionalist discourse in India; just as efforts to recover the engaged historical Jesus in the U.S. have emerged to try to break through the fundamentalist distortions of Christianity into 'end time' mythologies.[16] But the omnipresent poverty of millions of Indians, and equally omnipresent sanctifications provided by ashrams, temples, and fundamentalist organizations, remains a mysterious 'text' for Indians themselves.

As India modernizes, it is de-traditionalizing; but as this impacts on people there is a simultaneous re-traditionalization of everyday life, taking different forms, in reaction. This can vary as per place, caste, class and religion; but these reactive patterns are present and have spawned both the Hindu fundamentalist movement, and other behaviors. For example, less participation in the diversity of community festivals and more identification with one's religious origin.

Sacred traditions are ritually practiced in everyday life in India, but do these religious behaviors correlate with awareness and actions as responses to the grinding human destitution visible everywhere? Do they illuminate, hide it or just make it possible to live along beside it in a callous fatalistic way?

Focusing just on Indian religious traditions, do they have a genuine concern for social justice? Is the fatalism and seeming indifference of many Indians to caste, gender and class oppressions implicit in the religious concepts of *Maya*, illusion, and *moksha*, spiritual detachment from this world? Do these religious orientations deflect social awareness away from human agencies and just presume it works out higher up – in the dynamics of the metaphysical order? If so, no one is directly responsible for social wrongs, oppressions and misery. *Karmic* determinism has those who experience suffering – well, they have to endure it, due to bad actions in previous lifetimes! Is this the way traditional India thinks – or rather – doesn't think? Is Naipaul right? India colonizes itself.

Sri Aurobindo saw India's mission to be the center of religious life of the world and its destined savior. As a result when he was offered the invitation to be the President of the Indian National Congress in 1920 he turned down the offer because he did not know how to harmonize it with spiritual life.[17] The pursuit of *moksha*, or liberation from the *samsara*, requires a disengagement from other life pursuits; that is from the *purushartha*s – namely, *kama* (pleasure), *artha* (wealth and power), and *dharma* (ethics and religion). Ordering this four-fold inventory as a hierarchy of life pursuits is the way India has understood its traditional culture, even if the ordinary person sees *moksha* as remote from the need to stay afloat in the world now.

But Gandhi sees harmonizing these human pursuits as the most crucial life choice and is critical of orthodox Indian religion and philosophy. This difference can be illustrated by a famous story: Gandhi sent Sri Aurobindo a request for a visit, Aurobindo is said to have replied he didn't have time to see him, nor did he have time to do more than put in a silent appearance three times a year for his devotees. Detachment is the prerequisite condition for the highest pursuit of *moksha* or liberation. As will be shown, Gandhi rejects this view.

Other contemporary interpretations of Indian culture disagree that India's mission is spiritual enlightenment by a different ordering of life pursuits. A recent demythologizing by Pavar Varma argues that what is most important to Indians is status in the hierarchies of power – especially recognizable status. In this way power and wealth seeking, *artha*, is more important than liberating knowledge. Consequently it is not the process or idea of democracy that appeals to Indians, but its rewards.[18] Contrary to the spiritual image, contemporary Indians are basically 'material minded' and 'it is the gods of prosperity and wealth', such as *Lakshmi* and *Ganesha*, that are the popular icons present in everyday places who show that material success is the primary goal.

Varma also claims that Indian culture is actually able to adapt to whatever the prevailing political economic order and its spirituality actually helps India to be compatible with this-worldly materialism. In fact the best hope for India is emergence of a pan-Indian identity that includes other communities such as the Muslims and orients all to the secular needs and pursuits.[19] On this account it is *artha* which really preoccupies most Indians and this is where India is going.

This view tends to merge with Indian secularists who are adamant that India's future depends upon 'secularizing common sense' and putting the religious and spiritual behind.[20]

In a different way Sudhir Kakar also converges with this assessment, by suggesting that Indians follow traditional patterns by accepting what has power now.[21]

An opposing view is Sunil Khilnani who argues that India is ultimately a moral order that cannot be changed by political regimes alone.[22] This would mean that *dharma* is the primary substance of Indian national character and the primary pursuit in Indian life despite all.

An anthropological approach that converges with Khilnani's is Axel Michael's claim that it is the identificatory habitus that is the frame that links all Indian culture together in a non-cognitive way. Perhaps this is the Indian exceptionalism; culture prevails over all other factors. Evidence of this is that even in the twenty-first century over nine-tenths of all Indian tourism is to holy sites. There is a basic habitus, or fundamental cultural frame, that seems to be shared by all, whatever their particular religious identity. That is why the caste system has also invaded Muslim communities.

Despite this ongoing dispute about the ends of India, the position of Gandhi, and his contemporary pragmatic followers, is very clear but not widely understood. Anthony J. Parel has persuasively argued that Gandhi held the view that without the transformation and harmonization of cultural ends no enlightened political reforms will ever succeed.[23] Not *artha*, or *dharma*, or *kama,* or even *moksha*, can be viewed as primary. Instead a constant harmonization is required. The term *purushartha* means that which is done for the sake of the spirit, or the immortal soul. All four of these forms of striving are the ways reason constitutes human existence in the interest of overcoming fate and karma. For Gandhi this is the foundational philosophical anthropology behind central Hindu sacred texts and is a dramatically different vision for spiritual regeneration.

Gandhi's truth experiments and the harmony of human pursuits

Gandhi's constant experiments to find harmonious order in the sensuous body, socially right conduct, and correct spiritual meaning of truth that incorporates them all, constitutes Gandhi's vision of a harmonized spiritual existence. Actually this is the regeneration strategy that Gandhi tried to affect over Indian life and culture. Gandhi was not a systematic philosopher, but as scholars absorb his now 100 volumes of collected works they are discovering a unity of thinking about the harmony of the four *purusharthas*. Gandhi is not doing something that does not already exist in the sacred texts; he simply brings it forward as part of his experiments in truth and his mission for the regeneration of India.

There is no one book on which Hinduism is based, it has a complex set of sacred texts that can be interpreted several ways. A contemporary view of Hinduism is Siddhartha's claim that:

> Hinduism . . . . is a spiritual laboratory that keeps itself open to both inside and outside influences, There is no single book, single messiah, single prophet or

> single belief system that holds it together. As a spiritual laboratory the one and the many . . . the immanent and the transcendent, the personal and the impersonal are all allowed to have their play.[24]

Whereas Siddhartha's 'Hermeneutics of Hope' is a fruitful principle for understanding the histories of Hindu social justice movements, how does this actually work in Gandhi's practice and thought?

Gandhi was striving to transform Indian caste prejudice and the exclusion of women.[25] But he was also centrally concerned with changing the Indian understanding of the pursuits of life. As mentioned earlier the *Purusharthas* include:

> *dharma* (the way of higher truths);
> *kama* (pleasure and art);
> *artha* (wealth and power);
> *moksha* (liberation).

All *Purusharthas* contain interrelated standards of 'truth' and each has to be tested, or in Gandhi's terms 'experimented' with, as living proceeds and as life circumstances change. The end is to maintain harmony.

The theory of harmonized *purushrathas* is Gandhi's philosophical anthropology in the sense of a new understanding of the telos of humanity. But it is also a reflexive reconstruction of Indian philosophy in the interest of the regeneration of Indian civilization. It is a lasting vision of how to pursue wealth and power without giving up beauty, ethics or transcendence.

The debate about the harmonization, or dis-harmony, of these four human pursuits is one of the central debates of Indian philosophy, Gandhi is a modern harmonizer who rejects the separation of the temporal and the eternal pursuits by rethinking how *moksha* retains its integrative role within the harmonized practice of the other pursuits. It shows Gandhi's foundational view in Indian philosophy which was much more thought out than people realize. He was not just a political genius, he was also a systematic Indian spiritual thinker and practitioner. Whereas studying the meaning of the great sacred texts is important, Gandhi shows these meanings also change. Specifically he names the changing meaning of sacrifice, no longer animal sacrifice, and asceticism, *sannyasa*, which his harmonization of the *purushartha*s would fundamentally transform. The complete separation of work from liberation is denied, an inclusive spiritualized work results. A very different type of virtue as a new Indian 'work ethic' results. Work is both elevated and embedded by a constant testing of how it contributes to the political and economic common good and to one's spiritual ends.

This differs from contemporary western culture, where secular work and wealth creation is central, to a view of work as concerned with spiritual welfare too. Work is conceived as in the spirit of ethical and political duty. Gandhi is adamant that duty precedes rights and refused to sign human rights documents for this reason.[26] Contrary to western political contract philosophy Gandhi argues that equal emphasis on duties, rights and virtue is essential to correctly ground a political community.

Work, religion and spiritual quests are inclusively dedicated to God, analogous to the Benedictine work is prayer ideal.[27] The bodily ego of desire and practice of work has to be harmonized with self-oriented higher ends. But since violence, *himsa*, is inherent in all living bodies, the restraints of spiritual harmonization yields non-violence, *ahimsa*, as an end in itself and as a principle for policy formation at all levels of social and political life. In this sense *satyagraha*, or truth force action, is an invention to deal with specific situations as a public form of *ahimsa*; other forms are also possible such as trusteeship – which is discussed below.

Work practiced as virtue incorporates non-violence practices and becomes a daily practice that includes contemplation and devotion to God. In so far as this is observed there is no ordinary worker but a spiritually enlightened and devout worshiper who is devoted to God.

Where orthodox Indian religion and philosophy elevates *moksha* as the ultimate aim, Gandhi is critical of the deceptions of yogis who speculate about the four stages of *moksha*. Gandhi sees these as spiritual fantasies, and the debate about living in this world after having attained liberation or *moksha*, as part of the weakening of Indian life that enabled a legitimating of caste hierarchy. Orthodox Hindu religious institutions have betrayed the Indian people in not representing how holiness of everyday life, centered around *artha*, is possible for all.

Here a parallel can be drawn to the western post-Plato debate about responsibility and enlightenment after leaving the cave allegory in the seventh book of *the Republic*. Those agreeing with Plato argued that those enlightened must return to the cave to help others turn around – versus those who made the 'great refusal', e.g. Plotinus, to stay out of the cave of illusions and false opinions and disconnect from the world. There is a 'great refusal' moment in India too.

Gandhi has a very rigorous test for yogis who claim primacy of knowledge about scriptures. That criterion is personally experiencing the truth they are interpreting. Nothing can be accepted as word of God which cannot be tested by reason or is capable of being spiritually experienced.[28] For Gandhi Truth is God, non-violence is the means, and the testing of the truth is the practice.

Truth is God is open to all faiths to be included in the quest, including atheists. But it is also a definition of the path and the means; for example, the famous verse that Gandhi recited in his daily prayers where *satya* is truth, or ultimate being in Sanskrit:

> From the unreal (*asat*) lead me to the real (*sat*).
> From the darkness lead me to light.

The meaning of *karma yogi*, or the path of action rather than understanding or devotion, can now be seen as the result of harmonizing the *purusharthas*. It is also why, while Gandhi accepts the Buddha as the major Hindu reformer, he is not enthusiastic about his rejection of *artha* and his emphasis upon emptying the mind rather than enriching it in prayer.

Gandhi's insights into the public truth testing of *satyagraha*, truth force, as the Indian way follow. Gandhi always claimed that *satyagraha*, or *karma yogi*, is the end and the means, consequences be damned: "*Satyagraha* strives to reach the reason through the heart. The method of reaching the heart is to awaken public opinion . . . which is a mightier force that that of gunpowder."[29]

Hence Gandhi's public actions became public theatre all over India.[30] It was an absolutely unique 'power' that Gandhi exercised over the impulses of millions of people; he electrified masses of illiterate Indians, who somehow were very aware of his *satyagraha* actions. The only word we have to describe this power is charisma, but somehow this seems not quite appropriate – Indians resonated with his spiritual practices in ways that were really about spiritual solidarity and community.

The achievements of these *satyagraha* actions for social change are more numerous, and more denied, than any other political practice. For example Martin Luther King, commenting on Gandhi's *satyagraha* asserts that "Gandhi is the first person in history to lift the love ethic of Jesus above mere interaction between individuals to a powerful social force . . . I [here] discovered the method for social reform that I have been seeking".[31] Other persons inspired have been Lech Walesa in Poland, Vaclav Havel in Czechoslovakia, Nelson Mandela in South Africa, Dalai Lama for Tibet, etc. Gandhi's vision remains a beacon for humanity but those who find their way to this way remain too few.

Gandhi claimed his life is his message, establishing a level of existential awareness that grabs our attention. He established seven different ashrams during his life time, and his intuitions about how to create consciousness changing solidarity and building bonded associations is outstanding. Gandhi transformed ashrams into spiritual training centers for both internal members and simultaneously created public forms to promote this moral imagination to wider public opinion formation. Gandhi self-consciously denied the western private–public segregation and transforms everyday living into an experiment in moral and *Swadeshi*- (self-reliance) centered learning. Indeed here the personal is the political; all the young professionals who came into Gandhi's ashrams had to face for the first time in their lives a responsibility to cope with dirty pots and the cleaning of chamber pots!

Swaraj, or self-rule: the key to the regeneration of India?

The idea of *Swaraj* is both a historical and a political-spiritual concept whose importance is not generally understood. First, it was the central slogan of the Indian independence movement and as such is a significant political notion for all political struggles for independence. But what is not grasped is that this concept represents an alternative to the western democracy or socialist ideals. Its history is the history of the transformations in the Indian independence movement and these changes are a record of a model for achieving independence.[32] India's consciousness crystallized around this notion in the course of the national liberation movement.

Swaraj means four things:

1 national independence;
2 political freedom of the individual;

3 economic freedom of the individual;
4 spiritual freedom of the individual as self-rule.

The positive role of the fourth dimension is that the fulfillment of the first three is a pre-condition for the fulfillment of the fourth moral – spiritual end. This is a clue to why Gandhi always rejected the coercive role of 'structured administration'; he did not want to replace one form of coercive rule with another. Consequently this is an ideal of liberation that is wider than western human emancipation. Gandhi was not a defender of 'received rights' without an organic relation to duties or *dharma,* morality. Freedom is ultimately linked to 'soul-force'.

Swaraj is a self-transformative activity, a mental revolution to experience inner freedom and our efforts to learn to rule ourselves. It is this *advaita* dimension of 'self', *sva*, where you and I are not other than one another – a struggle for the kingdom or autonomy of self. A very different dimension of freedom than the British notion.

Truth-seeking, or truth-testing 'experiments', were therefore involved in freedom and *satyagraha* was the mode of nonviolent political action implied by its realization.

Economic freedom meant freedom from poverty and the ability to enjoy the fruits of labor as well as protection for the growth of the individual. Gandhi's concept is focused on both the individual and the collective levels. What that means is not an imitation of western industrialization that sees the worker as a limitless consumer but an advocacy for village-based craft production as a protection of *Swaraj*:

> I do envisualize electricity, ship-building, ironworks, machine-making and the like existing side by side with village handicrafts. But the order of independence will be reversed. Heretofore industrialization has been planned to destroy the villages and their crafts. I do not share the socialist belief that centralization of the necessities of life will conduce to the common welfare when the centralized industries are planned and owned by the state.[33]

Swaraj was linked to *swadeshi*, or material or spiritual self-reliance. Although Gandhi had many high hopes, his wager was that self-restraint would be exercised by people themselves as the chief means to end misery.[34] His vision of village *Swaraj*, or self-rule, in a village republic, is a spiritual-democratic social image for India:

> My idea of the village *swaraj* is that it is a complete republic, independent of its neighbors for its vital wants and yet interdependent for many others in which dependency is a necessity . . . In a structure composed of innumerable villages, . . . life will not be a pyramid with the apex sustained by the bottom, but it will be an oceanic cycle whose center will be the individual . . . The outmost circumsphere will not wield power to crush the inner circle but will give strength to all within and derive its own strength from it . . .[35]

This is a very different vision of 'community' than western concepts of 'civil society'; everyone is their own ruler and governance is based on the control that people, as citizens, exercise over themselves. The wager was that movement from representative government to direct governance would transform both political, economic, social and moral-spiritual life. Politically Gandhi's thinking is in the interest of the last man, or an awakening of all, *sarvodaya*, not the British utilitarian ideal of the greatest good for the greatest number. The ideal of consider the 'last man' refutes that 51 percent of the electorate can dominate the other 49.

Gandhi self-consciously denied the western private–public segregation and transformed everyday living into an experiment in moral and *Swadeshi*-centered learning.

Gandhi's commitment to *Swadeshi*, national and local self-reliance, has several meanings in addition to the nationalism of the 'buy Indian goods' campaigns. It can mean that religious practice begins in the service to immediate situations and surroundings, to the exclusion of more remote goals or horizons.[36] That this attitudinal notion emerges in the context of Gandhi's reflections about the reasons for thinking that conversion to another faith is unnecessary is doubly significant; it implies that reform is always possible within Hinduism as well as within politics and economics. It also implies a way of being that brings attentions to the here and now in a place-centered way that is in line with moral economy noted above.

Spiritualizing wealth and economics: on Gandhian economics

Gandhian economics is not oriented to the increase of labor productivity but to full employment in the sense of universal right to life and livelihoods. Gandhi insisted that the gathering of facts and the building of the economy should proceed from the unit of village self-sufficiency. National industrialization supplements to this would be essential but the basic unit must remain the local.

For example, 'Food for all' was the principle of social justice.[37] In line with this Gandhi held that private capital must be held to a standard of state-regulated trusteeship. Trusteeship provides a means of transforming the present capitalist order of society into an egalitarian one and gives the present owning class a chance of reforming itself. Trusteeship derives from Gandhi's faith in the law of 'non-possession'; or the belief that everything belongs to God. Those who have more than their proportion are obligated to treat property as not determined by their selfish interests but by the common interests of humanity.

In another formulation; we don't really own what we possess, but we hold it in trust for the common good. Accepting trusteeship implies accepting great responsibility by those who have demonstrated skill in the use and development of resources. These people are the natural custodians, by reason of their competences, of the planet and social justice.

In this way Gandhi tried to image a spiritualization of wealth that would be an alternative to Marxist socialism and capitalism, one in which goods and service production would be guided by the common good and not personal greed.

One of the consequences of the trust idea in India and beyond begins with Vinoba Bhave who walked from village to village in rural India in the 1950s and 1960s asking those with more land than they needed to give a portion to the landless. He was not able to achieve his ambitious target of 50 million acres and ended with 5 million. But many of the new landowners became discouraged due to lack of tools and seeds, and having no affordable credit available to purchase these necessary things, the land was useless to them. This initiative was known as the *Bhoodan*, or Land Gift movement.

Soon after, the *Bhoodan* system was changed to a *Gramdan*, or village gift system, in which not less than 75 percent of the villagers gave up their right to ownership in the interest of the whole village. The village would hold the land and lease it as long as it was used correctly. However, this *Gramdan* ideal was not popular outside of tribal areas. Other gift movements that emerged after Gandhi – such as the *Sampattidan* (wealth-gift), *Shramdan* (labour-gift), *Jeevandan* (life-long commitment to the movement by co-workers), *Shanti-Sena* (peace-army), *Sadhandan* (gift of implements for agricultural operations).

Unfortunately, the *Gramdan* movement declined in the 1970s and its consequences have not been widely recognized. One application of this idea resulted in Gandhigram Rural Trust, GRT, at Gandhigram. Is the full story of post-Gandhi Gandhianism fully absorbed in India? I believe it has to begin with a recognition that Vinoba resolutely refused to combine his moral appeal with a campaign of active resistance.

However, these experiments with village land grant trusts, formed in India, has spawned a deep ongoing movement in the U.S. Bob Swann learned from Ralph Borsodi and J. P. Narayan about these movements and started a movement for Community Land Trusts in the United States.

> By establishing ownership of the land by the community, the land trust began to tackle the problem of property management by creating a new model of property ownership and tenure – a combination of private interests and community values. As a nonprofit corporation with the best interests of the community at heart, with people from the community on the board, the land trust will control the use of the empty land and empty homes. It will build homes for homeownership and be able to work with first time homebuyers and renters on credit problems, getting a mortgage, and home maintenance. It will develop commercial properties to enhance the quality of life.[38]

Today there are 1,200 land trusts that protect over 828,000 acres in the U.S.[39]

Testing Gandhianism: romantic idealism or seminal vision?

Have Gandhi's ideals of *Swaraj* and *Swadeshi* been effective in India after many socialist five-year plans and finally seemingly irreversible economic globalization in the form of deepening debt, growing direct foreign investment and gearing in of external WTO trade rules? The influence of Gandhi has been significant for India in many ways but how effective has it really been for institutional arrangements and procedures? Are we talking here of a founding father whose ideals, like Jefferson, are less and less in tune with the spirit of the times?

Of course it is possible to romanticize the rural villages of India as the realm of the authentic Gandhian pastoralism, as the sphere of independence which has government support for the local *panchayats* in ways that make local governance work. The realities are much more complex. But the problems of Indian society are not just problems of models of economic development but reach into the unknowns of how best to cope with the pathologies of caste society in a context of politically manipulated communal conflicts.

The debate within the congress party on the basic unit of government is pivotal, Gandhi had said:

> I hold without truth and non-violence there can be nothing but destruction of humanity. We can realize truth and non-violence only in the simplicity of village life and this simplicity can be best found in the *charkha* and what the *charkha* connotes.[40]

The decisive moment in the founding debate was when Ambedkar, as Dalit leader, who, on Nov 4 1948, fiercely assaulted the draft constitution by implying that the villages have always been passive evaders of domination and that:

> I hold that these village republics have been the ruination of India . . . what is the village but a sink of localism, a den of ignorance, narrow mindedness and communalism? I am glad the draft constitution has discarded the village and adopted the individual as its unit.[41]

Nehru was silent on the issue and so it passed.

Turning first to the institutionalization of decentralized governance, Gandhi's idea of *gram swaraj* was accepted in principle before independence and it was built into the centralized planning system, as the three-tier *panchayatic raj* system, by the second and third five-year plans.[42] In the fourth plan a specific micro-level linkage for decentralization was suggested; but without sufficient resource capacity these ideas were unrealized, and only centralized capacities were operationalized. When India accepted liberalization in 1992 there was a silent passage of the 73rd and 74th amendments to the India constitution. These amendments consolidated the foundations for local democracy.[43]

One of the first inaugurations of decentralized planning at three levels was begun in Madhya Pradesh in 2001 but fiscal constraints limited the village level capacity and overlapping 'user', common property committees, formed by state governments weakened *panchayat* processes. The *gram swaraj* system is to be a convergence of civil society and state sphere and works best where there are proactive NGOs and bureaucrats who understand that it is not just a state institution and that people are solutions not problems.[44]

As L. C. Jain remarks: ". . . 55 years after Independence there is not a single village out of 250,000 villages which is self-governing."[45]

The central dilemma is put clearly by Jean Dreze and Amartya Sen: "Local democracy is sometimes treated as synonymous with 'decentralization', but the two are in fact quite distinct . . . . in situations of sharp inequalities, decentralization sometimes heightens the concentration of power and discourages rather than fosters participation among the underprivileged . . ."[46]

There is a difference between income inequality and social/economic inequality. Social equity, achieved by social movements to support education, health, welfare, etc. has had astounding results – such as in Kerala. Several states of India have achieved a pragmatic synthesis of Gandhi and Marx which many Indians claim is consistent with the new ideal of *dharma*.

For example, Swami Agniuesh proclaimed at the 2004 World Social Forum in Mumbai, that 'Vedic Socialism' was essential for the *Bandhua Mukti Morcha*, the movement against bonded labor, or the entrappings of people in debt slavery.[47] The same pattern of predatory financial entrapment and the creation of debt slaves is operating in the U.S. in credit card, student loan and sub-prime home mortgages, but where are the liberation movements here?

Building local association for supporting of local communities is the crucial piece in realizing local self-reliance.

Realities of the Indian informal sector

The fact that huge numbers of people are still in 'the informal sector' is the India story; Barbara Harriss-White claims that 88 percent of India is still struggling and squashed by the intermediate classes – small land owners, money lenders and corrupt civil servants. Approximately 74 percent still live in rural areas and 14 percent in small municipalities. The consequence are that these intermediate classes have the ability to neutralize most progressive legislations that would disrupt their advantage in the accumulation of wealth or reverse the perpetuation of traditional and economic status.

These intermediate classes in the rural and small towns seal in the poor, struggling workers and subsistence people into a prison of debt, dependence, caste hierarchy and patriarchal prejudice. As Arundhati Roy so elegantly put it, India doesn't live in the villages, Indians die there.[48]

Driving all economic planning are the modernizing forces that are intent upon disembedding the agricultural sector and reducing it to a much smaller proportion – some name it as 20 percent instead of the current over 60 percent! Current advocates of the "second wave" of the green revolution are succeeding in forcing farmers to become more and more individualized as agricultural producers. Greater uses of fertilizer, pesticides, irrigation, hybrid seeds increase the cost and the risk of farming that correlates with the estimated 100,000 farmer suicides in the last 10 years.

The older safety nets of co-operative sharing in rural villages are being displaced by the commercializing trends and these are made more risky by climate, free trade, credit, upgraded technical knowledge, etc. Farming is no longer seen as the idyllic Indian profession but a very high pressured one with many losing out and being excluded from the land and having to become part of the internal migrations of poor Indians who go wherever there are wage opportunities in construction, road building, seasonal labor, or whatever. Returning to original villages as long as there are family connections, this movement of internal migration increases more and more. As the cities fill up with slums they become more hostile to rural immigrants. All of this is worsened by agriculture becoming less and less of the national production output and market fundamentalists less and less sympathetic to the massive rural poor who have no place.

All that is needed for elimination of poverty is, as the International Labor Organization's (ILO) 2004–05 World Employment Report indicates, that the 550 million people working in poverty are able to get more productive work. It cites the 1978 rural reforms in China which entailed a shift from collective farming to household farming which resulted in increasing agricultural productivity and town and village enterprises. And L. C. Jain cites Amartya Sen who also argues that if India could complete the land reform process, which was fairly complete in West Bengal and Kerala, it would unleash the energy essential to lift India out of poverty. The world report shows that labor based projects are often superior to equipment based ones.[49]

But the current realities reveal that agricultural development that tries to modernize agriculture by turning farmers into entrepreneurs, disconnected from the community, does not work. The farmers who have committed suicide in India leave behind destitute families that inherit their debt and their shame. Why has this happened?

The underlying reason, when all factors are considered is not the climate induced failures of crops – although this is a triggering mechanism. It is the forced dis-embedding of agrarian life from the sharing of village life to a more privatized and much more risky entrepreneurial role.[50] Co-coordinating green revolution seeds, chemical inputs, irrigations, banking, market timing, etc. into a pressured lifestyle is increasingly losing its appeal in rural India. Add to these increased risks the realities of differential caste access to resources, the terminal choice of many farmers is clearer.

There are fewer places to go to fail: word of hostility to immigrants in the cities is widespread and internal migration to work sites on roads or construction is more and more the only alternative – with the possibility of returning to the home village as an ever present hope. As WTO forces more food commodities to be opened to imports, the risks of prices undercutting the growth of cotton, sugar, spices, crops also increases.

Even with sweeping legislation in an election year – such as the extension of the Rural Employment Guarantee Act, NREGA, to all 608 districts the government has opened foreign direct investment into the retailing sector which, as L. C. Jain asserts, will throw more people out of work than the NREGA can help.

So the problems of India are massive and no simple solution presents itself.

But there are many small scale models that have great promise and I will end this chapter with one such example.

An alternative strategy to transform rural communities

We visited a very aggressive organization that has challenged and partially neutralized caste dominations in 913 rural villages: the Agricultural Development And Training Society ADATS (http://www.adats.com/) in Bagepalli town, 100 kms north of Bangalore. ADATS is a rural development organization working with 38,344 small and poor peasant families in 5 northern taluks of the Kolar district, Karnataka for the past 30 years.

Their learning curve – accessible on the web – is actually a record of changing caste-class-state relations in their area. This area is a dry land region just south of the Rayalaseema desert belt and subject to recurrent droughts, the last one lasting 4–5 years. The land is rocky, has very thin soils and only small rain-fed tanks, making agriculture hard, and crop choice very restricted. These realities force many to migrate to get seasonal work, or starve. Given this ecology, and the caste situation, the landless poor have had few options – in the past.

ADATS interventions begin by creating *coolie sangha* units in villages in a three-phase process over nine years. They carefully document (on the web) their every action and ongoing self-evaluations in providing protection from violence, enabling credit, getting government resources, winning local elections, etc. Indeed they have used the web to inform the world, and their funders, about their success, their strategies and their incredibly aggressive learning process. The following principle is forwarded as they form *coolie sanghas* in resistance to caste-class forces in rural villages:

> Persons belonging to lower castes must realize that it is not what 'others are doing to them' that can be changed, but what 'they permit others to do to them.' Then they can shake off the psyche of being manipulated. When that happens, there will be dramatic demonstrations of tangible change.
>
> (http://www.adats.com/home/results)

Slowly they build *sanghas*, or cross caste solidarity groups, that work together to achieve seemingly impossible goals of blocking upper caste manipulations, collectively access state resources, enable coolie women to succeed at family and social participation, foster diversified income flows, conserve and cultivate coolie lands, and help form coolie coalitions across all divides. ADATS is an incredible organization that exemplifies a social learning organization that systematically creates more effective staff and integration of social, political and ecological actions.

The intense efforts of ADATS, lead by a very astute leader Ram and his chosen family:

> [We] . . . take into account the added influence of the dominant societal trend of capitalism which, in some ways, has gained an entry precisely because of

> our anti feudal work. This is a very serious countervailing force because while it stands counter to the prevailing feudal value, offering a very attractive alternative to it, it is not, at the same time, compatible to our change oriented philosophy which rebels against both, the existing pseudo-capitalistic philosophies as well as against the capitalization process.
>
> (http://www.adats.com)

Despite their secular claims, they are not an NGO that uplifts caste workers into the market economy, although they train and enable many to work in nearby urban areas – a new level of mobility for those trapped in rural casteism. They also help train people to start local small business while introducing new technologies and techniques at every opportunity. For example, our visit witnessed the start up of the first of 12 biogas installations in a village where fuel is now the ever present cow dung. They form bonded groups and build social capital and political competences simultaneously – the deep identifications with the coolie *sangha* is clear in all interactions. They also bring into hopeless rural existence a proactive planning dimension since their communities are subject to conditions that can turn drought into famine. Now they have focused on the truth that they are deeply dependent on the skills and new techniques that can be mobilized for subsistence communities who may have to shift their locations at a later time.

The spirit of ADATS was revealed to us when we witnessed a youth training session in the martial arts, which happens regularly after the school lets out. The intensity of the proud children's faces as they performed for an impressive master revealed that they are learning how to protect themselves from violence outside, and hopefully the violence within too. The self-confidence shining from many of their faces was beautiful to see.

Here is a model for how Indians can create local social movements, and the real hope is that they can be lifted to other political levels too. ADATS' overtly aggressive procedures are important to watch. Can they succeed in forming wider political associations that go around the omnipresent conflicts of religious identities?

Part III

Alternative economies

6 Foundations of economic cultures

Secularization and remembrance of 'the other west'

Kenichi Ohmae's celebration of global expansion as a 'Borderless World' is followed by a book entitled *The End of the Nation State*. This sequence deepens the view that old political institutional arrangements are obsolete and globalizing markets and information revolution are the new mechanisms for development and consumer liberation everywhere.

For Ohmae this globalist revitalization also deepens economic freedom as religion and political power wanes: "When GNP/person gets up to around $10,000 a year, religion becomes a declining industry. So does government."[1]

Ohmae and other economic realists presume we are at a point where the expansions of capital and 'development' justify undermining traditional obligations and reciprocal practices. The new world order brings the superior powers of technology, wealth creation and consumerism into the reach of many in ways that de-traditonalize all social life and de-mystifies any spiritual justifications for the sacred order of nature and community.

Another interpretation is that there is a loss of remembrance that accompanies the liberations of modernity. Something like social amnesia, or public forgetfulness, accompanies absorption into progress. There is a strange disappearance of essential human suffering and sacrifice that has led to modern gratifications. New levels of material satisfaction, once attained, forget the path of their emergence. Milan Kundera's maxim that "man's struggle against power is the struggle of memory against forgetfulness",[2] is the principle that informs this inquiry.

For Illich and Gandhi remembrance of vernacular domain and self-rule (*swaraj*) are the common good for social persons and a harmonization of interpersonal and sacred obligations. They are the sources for a spiritual culture free from the disembodiments of economism. This co-original concept of the free person and free associations critiques western instrumentalism and the dogmatization of their own traditions. Illich and Gandhi are model critical traditionalists.[3]

But critical traditionalist remembrance and reconstruction can also be applied to the buried over traditions of the West; 'the other west'. As Illich revealed, the modern west has not absorbed its own institutional sources, starting with human faculties that are devalued in an information-and theory-oriented technical world.

There have always been western counter-currents to abstract theorizing. For example, the Ancient Greek tragedians' resistance to Plato's unified idea of the Good; performances of tragic drama were public reconciliations with contradictory social expectations. Or the resurgence of Civic Humanism in the fifteenth century that stressed deepening participation in the webs of social life and identified rhetorically sensitive language as a returning to common sense – the real source of human solidarity.[4]

Later articulations of 'common sense' by Vico and Shaftesbury constitute the 'other' western tradition:

> According to Vico, what gives the human will its direction is not the abstract generality of reason, but the concrete generality that represents the community of a group, a people, a nation, or the whole human race. Hence the development of this sense of the community is of prime importance for living.[5]

Common sense included the general good of humanity, the love of community, and natural affections of the heart. 'Knowing' here is always about the concrete moral and historical existence, not theoretical universals or methods ensuring certainty. It is about the virtues of the heart and not the head, about wit and humor and joys of living. It demands a 'generative method' as against a mathematical and rationalist one "so that justice can be planted like a living shoot".[6]

In Germany, Immanuel Kant insisted upon methodical thinking in the human sciences and buried over this common sense humanistic tradition. Thereafter, the evolution of common sense is connected with the concept of 'judgment' which can only be improved by learning from practice. Hence conviviality has many names before Illich's reemphasis, such as joy of living, good sense, common sense and moral proportion.

After the twentieth-century wars, advocacy to reunify social community against commercialization was suggested by Robert Nisbet's *The Quest for Community*. He argues that the stress on the individual and the state has not created an order that serves the fundamental human need for meaning:

> Material improvements that are unaccompanied by a sense of personal belonging may actually intensify social dislocations and personal frustrations . . . (the old laissez-faire) . . . as a policy . . . failed because its atomistic propositions were inevitably unavailing against the reality of the enlarging masses of insecure individuals. Far from providing a check upon the growth of the omnicompetent state, the old lassize-faire actually accelerated its growth. Its indifference to every form of community and association left the state as the sole area of reform and security.[7]

Out-of-date social theory is today dead on target. Nisbet in remembering the values and institutions that formed 'individualism' makes a judgment that social life can only be free if it continues to be based on a social – not an economic ordering. Elevation of the material over the moral can only create an inversion that leads to the demise of both. People derive their meaning only from the shared experiences in social groups, voluntary associations and communities of purpose and therein lie the foundations of freedom.

Contemporary quests for community include the intentional communities' movement, eco-villages, and co-housing movements each of which is a fascinating story of retreat from social privatizations to search for communal meaning. These quests for community in a commercial world have some good results and are growing. But internal debate continues; the poles of this communal discourse is the dilemma of sharing commonly owed property or sharing privately owned property such as co-housing and eco-villages, or a combination, such as in community land trusts where only the land is in common.[8]

Spiritually-based communities are also thriving, such as the Bruderhof Community who share all things in common and do not hold private property. No member receives a salary or has a bank account; income from all businesses is pooled and used for the care for all members, and for various communal outreach efforts. The Bruderhof is a peace church, members do not serve in the armed forces and model a way of life that removes the social and economic divisions that bring about war. Their end is to create a new society where self-interest is yielded for the sake of the common good. A recent book about them is entitled *The Joyful Community*.[9] Other peace churches are the Brethren, the Mennonites, Amish and the Religious Society of Friends (Quakers).

Another contemporary spiritual community more consistent with modern individualization is the Findhorn Community in Scotland. The Sirius Community in Massachusetts is also oriented to enabling persons to find meaning in shared spiritual and communal projects.[10]

Another source for oppositions to commercial materialism and transcendence are aesthetic quests to unify art and life. For example Owen Barfield's 'aesthetic participation' that images going 'beyond civilization' to a more individuated person.[11] Public aesthetic rebellions such as the antics of the 1960s Provo's and Diggers, or more recent actions by the Zapatistas and White Overalls dramatize radical politics as imaging the joy of living.[12] These aesthetic enactments, which were once part of all ritual and public cultural play, get buried when competitive lifestyles substitute conspicuous consumption for community. The social losses of privatized consumerism have to be confronted before the potentials of a shared moral economy can be recognized.

Examining the debates about reciprocity and gifting as the foundation for cooperative practice is a starting point.

Economistic reductions of reciprocity and gifting

The economistic image of the world as systems of goods that has calculable interactions obeying a gravity-like force of self-regulating efficiency is a mechanical system devoid of gifts. Justifying this system includes attempts to incorporate the 'gift' into this market world. Successful inclusion would have deep consequences for understanding human personhood and society.

Polanyi's economic anthropology asserts that gift giving is the basic reciprocal form of exchange, not only in pre-state social integrations but in all forms of social life with other organizing principles of exchange – such as redistribution, householding and market exchange. In this way Polanyi asserts that economies are always situated in social relationships.

Giving and receiving are reciprocity mechanisms that initiate and consolidate social relationships and identity formations in an ongoing way.[13] Most contemporary discourse about the 'gift' returns to the seminal interpretation of Marcel Mauss who created a polarity of gift and commodity exchange not only as an anthropology of non-modern social life, but also as a critique of the dominance of market mentality too.[14] Mauss' work has been subjected to intense debate; one recurrent theme is the attempt to expose the gift's obligatory side by reducing all voluntary spontaneity to forms of self-interested instrumental action.

On this view commerce applies to all social interactions; reciprocity as a norm is transformed into instrumental exchange, mirroring market logics. Gifts are ultimately a disguised form of debt creation, creating obligations that supposedly stabilize social exchange and create social bonds. Logically, the free gift is annulled each time an obligation for a counter-gift is set up, and the act of giving becomes an anomalous concept. 'Giving' is reduced to its latent economic interests: thus giving poisons itself.

These interpretations are examples of the reductive economism that haunts all modern interpretations of human motives and behavior. Is it possible that gifts combine interest and disinterest, freedom and constraints, calculations and affirmations of risk and uncertainty in a holistic relation? Could it be if you start with modern western notion of the monadic individual you will always end in a reduction to economic logics?

The logic of gifts beyond economism

In debates about Mauss' classic analysis of the gift, objects treated as sacred are usually excluded and this secularizes giving to simple forms of reciprocal exchange. A secular suspicion is that gifting always conceals a power relation unless it meets seemingly impossible standards.[15] It must be:

- spontaneous and disinterested;
- unforeseeable and therefore a surprise;
- free and unconstrained.

However, there are pure cases that meet these almost impossible criteria. For example, the practices of highly conscious Jain renouncer communities in India aspire to eliminate obligation and maximize impersonality. Here ritual practices of gifts do not create obligations. 'Grazing' for gifts are for them self-conscious random wanderings into houses where brusque taking from family pots is done in tiny quantities, making the giver's role and reciprocity relation trivial. Working out these details of precautionary guidelines for free gifts has taken centuries and result in the elimination of the 'poison' of the gift. Such learning is spiritually inspired and based on eliminating certitudes and affirming uncertainty.[16] But it would be necessary to go into the narrative practiced by these renouncers to get the whole set of exchanging relations.

Since gifts to Gods, as sacrifices, were the most widespread ancient type of gift, secular evolutionary sidelining of this centrality enables theorizing to conclude with an economistic perception of human nature. But gifting is not temporal in a serial sense; gifts of sacrifice include transhistoric mythical dimensions. Sacred gifts are syntheses of the real and the imaginary and participate in the secular and the sacred.[17] In mythical 'exchanges' gifts are inalienable (not reducible to exchange logics) because they are embedded in cultural narratives that take into relational account human origins and ends. These relations are ritually regulated as well as uniquely and spontaneously innovated in diverse contexts of 'exchange'. Gifting discloses, and also denies, the superhuman origins of human culture but in doing so it is a relatedness that cannot be reduced to relations between man and nature.[18]

Gifting is a moment of human questing for transcendence, while tied to specific narratives and practices of the giver, it aims for relations to other levels of participation; for example with the dead who have to be treated as part of the social context. In this sense gifts are expressions of relational intentions that symbolize the present, but also signify transformations of 'otherness' that include love, piety, charity and solidarity. This is a logic that does not reduce to individual instrumentalism; gifting aspires to transformation, as in the consecration of bread and wine in communion enabling participation in the social body of Christ – as the transgenerational Christian community.

What has to be explained here is the secular reduction of exchanges to a detached, disembedded and independently willed 'individual'. If we learn anything from this debate about gifting it has to be, as Louis Dumont suggests, that we cannot use the normal distinction between subject and object. We have to let go of this epistemological focus on certainty and come to see that boundaries fluctuate as the case may be.[19] This goes into philosophical issues beyond our concerns here. But it may be enough to note that Jürgen Habermas also rejects the subjectivistic framework of modern philosophy and bases his philosophic method on the linguistic inter-subjectivity of communicative action. Emmanual Levinas also rejects the subjectivistic framework and makes ethics the prime framework for philosophy beginning with the primacy of the 'self–other' relations. Both of these contemporary philosophers are moving beyond the enlightenment paradigm of subject-centered reason, and submit complementary reasons for why the unifying power of the sacred cannot be terminated by secularization.[20]

But returning to the gift discourse, Helmuth Berking interprets the origins of gifts as derived from rituals of food distribution that go back to sacralized killing and distributing of food. This implies a fundamental life-oriented spiritual practice; the gifting of food is inherent in the table grace, the last supper, the church supper and in 'give us this day our daily food' in the Lord's prayer. God, as life, is the addressee and source of the gift of food.

Gift rituals, and religious gift practices, are oriented to seeking wisdom, peace, discernment, prophecy, faith, miracles, healing, aesthetic dramatizations, etc. Most significant today, I think, is the avoidance of social violence and illustration of this can illuminate how ritual practices, as felt performances, still have relevance.

Berking relies on Rene Girard who tells us that all primitive and ancient communities created ritual practices and/or religious imitations of violence in order to maintain a lease on violence.[21] In local purification practices, a social art/craft of violence control is created that tricks violence into spending itself on victims whose death (real or symbolic) provokes no reprisals.

On this account the social wisdom of later religions was to reduplicate the sacred epiphany of the founding divinity by re-enacting the actions that brought violence to an end. From this perspective primitive sacred participations, Ancient Greek tragedy, and religious rituals of symbolic victimage are all socio-cultural institutions that prohibit violence by providing a mimetic catharsis that re-enacts the original events of violence.

These ritual innovations as re-enactments are not universal but local and last only for the time that the cultural institution remains a stabilizing differentiation and/or hierarchical reconciliation of conflictual differences. In primitive dance societies, or a cycle of dramatic festivals, or even in monastic reforms, the social potential for expressing conflicts is a permanent possibility built into the liturgical resources of every culture.

Today, cultural capabilities to express aesthetic reconciliations of conflicts in public life are ongoing but much diminished. Opposing ecological degradations and externally imposed colonizing developments results in imaginative groups creating public drama that are equivalent to traditional ritual protections against violence such as the 'all species' parade in San Francisco,[22] or enactments of street theater such as Bread and Circus and the San Francisco Mime troupe. In a different medium, new applications of Joseph Beuys' social sculpture creates participatory environments that stimulate insights into social justice or ecological crisis.[23] Another is the all night sacred music festival at Fireflies Ashram in India.[24]

Under the light of totalizing reason, harmony and peace are conceived as incompatible with symbolic remembrance of the tragic disorder and events of violence. Thus Plato turns out the poets from his utopia in the hope that excluding the representations of tragic violence would also eliminate their appeals. The logic of gifting and the logic of aesthetic and religious drama[25] is ultimately a form of participation in symbolic events that transform self-understanding – they cannot be reduced to instrumental exchanges between monadic individuals.[26] As Ivan Illich has claimed (see Chapter 4), this reductionism results from the disembodiment of sensibility that accompanies the cultural dominance of secularizing science. Seeing has become a passive experience; to repeat a TV news slogan, we 'watch the world watchers watch the world'.

From moral economy to a more reflexive individualization

In many traditional cultures gifting and sharing practices were understood to reduce envy and increase community building. This continues today with faith-based communities whose self-understanding obligates them to help the poor and desperate, and do so without expectations for public recognition or fame. The real rapid responders to Katrina, and other disaster situations, were the faith-based citizen groups who do not pay attention to public recognition. Another first responder to Katrina was Wal-Mart and that has been broadcast everywhere.

Reciprocity as gifting remains a form of social sharing as the exchange of blood, organs, semen, and time, as well as the sharing of art in public museums, or parks. In the West, we have been socialized to think possession and private property, but according to Helmuth Berking, through individualization we also become more reflexively oriented to sharing, fairness, and justice. Berking views the change of the norm of reciprocity from sacrifice, to debt, to duty and now to the separation of gratitude from traditional obligation, or simply interpersonal 'thanks'. The emotional and interactive meaning of modern exchange has become less determined by traditional motivations and more merely personal and this implies a transformation of contemporary moral economy: "Gift-giving is on the increase. The staging of the non-everyday, the intensification of the anti-economic is constantly expanding. Reciprocity is gaining ground as a protest against (economic) equivalence."[27]

A correlation emerges between greater individualization and reflexive orientations to community, love, friendship, trust, solidarity and empathy. What was once conventional behavior has become supplemented by post-conventional reflexive orientations to these traditional ends. The view is also argued by Robert Wuthnow[28] and David Korten[29] that most highly individuated persons are more likely to value doing things to help others! The 'altruism' of traditional practices is migrating into a reflexive 'subjective ecology' that has been de-traditonalized and yet re-moralized.

Social sharing and commons based peer production

The giving of hospitality is a primary model for the gifting practices of cultural groups. Hospitality to strangers is a strong norm from Judeo-Christian and Greek origins. 'Give me hospitality' is also an open sesame in many traditional worlds. The hospitality principle would actually be a more viable foreign policy than power politics that threatens pre-emptive strikes.[30]

Gifting and hospitality has always emerged in food situations from communal meal rituals to soup kitchens. But it takes an innovative form in the D.C. Kitchen where food gathering (from many sources) and redistribution pulls in homeless persons to cook the meals that then go out to many shelters and centers. Along the way this process gives the cooks in training a profession and the network becomes a self-regulating solution for many poor and deprived in Washington D.C. As the high point of American prosperity wanes, more service-learning programs have begun that bring volunteers together in ways that performs a public function – such as supplying food to the poor – and at the same time unites giving and job training for the out of work.[31]

A modernizing moral economy, as against those being rooted in commercial motivations, is increasingly about lifestyles. To this end new sets of sharing possibilities have emerged, such as new forms of auto share and bike share. Whereas these began in Europe much earlier, by 2005 there were 17 U.S. car sharing programs that include 91,995 people.[32]

Exciting new models of sharing that emerge from contemporary technologies abound such as file sharing, the Open Source movement, Linux, Napster and Wikipedia. This form of sharing reveals new potentials for production and creativity. In these and many other forms of post-materialism open sharing is beneath the screen mainly because there is no systematic way to see them as a dimension of modern economic behavior.

The growth of peer-to-peer forms of social sharing has accelerated and formed what Yochai Benkler calls a 'networked information economy' that he claims is building new social relations of mutual interest and mutual recognition.[33] He argues that commons-based peer production is now the most efficient way to produce, rather than the hierarchical corporate firm protected by intellectual property rights. The implications of this are very wide.

Benkler's book *The Wealth of Networks: How Social Production Transforms Markets and Freedom* explores the potentials of greatly enhanced individual capabilities and the new freedoms that it makes possible. For example, current struggles to open decentralized broadband use of telecommunications is building on the experience gained in the open source software movement to work around the barriers set up by exclusive property regimes. Of course this is being resisted by the massive force of corporate interests.

> The outcome of the conflict between the industrial information economy and its emerging networked alternative will determine whether we evolve into a permission culture . . . or into a society marked by social practice of non-market production and co-operative sharing of information, knowledge, and culture of the type I describe throughout this book, and which I argue will improve freedom and justice in liberal societies.[34]

Networked environments make possible a new way of organizing production:

> . . . radically decentralized, collaborative, and non proprietary; based on sharing resources and outputs among widely distributed, loosely connected individuals who cooperate with each other without relying on either market signals or managerial commands. This is what I call 'commons-based peer production'.[35]

Applications of this form of production to food security, knowledge production and utilization, medical and cultural creations is possible and constitute a crucial set of tools for poor countries and communities. These forms of social production and sharing patch together public, private and individual capabilities in ways that are more efficient forms of allocating human creativity than market oriented ones. Moreover, this form of social production creates opportunities for a more autonomous and a more critically engaged discursive public – for example, the supplementary role of the blogosphere in getting out stories and information that is hidden by the dominant media monopolies.

A new institutional ecology emerges where a networked information economy is operative. Such an institutional ecology would be non-market forms of co-operation that improves capabilities of organizations and individuals to directly participate in public debates. It also gives new opportunities to supposedly obsolete forms of production – such as networks of small farmers and artisans who can form fair trade virtual organizations that enable them to be competitive.

The emergent potentials of information-based production and distribution shows that other forms of socially based forms of production can be regenerated and expanded. For example, 'Aid to Artisans' that offers assistance to artisan groups worldwide. Through collaboration in product development, business skills training and development of new markets, livelihoods and community well-being can be secured that also preserves artistic traditions.

Co-operative economies: yesterday and today

An alternative path, not taken by the dominant economics theory, was the creation of federated co-operative movements of producers, consumers and credit that enabled communities and municipalities to resist wider market dislocations and sustain their local economies and ecologies. As Jane Jacobs has argued, the response of many city regions to the expansion of the market system was, and remains today, a shield to globalization and an affirmation of their own cultural practices and socio-economic arrangements.[36]

A contemporary form of this alternative socio-economic integration has been documented by Robert Putnam who has shown that in northern Italy region of Emilia Romagna there are many co-operating networks of small locally owned firms: local ownership is the key.[37] The density of co-op and small businesses is so great that one of every 10 people works in a co-operative business in a 4 million person area. The region's economy has been so successful that it now has the highest income per person in Italy, the lowest unemployment rate and the highest citizen satisfaction.[38] The city of Bologna is the capital of this world model for municipal-centered socialism. Over 80 percent of social services are decentralized to social co-operatives. In this city region reciprocity is a living principal for every business; not only is trust so high that legal fees are marginal, but the quality of commercial products are actually perceived as relations between people. Professor Stefano Zamagni states that "labor is an occasion for self-realization, not a mere factor of production."[39] This is indeed a market-centered economy where capitalism takes a backset to reciprocity, trust and quality production. How it evolved is one story but its importance here is that as an economic culture it is outstandingly different. That there is co-operation between the Left and Christian co-operative confederations, like that in Kerala, India, is significant. In this city region the political arrangements have been reversed from serving large corporations to creating an economic culture where citizens are aided to learn how communities can invest, contract, zone, tax, lobby and thus learn how bottom up politics can influence and restructure national, regional and local economies.

Such federated co-operative movements of producers, consumers and credit organizations enable communities and municipalities to resist wider market dislocations and sustain their local economies and ecologies. These co-op networks are the reciprocal economics that have generalized the gift economy. Co-operatives are everywhere, and yet not very well known to the mass consumer or capitalist worker.

Let's begin with their history as a response to the centralizing commercialization.

In England and France in the 1830–40s, 300 co-operative societies were organized by Dr. William King who argued that "cooperation is the form of production peculiar to labor". Or the Rochdale Weavers who demonstrated, circa 1844, that a social venture could amass capital that could be used for community prosperity. The fact that Rochdale eventually enlisted outside investors identifies the vulnerability of co-operatives to the problem of capital formation and to the systemic problem of sustaining co-operative economies. They require institutional support of one kind or another, and they cannot subsist in a hostile capitalist institutional order.

The co-operative movement was greatly facilitated by the passage of the Industry and Provident Society acts of 1852, which were aided by the support of John Stuart Mill. These acts gave co-ops limited liability status and the ability to issue shares; by 1865 there were over 100,000 people in co-ops in England. The success of this movement was aided by the co-ops paying a quarterly dividend of 4 percent per quarter encouraging direct investment in these social enterprises.

The primary focus of these English co-ops was to provide food, but the purchasing power of this network was used to buy from co-operatives up the supply chain from farm to granary to bakery. Collectively they formed a federated co-operative system; an 'organic co-op society' within a market society.

Today the advantages of a federated co-operative network are promoted by the innovative successes of Mondragon collective which are:

- unifying the roles separated in a commercial firm – worker, manager and owner;
- boosting the productivity of participating workers while maintaining or increasing profitability.

Worker participation and ownership form an economic democracy that has been seen as the real market economy, since the capitalist economy becomes controlled by massive monopolies. In a real economic democracy it is precisely the capitalist who is unnecessary, and yet the evolution of control over the worker has been justified in many ways as Stephen Marglin explained earlier.

Advocates of the economic democracy strategy are effusive about the possibilities of this model, if it can be maintained as a democracy.[40]

The fact that the Mondragon has become a multinational with seemingly profit-oriented goals is deemed correctable. But the fact that the successful models have solved the capital supply problem in different ways is important to understand, because that is the major criticism of alternative economies.

Internal self-financing such as the Mondragon collective, or union-sponsored capital funds such as in Quebec's Solidarity fund, or the Vancouver City Savings Credit Union, or government-aided financing such as in the northern Italian municipalities, or the participatory budgeting procedures in Brazil or Argentina, are all possible models for financing. More examples of alternative capital formation processes can be found in Chapter 8.

The Seikatsu Club Co-operative Union in Japan claims that it is the most advanced co-op in the world since they have spawned several movements as they developed. Starting as a consumer union by buying large quantities of safe quality foods and distributing it to their Hans, or groups of families, they soon moved on to recycling used oil and producing their own soaps. In planning for fresh wholesome food they pre-order basic food stuffs from many organic and environmentally screened producers for a traditional menu; no processed foods allowed. From a food co-op to producer co-ops they went on to become an active environmental movement too. As they learned about the political blockages in their way they moved on to become a political movement as well, electing many mayors and local representatives. Other dimensions developed along the way such as community-based care for elders, child care and the formation of workers collectives where their workers own and manage their own enterprises. Started by women and run largely by women this is a very savvy and far-sighted movement that is an international model for co-operative economies and deserves the Right Livelihood Award they received in 1989.[41]

Other innovative co-operative arrangements for producer co-operatives are the Briar Patch Collective in the Bay Area of California, Co-op Atlantic in Atlantic, Canada, etc., or Co-op America that helps consumers and producer co-ops see what is the meaning of green consuming. More than 750,000 cooperatives now serve some 760 million members in more than 100 countries.[42]

A central debate in the co-operative movement is illustrated by the European Union investing in the social economy in order to bring in excluded sectors and to create jobs. This top down investment strategy is opposed by the associations of European co-operatives who are adamant that the social economy be built from the bottom up in order to introduce the 'social' into the economy by generating solidarity. They believe that efforts to centralize and regulate a wider set of social economy enterprises and associations would undermine a 'social economy' as a co-operative sector of the private economy. These co-ops distinguish between co-operatives and the wider organizations that the E.U. would form in order to reintroduce solidarity into excluded groups as well as solve problems of national development:

> Co-operatives are private enterprises founded voluntarily by their members. It is the task of these enterprises to provide services that will benefit the members. The members jointly own the enterprise and they are responsible for it: they provide the capital and are the underlying organizational force, they make the decisions and are the recipients of services.[43]

The claim that associations of independent co-ops can sustain themselves and do not need government grants is the crucial point. They aspire to be, if you will, a non-governmental form of socialism.

Sustaining traditional art-craft-body knowledge systems

In 1819 Robert Owen republished John Bellars' 120-year-old plan for setting up Colleges of Industry and used it to promote his own movement in Lanark County, England. Owen claimed that he had discovered the 'nucleus of society' in his village communities. Owen alone, Polanyi claims, saw the problem of economic society; namely that what appeared to be economic solutions to poverty were not, because the problems and solutions were basically social. In retrospect Owen understood that the social nature of mankind would not be satisfied by purely economic integrations:

> The new market institutional system was the destruction of the traditional character of settled people . . . and their transmutation into a new type of people, migratory, nomadic, lacking in self-respect and discipline – crude, callous beings of whom both the laborer and the capitalist were an example . . . (In the new economic society) . . . a principle, quite unfavorable to individual and general happiness, was working havoc with his social environment, his neighborhood, his standing in the community, his craft, in a word, with those relationships to nature and man in which his economic existence was formerly embedded.[44]

As long as people had an embedded social status they could resist the atomizing market homogenizations, as well as maintain their own vernacular learning practices.

Vernacular stocks of knowledge about horticulture, healing, work and socio-political organization remain the basis of a lived world in indigenous, subsistence and traditional worlds. Interventions of expert knowledge systems of agronomy, forestry, mass production, scientific management, and impositions of western democratic models, into these worlds is dubious and dangerous. If chosen it has to be done in ways that supplement and do not negate successful vernacular domains of social and substantive economic subsistence.

Many efforts have been made to create store houses for indigenous knowledge with the expectation that it can be transferred to other places with good results. But it is not clear to me that this effort has been fruitful, partly because each set of knowledge is really context specific.

A different and more fruitful approach has been focusing on mutual learning processes from the viewpoint that all cultures have art-craft-body components as well as systemic head-oriented knowledge; focusing on balancing this learning is more relevant. Whereas expert knowledge systems present themselves as universal forms of knowledge (e.g. science, logic, theology), traditional knowledge is implicit, personal and contextually dependent (e.g. craft, art, practical common sense). Each culture then combines forms of knowledge in different ways that change over time and have different epistemologies, forms of transmission and innovation and differing power relationships in all these dimensions.[45]

A comparative approach to different socio-cultural contexts describes different ways of mixing disembedded universalisms and practical body-centered intuitive competences. Whereas Karl Marx could express disdain and impute the label of 'petty bourgeois' to all artisans and subsistence 'workers' who resisted integration into factories or the market economy, this can now be seen as an evolutionary prejudice.

Stephen Marglin's reflections on the origin of these types of knowledge distinguishes between the human capability for integrating contextual judgments (being able to integrate parts into a whole) and the separate ability to decompose operations into detailed parts – an analytic ordering competence that is not contextually bound. Citing the book by Oliver Sacks *The Man who Mistook His Wife for a Hat*, Marglin defines[46] contextually embedded knowledge as an intuitive and yet practical way of creating or making, as against logical deductions from self-evident invariant axioms or principles that are independent of contexts. These distinctions do not privilege experts but indicate that traditional, non-analytic ways of knowing are essential and are ultimately embedded in the human body's capabilities 'to put the puzzles together', and not in two different types of cognitive analysis. Learning to ride a bicycle or dance or cook are learning processes that are 'in the body' and we can do it again.

Today we are reminded again and again that body-based competences are relevant and can't be dismissed or replaced by theoretical knowledge. Backing off of the prejudices of the evolutionary superiority of western cognitive knowledge is on the agenda for sustainability strategies today. Opening up to mutual learning processes is far more productive. This is especially true of knowledge about the earth and what is essential to live sustainably.

7 Substantive economic cultures

Better indicators to the inseparability of ecology and equity

In India, human communities are interconnected with the viability of local ecology and local agriculture – because that is where over 70 percent of its people reside. Despite recent high growth rates the fate of India is still connected to its agrarian crisis. Will economic freedom resolve this problem? Here India is the point society for the world as a whole.

Unlimited economic growth continues to be taken for granted and India is proceeding without adjusting its 'inclusive growth' to ecological equity. Sustaining local ecologies and supporting rural communities are inseparable and not adequately measured by the dominant economic indicators. Perhaps the most succinct way to establish this is a series of overlapping points made by leaders in ecological economics:

1 Partha Dasgupta, economist at Cambridge, argues that without subtracting the degraded natural assets from economic indexes the results are highly misleading; the inclusive wealth of countries goes down as their GNPS go up.[1] Degradation of fresh water, soil, forests, estuaries, rivers, etc. destroy available natural assets and actually reduce the value of existing wealth.
2 Anil Agarwal, founder of the Centre for Science and Environment in New Delhi, suggests that there are two GNPs: there was Gross National Product but also Gross Nature Product. There was an inverse relationship between them. As one went up, the other went down! Hence we must learn to recognize that a standing tree, if its ecological role as a conserver of soil and water is taken into consideration, is three times more valuable than its worth as timber – which is all foresters and 'developers' see.[2] He makes an aligned case for measuring poverty in a predominantly agrarian society in terms of biomass used per person, rather than income, which is an inadequate yardstick. This represents wealth more accurately than earnings in rupees.
3 Herman Daly's *Beyond Growth* defines 'throughput', or the quantity of materials and energy used per capita as a new indicator that has great promise if it is used in decision making. Ecological economics aspires to change by defining the problem of sustainability in terms of maintaining the quantity of economic

throughput between the absorptive and regenerative capacity of the earth. The alternative is a focus on qualitative intensive 'development'.

4 The expanded ideal of inclusive, or actual wealth, of countries, then becomes a better standard for measurement of growth. However, the only recognition of the impact of 'throughput' or material flows of biomass per person is in incorporation of ecological economics into national reports, as is being done in Europe. For example, the Human Appropriation of Net Primary Production of biomass (known after its ungainly acronym, HANPP), is also gaining ground. Statistical offices like Eurostat are now disclosing figures on material flows for EU countries between 1980 and 2000.[3]

5 Paul Hawken has been a leader in trying to change the relation between business and the environment. In a series of books he has evolved a concept of 'comprehensive output' that takes into account all costs of economic projects to all parties, not just the stockholders. Together with Amory and Hunter Lovins, their book *Natural Capitalism: Creating the Next Industrial Revolution*[4] defines the services of nature as 'natural capital' that is being depleted. Therefore increased resource productivity, redesigning industry with closed loops and zero waste, shifting from the sale of goods to the provision of services and reinvesting in the natural capital are the priorities for a sustainable industrial economy.

These corrective concepts and indicators define ecological equity and demonstrate that very different approaches are needed for substantive economic cultures. Many NGOs, and a few corporations, are showing the way to practice this. For example, numerous groups are preserving and multiplying indigenous seeds against the tide of agri-business hybrid seeds. Another example is alternative development projects that take up the cause of preserving and harvesting more water capacity in households and villages in India and beyond.

The *Nayakrishi Andolon*, the new farming movement, in Bangladesh enhances the efficiency of land, water, biodiversity and energy and has spurned chemical agriculture. They have established their food products as highly valued organic alternatives in a region that has had massive pesticide use. Experimentation with multiplying varieties of papayas, jackfruit, rice, bitter gourd, beans, etc. allow them to be more flexible in providing products adjusted to weather and regional differences.[5]

Vandana Shiva's Research Foundation for Science Technology and Ecology initiated the *Navdanya*, the nine seeds movement, in India that stores seeds and promotes records of biodiversity to document the resources and knowledge of local and regional communities. Going along with these activities are efforts to bring pesticide-free products to the urban consumer, especially the endangered grain crops that face regional extinction. Shiva's group sponsored the *Bija Yatra* campaign that creates public awareness of the threats of the WTO intellectual property rights, while also advocating farmers' rights, as another dimension of this movement.

Banking on Seeds, or the community seed network, organized by the Green Foundation in India asserts that over 60 percent of the world's agriculture is farmed by traditional and subsistence farmers. Saving traditional seeds in the face of the hybrid 'green revolution' seeds is a matter of survival for small farmers. They have also innovated a 'bio-bomb' that is a pesticide made from bitter leaves and put in a sack where the water enters a paddy field.

The Central Himalayan Rural Action Group (CHIRAG) has been very successful in 163 villages increasing soil and water conservation techniques by vegetative and physical means, creating community forestry, alternative energy, animal husbandry and drinking water are all part of the watershed integration innovations they have used to mobilize villages. How to keep up with the massive explosion of different citizens' groups around the world and the innovative ideas that they are creating and applying is daunting. Paul Hawken's Natural Capital Institute in California has created a data base of civil society organizations around the world. It is the largest database in the world dealing with groups in 243 countries, territories sovereign and islands – The World Index Of Social and Environmental Responsibility http://www.wiserearth.org.

The Bioneers's ongoing conferences, organized by The Collective Heritage Institute in the U.S., bring together scientific and social innovators who demonstrate practical models for restoring the earth and communities. Bioneers are biological pioneers who are working with nature to heal nature and image a spiritual connection with the living world. The yearly conferences have been imitated in many parts of the country and beyond, and as a unique combination of social justice, sustainability and scientific mix. They focus on devising strategies for restoration based on nature's own operating principles.

One of their concepts and tools is 'biomimicry', an approach to the study of nature, its models, systems, processes and elements. It imitates or takes inspiration from them to solve human sustainability problems, since nature is imaginative by necessity and has already solved many of the problems we are grappling with; animals, plants, and microbes are the real engineers. They have found what works, what is appropriate, and what lasts here on Earth. The real news of biomimicry is that after 3.8 billion years of research and development where the failures are fossils, what surrounds us is the secret to survival. Janine M. Benyus' book *Biomimicry* explains that:

> Like the viceroy butterfly imitating the monarch, we humans are imitating the best adapted organisms in our habitat. We are learning, for instance, how to harness energy like a leaf, grow food like a prairie, build ceramics like an abalone, self-medicate like a chimp, create color like a peacock, compute like a cell, and run a business like a hickory forest. The conscious emulation of life's genius is a survival strategy for the human race, a path to a sustainable future. The more our world functions like the natural world, the more likely we are to endure on this home that is ours, but not ours alone.[6]

Starting from a thermodynamic modeling of nature, an ecological movement called the 'Natural Step' (NS) was developed in Sweden by Dr. Karl-Henrik Robert, a research oncologist. He built a consensus for scientifically-based sustainability that provides a comprehensive understanding of the natural cyclical processes needed to sustain life on earth. This framework has been promoted as a guide for businesses, communities, educators, government, and individuals for long-term sustainability. The four system principles are:

1 Nature cannot withstand a systematic build-up of dispersed matter mined from the Earth's crust (e.g. oil, minerals, etc.).
2 Nature cannot withstand a systematic build-up of persistent compounds made by humans (e.g. PCBs).
3 Nature cannot take a systematic deterioration of its capacity for renewal (e.g. harvesting fish faster than they can be replenished).
4 People must not be forced into conditions that systematically undermine their capacity to meet their needs.

These steps have been applied by:

Electrolux, Sweden Adopted the NS framework after it lost a multi-million dollar contract because it did not offer a refrigeration system without chlorofluorocarbons (CFCs). The company used TNS framework to phase out CFCs and won back that customer. Went on to develop washing machines that use 12 gallons of water instead of 45, substituted canola oil for petroleum-based oil in its chain saws – all the while reducing total energy consumption and hazardous waste.

IKEA, Sweden the largest furniture company in world, adopted the NS framework in 1991 in response to consumer pressure against rainforest wood. A four-year environmental plan called for TNS implementation throughout the company. IKEA began by redesigning one furniture line to eliminate metals, persistent glues, toxic dyes, reduced energy consumption and increased material efficiency. IKEA is now more profitable.

Interface, U.S. a Georgia based flooring company. Became the first U.S. company to adopt the TNS framework. The goal was to produce zero waste, and to 'never take another drop of oil from the ground'. Innovations include leasing carpets instead of selling them, powering a factory with solar energy. Design and manufacturing improvements have saved the company $50 million. Sales have grown $200 million, without increasing consumption of earth's resources.

Note that although the first three principles are natural science based, the fourth leaps to normative concepts such as 'justice' and 'fairness'. How to justify norms is not the same thing as establishing natural limits with facts. This requires historical justifications of normative frames. Therefore it is essential to review the normative frames that have emerged to protect equity and agrarian sustainability.

Customs in common and the wisdom of commons

A classic "commons" is an unwritten customary agreement that provides sufficiency limits for those who share the use of an "indigenous resource" essential for life, such as water use, irrigation networks, forests, biodiversity, mineral or wildlife access, or even use of open or city spaces, indigenous seeds, silence, etc.[7]

Using the model of local-regional sufficiency *The Ecologist*, in their response to the 1989 Brundland report *Whose Common Future?*, argued that 'commons' can be imitated and renewed everywhere. Of course reclaiming the commons will be realized in different ways; for example, in the U.S., community support for local agriculture, or formation of local currency systems permit local exchanges to support people and community rather than the single goal of maximizing profits.

Impositions of market logics maximize the single goal of profit realization which in the context of a forest disvalues its multiple uses that are central to the meaning of sustainability.[8] In contrast the Chipko movement, and others in Southeast Asian forest communities, have shown a practical rationality that derives from women's knowledge of life sustaining practices. Vandana Shiva, as a leading eco-feminist, is clear that protecting and regenerating this local knowledge are the essentials for sustainable communities and she hopes the West will wake up and learn from these traditional commons cultures.

A commons protects against scarcity of essentials for life and guarantees access for members' subsistence. The normative logic of the commons is the opposite of the modern economic scarcity postulate in that it secures 'enoughness' or 'sufficiency'. For example over 90 percent of inland commercial fishing is still regulated by informal commons' agreements of the participants. Commons is the protection that many people, especially the 'poor', have to resist formal legal enclosures that accompany state or market formations. As mentioned earlier, agro-business corporations promoting genetically modified seeds have been met with the regeneration of indigenous seed banks that are operating on commons' principles.

Enclosures of land, by autocratic fiat or credit dispossessions, forced labor or taxes, since the seventeenth century in England, have always undermined established commons for economic wealth creation for the few. Forced scarcity, as the 'whip of hunger', has been used to form 'labor markets'. Imposed economic development and professionalizations of knowledge also fragment customary agreements and local self-rule by the imposition of 'individual property rights'.

What is de-valued in official enclosures are the local vernacular customary norms that have enabled herbalists, horticulturalists, women's knowledge and local craft enterprises to maintain their substantive sustaining role. Gusteva Esteva argues, echoing Ivan Illich, that "disvalue is the secret of economic value and it cannot be created except with violence and in the face of continuous resistance." He goes on to say: "Establishing economic value requires the disvaluing of all other forms of social existence. Disvalue transmogrifies skills into lacks, commons into resources, men and women into commoditized labor, tradition into burden, wisdom into ignorance, autonomy into dependency."[9]

Modern idealizations of theoretical rationality and the application of methodologies insisting upon certain knowledge constructions, sidelines focusing on common sense practices or the cultivation of judgment.

The labor historian E.P. Thompson views the moral economy, or a 'customs in common', as a corrective to the theorizer's propensity to confuse 'real abstractions' for living sociality.[10] In response to critical theorists, who take theory integrations as cognitive advances that are essential for emancipation from social necessity, Thompson is clear that concrete practices are the real object domain for critical thinking that can recognize distortive, from humanly possible, social arrangements. He indicates that 'commons' are omnipresent realities – not only in past worlds but in the contemporary world too.

Concepts used in commons spheres, in general, have to be formed from the ecological and political relations themselves and not from industrial or post-industrial productivity interests. For example, the concept of the 'Multitude' forwarded by Michael Hardt and Antonio Negri[11] misses the mark. They aspire to reconceive class analysis on the basis of a vague notion of 'immaterial labor' that perpetuates labor theory while claiming to transcend it. The concept of 'peasant family economy' recognizes all the mixed economic relations they attempt to describe and identifies its unique substantive economy functions.[12] While their analysis of the war system of empire is brilliant, they are totally out of touch with the realities of rural and agricultural existence and take the analysis of maximizing economics too literally.

Getting out of the urban centers and receiving hospitality in subsistence worlds might be an antidote to super 'progressive' left theorizing. Toward that end consulting fair trade tourism groups – accessible on the web – which are set up to take interested people to meet rural groups in reciprocal exchanges, is an open opportunity.

Localizing cultural affirmations in a globalizing world

Rather than be pushed into catch-up development, many communities and regions that retain some arrangement of 'sufficiency', or 'enoughness',[13] represent alternative economic cultures. The wisdom of these arrangements is denied by modernizers, which sees them as not oriented to greater productivity and therefore as having deep limitations for attaining the 'good life' in the modern consumer sense. Documentation of customary vernacular organizations is a different research program, as Veronika Bennholdt-Thomsen and Maria Mies have shown, that documents how subsistence alternatives to modernizing logics are viable options today.[14]

Luis Lopezllera Mendes is a grass roots leader of a network of Mexican community organizations whose newsletter names their project *La otra bolsa de valores* – The Other Stock Exchange. This is a metaphor for an alternative credit plus system where network help is a 'hammock' and takes the shape of whatever the user needs. Mendes says we must look to indigenous people for a model. They survived 500 years of conquest and we can learn from them a new way of looking at time and space. Perhaps we could recover their rhythms and learn to think of space as a 'bioregion', or a sphere of life that has an order in itself that we have to learn to live within. Indeed this is an appropriate substantive economic concept and the name of a relevant social movement.

Bioregionalism, originated by Peter Berg and Raymond Dasmann in the early 1970s, is another vernacular domain strategy. Reinhabiting ecoregions by relearning how people who lived there for many generations survived is the goal. Modern communities can be helped to regain their sustainability in particular bioregions too, when citizens become aware of the living and integrating qualities of their place. The Bioregional movement in North America advocates demarcating political regions in watershed or related ecological ways. Bioregionalism refers to living a rooted life by participating in the ecology, economy and culture of the place you live. It would be a real breakthrough if all local historical societies went beyond glorifying past 'founders' and bridged the gap to subsistence groups in the past. Bill McGibben's *Deep Economy* expresses a version of this philosophy and practice. Tom Berry's *Dream of the Earth* is also attuned to this thinking.

More recently, Luis Lopezllera Mendes stated that the movement of recent history in Mexico is from poverty to misery to chaos and that the old national liberation movements have been replaced by movements for local-regional autonomy. In order to preserve their cultural identity and environments, the first goal of current actions is to de-link, as much as possible, from the development paradigm and at the same time to link peasant/indigenous communities to the urban middle class to sustain cultural and historical values, as well as livelihoods. Mendes argues that intellectuals have got to go beyond Antonio Gramsci's notion of an 'organic' intellectual who defends people's rights to become innovators of the new institutions and local economies that can increase people's might. To do this requires inventing new ways to overcome imposed economic development while involving people in substantive economic alternatives.

Efforts to regenerate and renew traditional practices from within; that is, to view traditions as open books not closed systems, that can be made more adaptive to contemporary circumstances, has been promoted by the International Network for Cultural Alternatives to Development (INCA(D)) network founded by the Montreal Intercultural Institute.[15] Their mission is to search for and help facilitate cultural alternatives to economic development, or what I have called substantive economic cultures. Their journal *INTERculture* is a treasure house of additional examples of what Ashis Nandy calls 'critical traditionalism'. That is the effort of third world people to understand their own situations in their own terms while revising their traditions and incorporating what is judged appropriate from the modern world.

This INCA(D) network perceives the westernizing economic globalization process as destructive to local cultures in ways that create poverty, dependency and ecological degradation. Forced integrations into the world economy is a shipwreck for marginalized cast-off's and an endless struggle for survival. However, looking carefully, it is often the cast-off's that invent – with different logics – other paths for human existence/subsistence. INCA(D) is preoccupied with learning about and facilitating these spontaneous self-organizations of the excluded.

Serge Latouche, a French member of INCA(D) has stated their critique of economism very directly:

> It is necessary to set different meanings at the center of human life, other than the expansion of production and consumption. We aspire towards a . . . world

> where the economy would be put back where it belongs, as a simple means of human life and not as an ultimate end, and in which one would renounce this kind of uncontrolled drive to despair.[16]

'Globalization' is a complex of economic, technological, political and social flows that can destroy local social and cultural arrangements if not screened carefully. Helena Norberg-Hodge in *Ancient Futures; Learning from Ladakh* records how she helped form an ecological group that screened out inappropriate technological transfers. All communities who are impacted by global financial integrations need countering alternatives that enable them to defend themselves. In some case it is global outreach – which was done by the Zapatista's in Chiapas who used the internet very effectively to broadcast their situation. An outstanding model here is the incredible networking achieved by the world's indigenous peoples who successfully pushed a 'prior and informed consent protocol' at the United Nations.[17]

Images of idyllic vernacular villages not affected by complex society, or wholesale denial of the relevance of human rights, are an unnecessary nostalgic purism. The idea of mutual learning is a much more fruitful approach if the right institutional forms are created to enable this form of local-global learning. Since the indigenous peoples have learned how to connect and advocate their interests globally, other groups can do so too. An example of this form of learning follows.

Frederique Appfel-Marglin's *The Spirit of Regeneration,* a study of PRATEC (Andean Project for Peasant Technologies), in Peru is a revelation about third world trends. PRATEC began as a project when development professionals recognized that the green revolution was not as fruitful as regenerating traditional Andean horticulture. By affirming peasant horticultural knowledge, rather than modern expert agronomy, they came to understand the Andean world was not primarily as a world to 'know' but a world to live in, to participate in, and to collectively construct. The founders of PRATEC saw that the introduction of hybrid seeds, and the technical packages of the green revolution, not only interrupted the regenerative cycles of the local cultivars, but their culture as well.

Despite the fact that with chemical fertilizers and pesticides, irrigation and hybrid seeds, two or three crops could be raised in a year, they choose to accept the one or two raised by traditional horticultural practices. The technical path destroyed the cycle of rituals and destroyed the reciprocities of regenerating biological and cultural worlds together. The green revolution transforms peasants into individuals dependent on the market rather than on each other, nature, and the *huacas* (deities). The penetration of the green revolution broke the natural creativity of the peasant communities, losing all holistic meaning and social cultural identity too.

The members of PRATEC began deprofessionalizing themselves and learning how to act and write from within the Andean collectivities, and they came to know with clarity the impossibility of participating in the Andean collective actions from within their professions.[18]

Mutual learning is the model of learning recommended by those aware of alternative development capacities. Mutual learning centers for horticulture and healing have been established in South America and India. But they involve a de-colonization of the professionalized mindset as essential for participation in other cultural contexts. At the same time modern technical knowledge makes other contributions, including legitimating traditional agriculture's carbon-saving reductions of green house gas emissions.

De-colonization is not to preserve traditional culture but to allow a space for organic growth of indigenous cultures – not to totally stop economic growth or the consumption of material goods, but in the absence of real redistribution in the poorer nations, to decouple the introduction of technologies, including social technologies, from their destructive cultural and political consequences.

The superiority of peasant, or local agriculture: an ongoing truth

Every modern national economy has historically followed the path which begins with agriculture being the main source of income for the majority of the population and ends with agricultural employment being a very small fraction of the total labor force. This point is especially acute in today's India where the industrialization of agriculture is creating a mass of displaced people with no place to go.

Robert Rodale urged that 'regeneration' was going to be the big idea for our time.[19] Given the degradation of the earth, 'regeneration' is the appropriate term for responding to the disturbances in ways that improve the productivity of natural assets. In the U.S. it was the Rodale Institute in Emannus, Pennsylvania that took the lead in conversion from high energy to low energy organic farming. Robert Rodale was central in getting organic agriculture recognized as legitimate by bringing together outstanding organic farmers who instructed other farmers in these techniques, and at the same time running sessions in the Congress about these issues for both parties. Rodale also had, in the 1990s, 24 different magazines that got the word out about the interconnections of organic farming, health, sports and well-being.

There is a tragedy shaping around farming and food today and therefore an appropriate voice comes from A.V. Chayanov, a Russian agricultural economist who tried to influence the industrial debate in Russia in the late 1920s and was sent to his death in Siberia for his dissent. He rejected the class division analysis of the family farm and treated it, as Polanyi does, as a house holding organizational principle that has many advantages as long as the informal sector is not integrated into the market economy – or into state collectivist planning.

In *The Theory of Peasant Economy* A.V. Chayanov showed that the costs of production on a peasant farm are lower than on a capitalist farm and ultimately more productive in balanced agricultural output than the collective farm or, today, the agribusiness plantation.[20] Peasant farms, in their substantive contexts, have multiple yields that make them superior ecologically and in terms of diverse food production locally. Projecting economic liberal theory, or Leninist development theory, into these embedded economic contexts becomes distortive because it assumes production imperatives that do not recognize motives and institutional operations of a subsistence family farm sector.[21] This suppressed theory applies to informal family farm sector in many contexts and is still being disputed by modernizing perspectives.

There are many other voices who speak for the wisdom of local agriculture – such as Wendall Berry, Mia Mies, Mark Richie, Jim Hightower, Joan Gussow, David Korten, Michael Pollan, etc. Each of these has argued for the ecological and social superiority of local agriculture. An outstanding example is Wendell Berry, a Kentucky poet-farmer, whose book *Unsettling of America* records the demise of the family farm in America as paralleling the rise of the land grant college that diffused agronomic knowledge and pulled the family farm into the productive market system. In a recent essay on 'The Agrarian Standard', his prose continues this message in a startlingly clear way: "Industrialism cannot understand living things except as machines, and can grant them no value that is not utilitarian, it conceives of farming and forestry as forms of mining . . ."[22]

Berry makes an analogy between the colonial domination of the European monarchy and the contemporary corporation and proposes they are both inherently violent. Agrarian farming is the proper use and care of an immeasurable gift and this cannot be done within an industrial form.

Berry spoke at the post-earth summit conference 'From Rio to the Capitals' in his home state of Kentucky and presented a direct challenge to corporate agribusiness and government elites in the audience. Asserting that the spirit of democracy is best represented by plain talk, Berry stated that the truth of farming in the United States had been skewed by the domination of 'free trade' WTO rules that have placed communities everywhere under the same economic forces and have undermined agriculture and rural communities in the United States. The farm population in the United States has declined from more than 30 million in 1940 to less than 4 million today. In the decade of 1980–90 alone there was a decline of 31 percent of the farming population or 1,746,320 people.

Appropriate forms of governance to sustain the family farm and food safety can only come locally from skilled and highly motivated farmers and informed local consumers – not from global trade rules, speculative investors or bureaucrats. Berry claims we must realize the hope for a sustainable food economy is represented by no political party or spoken for by no national public officials of any consequence. Like the proponents of American independence at the time of the Stamp Act, citizens must take action – but unlike that time there is no need for a national organization. We must shorten the distance that food is transported and this can be done by co-operation among small organizations, conservation groups, churches, consumer co-ops and organizations of small farmers. This vision for the future is based on direct people-to-people actions, co-operative associations and the competences of local farmers and consumers.

Small farmers today are desperately seeking a niche to survive; selling their produce at multiple farmer's markets supports some. Pulling more people into community support for agriculture (CSAs) is a common cause. Food safety concerns can help in a country where 5,000 people have died of salmonella and 30,000 became ill in the last year. Only when people become aware of health risks and the dangers of international food trade will the importance of local agriculture dawn on many consumers. A way for consumers to find local foods is foodroutes.org.[23]

Capacity building in active communities

Amartya Sen has an approach to providing tools that enables social groups and institutions to deal with their own problems which he calls 'capacity building'. This concept can be used to describe what has been happening where community initiated actions are solutions by the communities themselves. Stories of towns that achieve these kinds of self-activated capacities include Curitiba, Porto Alegre, Portland Oregon, etc.

Small farming towns in Pennsylvania, have banned large agribusiness corporations from dominating their land use and local markets.[24] They consolidated their base as a political community first before they acted together to protect their local economic capacities.

The E. F. Schumacher Society in Great Barrington, Massachussets promotes the creation of local currency systems that form a capacity for local exchanges to reduce the cost of life and give unemployed people access to wages and small job opportunities. Local businesses that accept the currency help build greater affinity between citizens of the region and their local merchants. Individuals choosing to use the currency make a conscious commitment to buy locally first, taking personal responsibility for the health and well-being of their community.

Municipal discourse about developing local assets creates the capacity for ambitious regeneration of local economies; as does forming local non-profits for providing services, or 'for-profit' co-operatives and service companies to supply alternative energy, recycled materials and communications services, as will be discussed in Chapter 8.

Securing communities and households in poor regions requires that people in the 'informal sector' receive some kind of capacity to survive in a widening commercial system. This requires non-colonizing help from government, such as the National Rural Employment Guaranteed Act (NREGA) of 2005 in India which secures 100 days of work per family per year.

Unfortunately official policy formations seldom include community actions but instead design new managed systems of services to deal with social problems. In response, citizens group's advocacy of rights to services by those excluded or marginal is crucial. 'Community' action is usually not on the map of policy options so community groups have to end up acting on their own.

Capacity building in a poor Chicago community that was experiencing too many unaffordable visits to the hospital initiated a community research group about the types and reasons for hospital visits. Learning the frequency and locations of traffic accidents, incidences of dog bites and increases in childhood asthma, etc. lead to community deliberation and actions: new traffic signs and patterns, new methods of dog control, and most interestingly a roof top hot house vegetable garden that provided malnourished children with fresh vegetables to deal with undernourished vulnerability to asthma. This hot house experiment had positive unexpected consequences of bringing in a new source of income and gave elders, who took over the hothouse, social recognition. Such community problem solving is often displaced by professional services – including NGOs that aspire to sustain themselves first and enable citizens or poor people afterward.

Urban poor community groups need professional help to build their own capacities to deal with local problems. The Washington Greater D.C. Care[25] organization builds capacity for citizen and NGO groups by organizing volunteer time, skills, goods from professional and business corporations. D.C. Care also helps create capacities for learning and political action in the community and city itself. Organizing a citizens academy that enables group leaders to access advocates in the local and national governance and point them to the meetings and public events where they can get their interest heard. Creating financial literacy training for citizens and groups, while trying to make this integration of knowledge capacity into the community a learning demand that comes from the communities themselves.[26] Providing non-monetary resources to the community is their goal.

Capacity building includes jump starting literacy programs in the communities that are then ongoing. The Time-Dollars local currency, in one of its many applications, identifies people on the block that have time and interest in providing aid to those who need to learn to read. Edgar S. Cahn's *No More Throw-Away People: The Co-Production Imperative* is an inspiring account of the time-dollar local currency system that is a fountain of innovative thinking.[27]

Instead of forming new self-help groups or experts to deal with problems of the informal sector, 'community guides' that enable communities to build capacity are emerging everywhere spontaneously. For example, David Schwartz in *Crossing the River* records his role as identifying community 'askers' who enable community solutions for impossible problems of disabilities that could not be afforded by the poor families.[28] Community guides know the latent hospitality capacities of the community. The revolution in community that Swartz records is amazing and beneath the screen.

Recently, community guides have been called 'social entrepreneurs'; naming them with the dominant business virtue makes them officially respectable. More recently professorial academics have re-discovered these dimensions of social life and named them Social Capital (Putnam), Social Trust (Fukuyama). But the message of community capacity building is that people must do it themselves and professional interventions can only create a hierarchy of dependence. People are doing more and more for themselves, for example voluntary simplicity groups meet in many places to strategize about simpler lifestyles, increasing the capacity of households to reduce costs.

Another active capacity building dimension was pioneered in Woburn, Massachussets after experiencing high rates of unexplainable children's diseases. Popular epidemiology learning was developed by highly motivated parents who got the records from hospitals and constructed a map that indicated that the town wells were the source of the problem. This is now recognized as 'local citizen epidemiology'.

8 Social learning for people's economies

Participatory learning for people's economies: the Grameen Bank and legal entitlements

Alternative economics can expand only if a social learning strategy gets it around and people become more aware and connected. Toward that end a perspective on social learning proposes there are two distinct forms of social learning; one describes how established institutions learn in contrast to participatory learning.[1]

Maintenance learning is oriented to instrumental problem solving essential to secure institutional goals and procedures. Participatory learning departs from people's place-oriented situations and from people's organizations focusing on community-based projects such as participatory budgeting processes in Brazil.

Goal-oriented learning reduces complex situations by implementing reality-simplifying structures of instrumental knowledge, such as applications of neoliberal economic theory as development programs.

A participatory approach proceeds by creating wider interpretive syntheses from many social interests in ways that reveal more interrelations of problems and permit many more people to reorient their actions on more fronts, such as the movement to relocalize agriculture. Rather than simply applying expert knowledge systems, participatory learning reconceptualizes and reformulates the problems on a wider scale.

While maintenance learning is good for maintaining obedience to authority, participatory learning stimulates socio-cultural renewal and revitalizes social solidarities. For example, the problem of poverty would be seen, not in terms of top down funding, but as requiring people's access to credit, such as was done by Muhammad Yunus as he helped form the learning process that became the Grameen Bank in Bangladesh.

Participatory learning unites thinkers and doers in ways that depend upon the only infinite resource we have; the human language derived capacity for insight into meaning. In this way substantive economies begin from insights into community and place relations and constitute a more radical response to national economic stagflation and limited job creation than external development projects.

The Grameen Bank reversed assumptions made by banking and development agencies about the capacities of the poor to tap into survival skills and motivations, and to repay loans. Muhammad Yunus has presided over a social learning process that reveals more about the relations of poverty, business and credit than was known before he took $27 out of his wallet to start the project in 1977.

Evolution of the field methodology of the Grameen Bank (GB) is a good example of participatory learning that has transformed passive suffering into pro-active creativity. An enthusiastic young staff continually refined an innovative field methodology that balanced humility and respect for the people's abilities, with educated awareness of social and cultural realities of borrowers. It was these methods which overcame the cultural resistance to women taking loans; the religious competences of the field workers enabled them to overcome local religious resistance.

Critics of the Grameen bank have fastened on the number of loans taken by women that are turned over to men, and on the seductive habit of taking continual loans that becomes another variety of debt trap. These criticisms have some truth, in that repeated loan taking is also economism. But this is secondary to the community building aspect. A poor Muslim woman comes out of the shadows of the household by the very fact that she takes a loan. She becomes part of an organizing process that widens her understanding and action capacities in many ways. This is real empowerment, and the loans also help undermine the predatory traditional money lenders.

During the mobilization of borrowers, requiring them to become familiar with the GB's 'sixteen decisions', the list of good practices that also functions as child bearing and dowry restraints, a savings mechanism and much more. Borrowers are tested on their understanding of the lending process as part of the preparation for receiving a loan. An initiation process of 7 training days is crucial for socialization into the status of borrower and peer group member. After that, the five person peer group has regular interactions with the Grameen outreach workers, who are careful to be helping workers and not self-important bank employees who demand luxury accommodations.

Yunus claims the central learning of the GB is that it frees credit from the bondage of collateral; credit is more than business, it is a human right. The GB revealed the way to create credit with the use of friends as equity and as a peer group backed up process for building confidence. As a learning process it begins with communicating belief and trust in the worth of those who have had no chance to use their intelligence for themselves.

Contrasting greed led enterprises with enterprises driven by a social consciousness, Yunus enlisted the compassion of workers and investors. They created a new kind of social business that is a model for people's economics.[2] But there are two dimensions here – one is a social economic one of enabling the poor to access capital to create their own livelihoods; the other is a social mobilization process that creates commitment, support and social identity formation in ways that were not present before. These innovations widen the meaning of business to 'social business' that builds community.

For the GB 'maximization of profit' has two parts, money and social returns. Without both there is no real profit. 'Social business' means investing in the social entrepreneurs who do the organizing and that profits can be made by owners of the micro business themselves. Ninety-four percent of the Grameen Bank is owned by the borrowers. As of March 2008, the Bank has 7.46 million borrowers, 97 percent of whom are women, and provides services in 81,574 villages, covering more than 97 percent of the total villages in Bangladesh. Yunus has overturned most of the assumptions previously held about poverty; banking experts who have tried to adopt Grameen process with older forms of equity fail.

Psychologically, GB formed by focusing on internal social recognition, and institutionalization of this recognition sustained high motivations of workers and peer groups. Banking became a means of community building in rural villages that had little active community. Beginning with the assumption that every borrower is honest, the bank built on trust – not formal process contracts – Grameen succeeded by building on interpersonal relations and not formal banking rules. It was often the borrowers who came up with solutions to problems and new innovative ideas for people to succeed at their projects.

This social focus redefined key concepts of economics across the board. Economists equate jobs with salaried or wage labor employment, but lending to the poor creates self-employment as a form of economic power which is at the same time social power. This is very different from hiring the poor in development projects. Top down official development projects, funded by private or public institutions, leads to 75 percent of the capital leaving the country to buy equipment, materials or expertise from the donating country. The remaining 25 percent, Yunus claims, goes directly to a tiny elite of national suppliers, contractors, consultants and experts. At best it builds infrastructure that helps the already established classes; little if anything trickles down to the bottom half.[3] Yunus would redefine 'development' to mean improving the quality of the poorest 25 percent of the economic hierarchy. GB eventually got its way in the ongoing struggle with the World Bank and government agencies, which had made the presumption that only they have the knowledge to make lending work.

The poor are poor, not because they are dumb and have no skills, but because they cannot retain the returns from their labor. Having the ability to control their capital enables them to use their survival skills to rise out of poverty. No job retraining is needed to uplift the poor, they can be very creative in their worlds. The assumption that they have to be 'upgraded' to be productive is an expert knowledge prejudice. That this program does not reach all in the village is a constant criticism; but the difference is the start of another set of community capacities that can benefit all.

GB now has many imitators, some fraudulent and predatory, but nonetheless there are parallel micro credit organizations all around the world. In the U.S. it faced unique barriers; only 10 percent of the population is self-employed and welfare rules rule out the poor getting loans. But these barriers have been worked around and now there are 500 organizations, united under the Association for Enterprise Opportunity (AEO), who report that U.S. micro enterprises have created an average of 900,000 new employments per year from 2000 to 2005.[4]

What is important about the GB is that poor people learn how to learn to help themselves. Comparing the GB methodology to another approach, which is the opposite, is Hernando de Soto's private property entitlement solution for poverty.

Entitling property in urban slums to bring the 'dead capital' into the formal sector in order to create security of tenure and release the liquid capital of untitled real estate promises is the key idea. But this promises more than most slum situations will permit. The 'Movement of Workers Without a Roof' in Brazil argues against individual land entitlements. They want communal and democratic systems of collective land tenure because this offers protection to the poorest and prevents 'downward raiding', in which richer people displace squatters once their neighborhood's property is formalized.[5] Making newly titled properties visible to official city tax collections and municipal utilities is a risk that opens the door for property buy outs by absentee owners. Urban poverty becomes more complex by an overcrowding of property hierarchies of client subordination.

Studies show that newly discarded public sector professionals and the growth of new small entrepreneurs are interrelated and results in driving down slum wages, while undermining capacity for joint community action.[6] Slum survival competitions increase as does an expanded underclass. The result forces greater ethnic fragmentations, fomenting situations of greater conflict. There may be regional situations where bringing pieces of urban land into the property system is useful for some, but for the above reasons it cannot be a general solution.

The worldwide appeal of de Soto's strategy is its convergence with the World Bank's policy of universalizing property relations while reducing the government's share, with the side result of dismantling informal group and union formations. De Soto's perspective fits the current western model of the expansion of property entitlements; but in the context of the urban slum the amounts of capital released and the hierarchies of criminal domination come together to make it a pseudo solution that validates western neo liberalism. It over simplifies and ideologically justifies the centrality of private property.[7]

This perspective now has U.N. sanction: Hernando de Soto and Secretary Madeleine Albright, the two co chairs of the United Nations Development Program's Commission on the Legal Empowerment of the Poor have announced a Report on this topic. Although it advocates wider legal entitlements that have great merit and go beyond property entitlements – they remain central. What is real in practice and what is ideological cover for 'economic freedom' in the western sense, will have to be tested.

But between Yunus's rural GB and de Soto's urban strategies for creating a people's economy there is an alternative approach that suggests a regional starting point is possible.

City regions and going local

How is it possible to override the mal development and dependency patterns that come with the internationally supported 'economic growth first' approach? As we have seen, thinking in terms of national economies yields knowledge that does not reveal enough facts about local/regional dynamics. How can substantive economics learn how to balance local/regional economics with societal arrangements?

A way of thinking about this issue comes from Jane Jacobs who claims that the real economic unit is the city region; its internal ecologies have economic implications. As a dramatic negative case, Jacobs recounts a report from Henry Grady, editor of a newspaper in Atlanta Georgia, speaking in 1880 about a funeral he attended in Pickens County, Georgia:

> The grave was dug through solid marble, but the marble headstone came from Vermont. It was in a pine wilderness but the pine coffin came from Cincinnati. An iron mountain over shadowed it but the coffin nails and the screws and the shovel came from Pittsburgh. With hard wood and metal abounding, the corpse was hauled on a wagon from South Bend, Indiana. A hickory grove grew near by, but the pick and shovel handles came from New York. The cotton shirt on the dead man came from Cincinnati, the coat and breeches from Chicago, the shoes from Boston; the folded hands were encased in white gloves from New York . . . That country, so rich in undeveloped resources, furnished nothing for the funeral except the corpse and the hole in the ground and would probably have imported both of those if it could have done so.[8]

Jacobs used this ironic story to identify a passive economic region, a concept that is even more relevant for regions impacted by global outsourcing today. Jacob's notion of a city region posits a form of substantive economics that begins from innovations in the cities. For Jacobs using the national economy as the unit for economic analysis was a fateful mistake.[9] Cities can transform the regional economy by regenerating five forces: cities' need for supplies, wealth of jobs, productivity improvements, transplants of work units, capital.

City regions can become dynamic centers that can learn to increase all these factors in a balanced way. As engines of growth, cities are the pivots for securing rural areas. The population of cities becomes a resource that reduces transaction costs, and lowers costs for services. Because city infrastructures are less expensive to create, business costs are lower. All these factors make lower prices in cities possible, if coordinated with rural areas. Regional production substitutes for imports by investing in the capacity to produce quality products locally; this organic self-learning system works in Northern Italy as described in Chapter 6. Jacobs also cites Tokyo's replacement of American bikes with their own technical learning and investments, but she could have also included Cuba.

The social ecology of a city region presupposes a set of neighbor communities that work together to achieve this end. Here Jacobs contrasts those motivated by a commercial ethic versus those who have a guardian ethic. This contrast also divides the 'third way theorists', i.e. those who see partnerships with corporations as optimal, from what we will call the 'Going Local' strategy.[10] The 'Going Local' strategy focuses on community self-reliance that ties personal responsibility, respect for others and harmony together with the ecology of place.

But contemporary forms of urbanization are deeply affected by global free trade and investment mechanisms. Many refugees from the rural areas come into the city to find work, and since this is happening on a world scale, the city has become a trap as well as the last ditch possibility for better economic connections. As discussed earlier, as of 2008 over half the human species are living in cities; not in secure situations, as Mike Davis has documented, but in urban networks that pull in the displaced from the countryside.

Michael Shuman's application of Jane Jacob's ideas projects a social economics that sees creating local solidarity and keeping money in local circulation as essential to encouraging local reinvestments, livelihoods and a dynamic economic life.[11] Shuman describes how community non profits, co-operatives and for profits, with residential restriction on stock ownership, can work together. He cites the model of the Greenbay Packers who secured their football team with regional limits to stock ownership. Community corporations, public and private, are the key to providing basic needs, e.g. energy, food, water, housing, clothing, that reduce imports, internalize external costs, provides ecological protection, and operates for local restoration and solidarity.

Shuman defines the alternative economic path as the end of 'TINA', or there is no alternative. LOIS, or Locally Owned Import Substituting Development, is the way of the future because of its economic advantages. The incredible subsidies of tax payer dollars that states and municipalities put out to lure large corporations to their region, only to be shocked when they move on, has gone sour. LOIS stays in the community, provides more job security and income without the danger of losing local capacities.

The economy of scale principle is true for mass manufacturing only up to a point; decentralized customized products and services are needed now. Small business is a good local economic multiplier, especially in keeping the tax receipts local, while decreasing dependency upon unnecessary commercial activity that leaves the region.

Shuman argues that the only way a community can get control over its wealth is to rebuild it from the ground up. His 'Going Local' strategy begins with a visioning procedure oriented to what is essential for economic sustainability, but argues that this is not sufficient. Communities should also create a local bill of rights that is based on a community survey of what constitutes basic needs and existing assets. Taking inventory of unused resources and current problems can be recognized as new business opportunities. Applying local indicators of sustainability can result in community report cards that report on co-operative efforts to restore commons' rights to water, safety, security, livelihoods, etc. Environmental initiatives can be reframed as contracts for community reinvestments.

The growing oil driven costs of wide distribution, and transportation make local production, and especially local services, cheaper. Instead of Wal Mart, Shuman claims that there is a 'small mart' revolution[12] that is being promoted by organizations, such as the Business Alliance for Local Living Economies (BALLE), and the American Independent Business Association (AMIBA) that are concerned with networking for local economy building.

Both Michael Shuman and David Korten serve on the BALLE board which now has 52 chapters around the U.S., representing 15,000 small businesses.[13] Driven by a conviction that a business can serve society by rooting it locally, where it functions within the framework of local values and accountability. When local citizens see the BALLE emblem on the shop window they can be confident that this shop is not owned by absentee owners. LOIS ultimately implies a 'revolutionary consumerism' that aims at democratizing production and consumption locally. Building local awareness of this becomes a consciousness multiplier in itself, not only does it create local pride but it also educates about the global economy. People can have a prime example of why local business is also taking responsibility for the north's ecological and economic footprint on the south. Locally informed consumerism can be presented in ways that go against the current thoughtless celebration of affluence. This can be promoted as one of the renunciations essential for a post carbon lifestyle.

Building a strategy of 'inter co-operation' is essential for a "no boss" co-operative movement that links consumer co-ops and local currency systems, worker owned enterprises, etc. These are the bases for a democratic and sustainable economy where there is no domination by capital. This overlaps and links the co-operative movement with the anti-sweatshop and -fair trade movements.

Strengthening local economies via alternative financial institutions

An enabling step toward this regeneration of local/regional economies is working with community financial structures that interrelate the many community financial services now existing. Community Development Financial Institutions (CDFI) exist and these can be expanded everywhere; 'anything that exists is possible', as Shuman is fond of saying. Examples are the early phase of the South Shore Bank in Chicago, or the Self-Help Credit Union in Durham, North Carolina or the Women's Self-Employment Project in Chicago or Working Capital in Cambridge, Massachussets

A strategy for expanding financial capacity more regionally is to integrate local financial institutions. Hence unions in Holland set up a financial institution (ASN) and convinced the Dutch Postbank[14] to administer a special fund run by ASN for investing in local needs industries. The Triodos Bank in Sussex U.K., looks for community projects first, and depositors afterwards. But ultimately political interventions that enable pension fund investments to be channeled into socially responsible investing and green purchasing will be the turning point.

Since financial services have moved from banks to mutual funds and pension funds, the hope is that public asset securing practices will be the key for local financing. For example, the California Public Employee's Retirement System (CalPERS) pension fund decisions performs a crucial role of corporate accountability and is helping organize a nation wide coalition for state treasurers to do the same.

The best hope for the future is the socially responsible investment movement which has expanded from billions in the 1990s to over 2.7 trillion dollars today.[15] The origins of this go back to renunciations by spiritual traditions; for example in the U.S. the 1758 Society of Friends (Quakers) refused to invest in slave holding enterprises. The movement reached a new level in the investment boycotts around

South Africa under apartheid and has expanded ever since. In India this movement is seen as continuing Gandhi's notion of "Trusteeship".[16]

Other forms for the democratization of wealth have been documented in Gar Alperovitz's *America Beyond Capitalism*.[17] He breaks down asset securing mechanisms into sectors. For example worker owned firms, and employee stock ownerships programs, ESOPs, which can take weak or stronger forms, now total 11,000 in the U.S.[18] Shifting ownership of assets to institutions for securing the economic situations of participants constitutes a major strategy for building economic self-development and self-determination capacity.

Both Shuman and Alperovitz agree that there is a middle ground between right and left in the economic experiments for citizen asset based wealth holding solutions to poverty and inequality. Democratic capacity building is often obscured by negative liberty arguments of the anti-public right and the anti-privatization prejudices of the left. But if the issue of democratization of ownership and enabled access to capital for the economically insecure is kept central, many already existing solutions can be supported by both political persuasions. Ultimately it is in everyone's interest to admit that, in some circumstances, the public and the private can be mutually supportive. Social co-operation is the secret of stability despite the extreme polarizations created by the current Bush regime and the wrecking of governance under his administration.[19] As Alperovitz reminds us, the founding ideal of America was 'equal liberty' not just liberty for the super rich.

Alperovitz cites John Dewey who had advocated an 'effective freedom', which required effective power to do specific things; a parallel concept to Amartya Sen's capacity building in *Development as Freedom*.[20] Alperovitz links these back to John Adams thinking about 'equal liberty' which includes an approach to the ownership of wealth that can be used today.

Len Krimerman critiques Alperovitz and raises the issue that all thinking about alternatives to capitalism has to face up to capitalism itself, and few manage to do. Krimerman, as founder and editor of *Grassroots Economic Organizing Newsletter*, has made available documentations of these alternative micro models for a long time and constantly raises skeptical issues concerning the whole project.[21] While many of the micro models can become authoritarian, the major problem is how can micro models become the basis for the whole economy? How can micro models learn to collaborate with one another? Krimerman suggests that Brazil has such a democratic innovation participatory budgeting.

Grass-roots-up participatory financial forms

In Porto Alegre, Brazil, the budgeting process begins at the local levels and goes forward as a participatory planning procedure. This is a model for fair and equitable investment for capacity building. With over 200 municipalities actively involved and now spreading to Europe and Canada, this process is a huge success in bringing excluded groups into the planning process. With this innovation, investing in ignored projects in poor neighborhoods that are essential for local infrastructure improvements, such as water and sewage, housing, education, day care, medical services, go forward. They bring expertise into the planning process in the public phase of planning, but not as a top down take over, or behind closed door deal. Details of this planning process are an impressive story of how to mobilize the most marginalized and poorest sectors into expressing their needs in public. Participatory budgeting is also a means of achieving participatory democracy and that it takes place in the context of public asset allocation is also significant.

The participatory budgeting process emerged in Porto Alegre, Brazil – the site of three World Social Forums in the last five years. The unique budgeting process in Porto Alegre shows that the slogan 'another world is possible' can actually work. Between 2000 and 2006, the total number of cities with participatory budgets grew from 200 to roughly 1,200 around the world.[22]

Beginning in Brazil in 1988 it has been very successful with a side consequence of eliminating corruption due to the open and transparent process of planning. Participatory budgeting works best where there are high levels of community activism to begin with, otherwise the ability to undermine the role of elected representatives doesn't work too easily.

Globalizing anti-globalization economies: solidarity economics, economic democracy and fair trade

An emerging strategy for globalizing economic democracy is the solidarity economy movement that was imaged in Peru in 1997 and catalyzed at the first Porto Alegre World Social Forum. The process, projected as a globalization of solidarity, was achieved by gatherings in Dakar, Africa, Asia, Europe, the Philippines, Japan and India. Many forms of alternative economic solidarity that already existed were brought together at these meetings – seen as a sharing laboratory for social innovations and leading to the theme 'sharing social solidarity'. The fact that it has many origins, many organizing events, and many appearances in international NGO meetings identifies it as a world social movement that demonstrates that 'another economy exists'.

Some say the Solidarity Economy (SE) was created by the Alliance for a Responsible, Plural, and United World from France, but other origins are claimed too. At the 2004 World Social Forum in Mumbai, India, the Global Network had grown to include 47 national and regional solidarity economy networks representing thousands of democratic grassroots economic initiatives worldwide. At the World Social Forum in Venezuela, solidarity economy topics comprised about one third of the entire events program.[23]

In 2007 at the Atlanta, Georgia, Social Forum in the United States, the Solidarity Economy Working Group reported co-operation from grassroots experiments from around the world and published the *Solidarity Economy: Building Alternatives for People and Planet*.[24] An interesting distinction between private, public and social economies is used to define solidarity economics which would be a cross sectorial strategy for linking all three economies.[25] A 'high road' advocacy for innovation and efficiency is used to define a truly productive economy. SE wants to avoid the financial engineering of the neo liberal economy and create an actual democratic economy.

The SE movement has many voices. I have chosen one participant from the 2007 Atlanta collection, David Schweickart, who defines 'economic democracy' as having three basic features: worker self management, markets and social control of investment.

These features allow for workers' participation and ownership, but totally change the economic parameters by creating a process that is not expansionistic and is self-limiting in size. While capitalism is characterized by private ownership, economic democracy abolishes private ownership of productive resources, and wage labor, but retains the market.

In Schweickart's model:

> Each productive enterprise is controlled by those who work there. Workers are responsible for the operation of the facility, including organization, discipline, techniques of production, what and how much to produce, what to charge and how the net proceeds are distributed.[26]

Decisions concerning distribution are made democratically, as are forming authority structures. Whatever internal structures are put in place, ultimate authority rests with the enterprise's workers, one person, one vote.

> Although workers control the workplace, they do not 'own' the means of production. These are regarded as the collective property of society. Workers have the right to run the enterprise, to use its capital assets as they see fit, and to distribute among themselves the whole of the net profit from production. Societal 'ownership' of the enterprise manifests itself in two ways:
>
> - All firms must pay a tax on their capital assets, which goes into society's investment fund. In effect, workers rent their capital assets from society.
> - Firms are required to preserve the value of the capital stock entrusted to them. This means that a depreciation fund must be maintained. Money must be set aside to repair or replace existing capital stock. This money may be spent on whatever capital replacements or improvements the firm deems fit, but it may not be used to supplement workers' incomes.[27]

Economic democracy uses the price mechanism because market competition resolves the problems of knowing what and how much to produce, which production and marketing methods are the most efficient and how to design a set of incentives that will motivate producers to be efficient and innovative. But 'profit' in a worker run firm is not the same as capitalist profit where labor is counted as a cost. For a worker run enterprise it is not a cost, because labor is not another 'factor of production' technically on par with land and capital. Workers gets all that remains, once non labor costs, including depreciation set asides and the capital assets tax, have been paid.

Economic democracy's enterprises will not relocate abroad, since they are controlled by their own workers. Finance capital will stay mostly at home, since funds for investment are publicly formed and by law are to be reinvested domestically. The capital assets of the country are collectively owned – and hence not for sale.

Another converging alternative economic vision, and network, that participates in SE, but has an independent origin is the Progressive Utilization Theory (PROUT) derived from the Indian philosopher Shri Prabhat Ranjan Sarkar. It is oriented to building healthy communities based on co-operative and ecological principles. From different cultural origins it is deeply involved in regenerating and sustaining a degraded earth and creating decentralized and humanly enriching democratic society.[28] At present it has a track record of many successes in Australia, Argentina, Europe, India, Venezuela and North America.

Another anti-globalization economic form that has emerged is Fair Trade (FT). As an alternative trade network, FT was innovated by the Mennonites in the 1940s and 1950s and expanded by European NGOs in the 1960s. Exports of coffee, cocoa, handicrafts, sugar, tea, bananas, cotton, fruit, honey, etc. have expanded rapidly in the last few years and in June 2008 it was estimated that 7.5 million producers and their families are supported by fair trade.

FT secures marginalized producers who otherwise would by eliminated by industrial markets as well as promoting sustainable forms of production. International distribution and labeling organizations have been set up and are now coordinated by an alliance (FINE) of four international NGO networks.

A example of FT that aspires to go beyond being fair is 'Just Change' which attempts to link producers, consumers and investors in a cooperative chain from India to Britain. Just Change seeks to link up producer and consumer communities such as community groups, cooperatives, schools, and faith groups who share a common belief in justice and equality. Just Change Trust has initiated the Just Change India Producer Company Ltd. whose members trade their products amongst themselves as well to external client groups. Currently tea, rice, coconut oil and umbrellas are the products being traded. These community groups have begun to trade directly with each other.

The significance of FT is that it demonstrates that consumers are in solidarity with producers who otherwise would be eliminated and it also registers a vote for organic products. It refutes economism because it is clear that compassion for the excluded by industrial markets is here to stay and is growing. Fair trade stores are open in many countries and expanding in the U.S. too. Google 'fair trade stores' and choose how you can become part of the growing support for artisans, farmers and help oppose sweatshops around the world.

Geonomics and earth rights and tax shift

Henry George remains an enigma to many economists and yet his 'Poverty and Progress' ideas live on in highly devoted adherents; some have now dubbed his thought 'geonomics'.[29] This refers to economic land values that are properties of the whole community and not owned by anyone. A large part of the wealth in a free market economy is captured by land owners in economic rents. Henry George considered this unearned wealth the root cause of poverty and a great injustice. Private profit is earned by restricting access to natural resources while human productive activity is burdened with taxes. Natural resources are given freely by Nature rather than being products of human labor or entrepreneurship. No individual should acquire unearned revenues by monopolizing commerce on land or any other mineral and biological resource.

Building on the thought of Henry George, Alana Hartzok[30] provides a model for how to enhance the democratization of asset wealth. She brings the issue of democratization of land assets to our attention as a primary sustainability goal. Documenting the inequality of land ownership and the large proportion of wealth that is generated by land rents, she restates the principle that comes from Tom Paine and Henry George: "Men did not make the earth . . . It is the value of the improvement only, and not the earth itself, that is individual property . . . Every proprietor owes to the community a ground rent for the land which he holds" (Paine).

These rights were originally protected by commons arrangements that were part of all traditional worlds, but in the money system era new accounting procedures are essential to retain this right. If we put a dollar value on the services that the earth provides it has been calculated that over 50 percent of the GDP derives from this source. Therefore it is everyone's birth earth right to share in this community asset.

Twenty cities in Pennsylvania, with Harrisburg as the best case, are applying the same split system for taxing land, while allowing improvements on sites in ways that promote the efficient and optimal use of the best urban locations. Sprawl and land speculation is stopped and accumulation of revenues for municipal investment increased. Application of this principle worldwide has the potential of resolving resource wars and eradicating poverty while enabling public and private asset creation. This is a sustainability tool that is especially effective against corporate globalization and can be extended to other aspects of the earth services such as water, forests, minerals, the atmosphere, electro magnetic frequencies, and even satellite orbits.

Appendix
The medieval origins of instrumental reason

Ivan Illich on radical contingency and the medieval coherence crisis

Illich's last book *Rivers North of the Future* begins with reflections on the crucial Christian notion of 'contingency' which expresses the ontic state of a world, which has been created from nothing, is destined to disappear, and is upheld in its experience through divine will. Although this radical thesis is difficult for the modern secular mind to consider, the consequences of the medieval debate that it fostered is very important for understanding the origins of modern instrumental rationality.

Illich cites the work of Hans Blumenberg whose *The Legitimacy of Modern Age*[1] views western civilization as grounded in the foundational search for certitude. Certitudes about creation and the end of mankind's salvation revealed by Christ were combined into an identity of ontological truth. Blumenberg asserts that this combination of Cosmogony and Christology came together to define a Christian idea of absolute certitude that was unique in human history.

But this Church 'property in salvation' culminated in an internal coherence crisis in the twelfth and thirteenth centuries. The medieval world's coherence was contradicted because the ends for self-fulfillment, salvation based on Christology, could not be fully reconciled with the order of the cosmos that had been developed through the entwining of theology and Ancient Greek philosophy. Incorporation of the newly re-discovered Aristotelian metaphysics into scholastic theology resulted in a fundamental *aporia*, or confusion. God's freedom could not be necessitated to redeem humanity; but there is a necessity to the Cosmos in Greek metaphysics. A gap opens between the God of redemption and the God of creation, the promise of Christology and the radical contingency theology of God's freedom.

This coherence crisis created intense internal discourse in the Church which resulted in two types of response. First, was the further codification of the church's historic role in administering its 'property in salvation'. The second was theological theorizing that was resolved by a nominalist critique of essentialism. The coherence crisis was resolved by the nominalistic beginnings of science, which for Blumenburg, are the foundations of modernity.

But according to Illich these new constructions have had perverse consequences that have helped shape modern pathologies. The corruption of the best is the worst.

To put it in simplistic terms, a theodicy of salvation was replaced by what ultimately became a secular theodicy of progress.

The rise of nominalism

The epistemological break that led, eventually, to the seventeenth-century scientific revolution was initiated by nominalism. In retrospect the fourteenth-century effort to sustain the cogency of theological absolutism as faith, while also securing the truth of objective claims about nature, had fateful consequences. While the discourse was to justify the reality of the scholastic world view, the result exposed its inconsistencies and resulted in a new epistemological principle of truth. The unintended outcome of this crisis in medieval theology, in the formulation of nominalism, was the emergence of an instrumental use of language that disconnected purely technical learning from traditional metaphorical analogies of natural theology. A brief reconstruction of this pivotal transition is necessary if we are to understand the medieval origins of instrumental reason.

Reconciling the Bible with the philosophical insights of the Greeks divided medieval Christian discourse into Augustinian Platonism and Thomistic Aristotelianism. A third and reactive position to both emerged in William of Ockham's nominalism as a resolution of the resulting disagreements of the first two traditions.

Augustine develops the Platonic theory of knowledge as a theory of the use of discursive reason and intellectual vision to discover immutable Truth. The human soul understands itself through its own self-understanding. In the intelligibility of the act of understanding the pre-reformation Christian vision ends.

Ockham splits the identity of Being and the action of Soul by starting with the separation of knowledge, as constructs in the mind, from the structure of Being. 'Knowledge' is not the intelligibility of the world gained by the activity of the soul alone, but it is a concept that 'stands for' objects in the world and about which we must enter into discourse in order to validate. There is no possibility of arguing from the structure of knowledge to the structure of nature since we do not know if nature is at every point intelligible. This new 'empiricism' ends by denying that there are any universals in nature at all, these are primarily the capacity of the mind to create concepts that stand for particular things.

Concepts, or mental universals, are the instruments that the mind uses in knowing the world, and they come naturally into the mind from particular things themselves. But they then require an analysis of the suppositional use of language in reference to domains of objects to confirm truth. Ontologically this means that only individual substances and singular sensible properties can be known as true. The status of empirical knowledge is not necessary, but is contingent knowledge of objects – to which the will must be applied to affirm or deny the referential claims. Here begins a new philosophic paradigm of epistemology that gradually replaces the classical discourse about substance.

Ockham's reinterpretation of Aristotle's logic resulted in a new epistemology which split philosophical analysis from theological disputation. The razor of

Ockham had shorn scholastic realism of its access to appearance; causality was reduced to observation of events, while the concepts of natural order and substance could not be defended as existents. This split the reach of reason and the scope of belief, as faith, into different spheres. The omnipotent God had been elevated so high that there was no way to maintain the certainty of intellection of the world.

Ockham's theories sweep across the fourteenth-century universities and become the common view despite official condemnations of this teaching. This was happening in a context where the conflicts of Church and State, Dominion and Grace, Papacy and Empire were the front stage events and these cognitive transformations were less visible but ultimately deeply consequential.

The search for new knowledge foundations, from the thirteenth to the seventeenth century, isolated the subjective sphere in a progressively more radical way. Evolution of the new science from Galileo through Descartes and Bacon can be reconstructed as a more and more strenuous effort to form a paradigm of justifiable cognitive truth whose canons are constructed by the methodical consciousness itself.

We have discussed the inadequacy of the subjectivistic paradigm of philosophy by citing Habermas and Levinas' critiques of instrumental reason in Chapter 6.

But Illich also argues that it changed the poetic and performative use of language and contributed to the disembodiment of sensibility.

Notes

Introduction

1 Chapter 2 discusses this origin.
2 S. Chen and M. Ravallion, 'The Developing World is Poorer than We Thought, But No Less Successful in the Fight Against Poverty', *Policy Research Working Paper 4703*, August 26, 2008. The World Bank has now corrected the poverty line from $1.08 to $1.25 per day!
3 S. G. Reddy, 'How Not to Count the Poor', in J. Stiglitz, S. Anand and P. Segal (eds) *Debates on the Measurement of Global Poverty*, Oxford: Oxford University Press, forthcoming.
4 J. Ghosh, '*Why We Can Not Feed Our People*', *Macroscan*, Feb. 5, 2008 http://www.macroscan.com/cur/feb08/cur050208People.htm.
5 Raj Patel in his book *Stuffed and Starved* (2007) says that "over the course of the 1990s, malnutrition INCREASED in India, and during that period the average calories intake declined among India's poorest. Today, Indians are suffering from inadequate intake of calories and micro nutrients of children under the age of three years, 46 percent are malnourished" (pp. 127–28).
6 K. Nagaraj, 'Farmers Suicides in India, Magnitudes,Trends, and Spatial Patterns' *Madras Institute of Development Studies*, March 2008.
7 A.R. Vasavi, 'Agrarian Distress in Bihar: Market, State and Suicides' *Economic and Political Weekly*, August 7, 1977.
8 An idealization is the process by which scientific models assume facts about the phenomenon being modeled that are false.
9 K. Polanyi, 'The Economy as Instituted Process', in Mark Granovetter and Richard Swedberg (eds) *The Sociology of Economic Life*, Boulder: Westview Press, 1992, pp. 29–52.
10 An economist who argues essentially the same point is J. K. Galbraith, *The Predator State: How Conservatives Abandoned the Free Market and Why Liberals Should Too*, New York: Free Press, 2008; a converging view is T. Frank, *One Market Under God: Extreme Capitalism, Market Populism, and the End of Economic Democracy*, New York: Anchor Books, 2000.
11 T. Frank, *The Wreaking Crew: How Conservatives Rule*, New York: Henry Holt and Company, 2008.
12 D. Rothkopf, *Superclass: The Global Power Elite and the World They Are Making*, New York: Farrar, Straus and Giroux, 2008. Rothkopf aspires to be the new C. Wright Mills but serves the class he is fondly describing.
13 M. Kohr, article in *The Star* (Malaysia) on the collapse of the WTO Talks on the Third World Network webpage, http://www.twnside.org.sg/ title2/wto.info/twninfo20080805.
14 D. Brooks, 'Missing Dean Acheson', Op-Ed page in August 1, 2008 *New York Times*.
15 J. Faux, *The Global Class War*, Hoboken, NJ: John Wiley & Sons Inc., 2006, pp. 160ff.

16 Returning from the 1999 Seattle meeting of the WTO ministers and surfing the web to see how the first world historic confrontations of the "third world" with the WTO establishment had been reported made me aware of lack of coverage in the press. Outside of a few brief instances of coverage in the *New York Times* and the *Wall Street Journal*, the vast majority of reports were about violence in the streets in Seattle. The teach-ins on substantial issues related to the 18 agreements in the WTO, held in colleges, churches, hotels and labor halls, were not mentioned. The radical re-regulation of world trade by these "free trade" agreements simply was not discussed. However, good analysis of these appeared in *The Hindu* and the *Athens News* and in media nodes such as the Third World Network in Penang, Malaysia. Again, as a college teacher I had the same experience that serious discourse about these issues is skipped in the newspapers and in our colleges. I constantly ask my students if the issues like the WTO or biopiracy are covered in their other classes and almost always get "never mentioned".
17 'Executive Summary', *Index of Economic Freedom*, January 15, 2008.
18 J. Gwartney and R. Lawson, with R. S. Sobell and P. T. Leeson, 'Economic Freedom of the World 2007' from the *Cato Store* Data from Economic Freedom of the World, available at http://www.Freetheworld.com.
19 J. Sachs, *The End of Poverty; How We Can Make It Happen In Our Lifetime*, Penguin Books, 2005, pp. 320–21.
20 J. K. Galbraith, op. cit, pp. 15ff.
21 G. Soros, *The New Paradigm for Financial Markets: The Credit Crash of 2008 and What It Means, Public Affairs*, 2008.
22 R. W. Baker, *Capitalism's Achilles Heel: Dirty Money and How to Renew the Free-Market System*, Hoboken, NJ: John Wiley & Son Inc., 2005.
23 John Bogle, *The Battle for the Soul of Capitalism*, New Haven: Yale University Press, 2005.
24 P. Dasgupta, 'Economic Growth Often Accompanies a Decline in a Poor Country's Wealth', *New Stateman*, Nov. 3, 2003, p. 29.
25 M. Hudson, *Global Fracture: The New International Economic Order*, new edition, London: Pluto Press, 2005; William Tabb, *Economic Governance in the Age of Globalization*, New York: Columbia University Press, 2004.
26 R. Weissman, 'Reclaiming Economic Freedom', January 24, 2008 http://www.multinationalmonitor.org/editorsblog.
27 L. Dumont, *Essays on Individualism: Modern Ideology in Anthropological Perspective*, Chicago: University of Chicago Press,1986, p. 260.
28 http://en.wikipedia.org/wiki/Ayn_Rand
29 J. Micklethwait and A. Wooldridge, *The Right Nation: Conservative Power in America*, New York: The Penguin Press, 2004, pp. 13, 46.
30 U. Beck and E. Beck-Gernsheim, *Individualization: Institutional Individualism and its Social and Political Consequences*, London: Sage Publications, 2002, p. xxi.
31 J. Habermas, *The Postnational Constellation: Political Essays*, Cambridge, MA: MIT Press, 2001, p. 79.
32 Ibid., p. 83.
33 D. C. Korten, *The Great Turning: From Empire to Earth Community*, San Francisco: Berrett-Koehler Publishers, 2006.
34 A. Nandy, *Talking India: Ashis Nandy in Conversation with Ramin Jahanbegloo*,New York: Oxford University Press, 2006, p. 125.
35 A. Nandy, *Time Warps: Silent and Evasive Pasts in Indian Politics and Religion*, New Brunswick, NJ: Rutgers University Press, 2002, p. 68.
36 A. Nandy, ibid., p. 103.
37 J. Habermas, Holberg Prize Laureate, 'Religion in the Public Sphere' lecture presented at the Holberg Seminar 2005.
38 C. Hedges, *American Fascists: the Christian Right and the War on American*, New York: Free Press, 2006.

39 C. Hedges, *I Don't Believe in Atheists*, New York: Free Press, 2008.
40 W. Wink, *Engaging the Powers: Discernment and Resistance in a World of Domination*, Minneapolis: Fortress Press, 1989.
41 C. Taylor, *A Secular Age*, Cambridge, MA: The Belknap Press of Harvard University Press, 2007, pp. 554 and 615.
42 In Chapter 4 this definition becomes more complex as Ivan Illich discusses the "loss of the flesh" of the world and the meaning of Christian Freedom.
43 "'Plastic words' are scientific terms that colonize vernacular language, because they disable everyday talk by replacing metaphor with exact meanings that imprisons perception by anchoring everyday talk in the need for expert help", U.Pörksen (a.1984) *Plastikwörter*, Stuttgart: Klett-Cotta, pp. 17, 37.
44 Quoted in David Ewart 'Synopsis of Charles Taylor's *A Secular Age*', http://www.davidewart.ca/2007/
45 Quoted in Fred Dallmayr, *Dialogue Among Civilizations*, New York: Palgrave Macmillan, 2002, p. 105.
46 J. Harriss, 'Institutions, Politics and Culture: A Polanyian Perspective on Economic Change', in M. Harvey, R. Ramiogan and S. Randles (eds) *Karl Polanyi: New Perspectives on the Place of the Economy in Society*, Manchester: Manchester University Press, 2007, p. 52.
47 See Mark Blaug's defense of the notion of a research program as more relevant for economics than the idea of a "paradigm". See Mark Blaug's *Economic History and the History of Economics*, New York: New York University Press, 1986, pp. 231ff.
48 J. Allard, C. Davidson, J. Matthaei (eds) *Solidarity Economy: Building Alternatives for People and Planet*, Papers and Reports from the 2007 US Social Forum, Chicago, ChangeMaker Publications, 2008.

1 Origins of idealization of the self-regulating world

1 J. G. A. Pocock *Virtue, Commerce and History*, New York: Cambridge University Press, 1985.
2 A. J. Bacevich, *The Limits of Power: The End of American Exceptionalism*, New York: Metropolitan Books, 2008.
3 J. G. A. Pocock, *The Machiavellian Moment: Florentian Political Thought and the Atlantic Republican Tradition* , Princeton, NJ: Princeton University Press, 1975.
4 R. Fallow, 'What is Republicanism, and Is it worth Reviving?', *Harvard Law Review*, Vol. 102, 1989, p. 1695.
5 A. MacIntyre, *Whose Justice? Which Rationality?* Notre Dame, IN: University of Notre Dame Press, 1988, pp. 256ff.
6 J. G. A. Pocock, op. cit., p. 49.
7 R. F. Teichgraeber III, *Free Trade and Moral Philosophy*, Durham, NC: Duke University Press, 1986, p. iv.
8 This reorders the twofold Aristotelian construction of social justice as "commutative" (what rightfully belongs to a person) and what is due a person according to relations between equals (distributive justice). In Hugo Grotius' amalgamation of distributive justice into commutative justice a new vision of the social order aimed at preserving a peaceful community emerged.
9 E. Rosenstock-Huessy, *Out of Revolution. Autobiography of Western Man*, New York. William Morrow, 1938, pp. 257ff.
10 A. Smith, *Wealth of Nations*, Chicago: University of Chicago Press, 1976 , Vol. II, Bk 4, pp. 29ff.
11 E. Rothschild, *Economic Sentiments: Adam Smith, Cordorcet and the Enlightenment*, Cambridge, MA: Harvard University Press, 2001, pp. 87ff.
12 Quoted in Albert O. Hirschman, *Rival Views of Market Society*, New York: Viking, 1986, p. 108.

13 H. Achterhuis, 'Scarcity and Sustainability', in Wolfgang Sachs (ed.) *Global Ecology*, London: Zed Books, 1993, pp. 104ff.
14 R. Hamowy, *The Scottish Enlightenment and the Theory of Spontaneous Order*, Carbondale: Southern Illinois University Press, 1987.
15 F. A. Hayek, *The Constitution of Liberty*, London: Routledge and Kegan Paul, 1960, p. 67.
16 J. Gray, "F. A. Hayek 'On Liberty and Tradition', *Journal of Libertarian Studies*, Spring 1980.
17 D. Korten, *When Corporations Rule the World*, West Hartford, CT: Kumarain Press and San Francisco: Berrett-Koehler Publishers,1995, p. 74.
18 E. Rothschild, op. cit., p. 141
19 P. Mirowski, 'Naturalizing the Market on the Road to Revisionism', *Journal of International Economics*, 2007. Mirowski argues that Hayek changed his approach at least three times in efforts to undermine socialism and that these approaches are inconsistent, and each is bound to fail. Hayek moves from an effort to use Austrian economics as the basis for critiquing socialism, to a critique of the abuses of theoretical abstractions, to an evolutionary theory that adds cybernetics and functionalist dimensions to the Scottish evolutionary model. But this does not stop those who share Hayek's project from seeing it all as one evolving and correct perspective.
20 Later theorists, such as Robert Nozick, have argued that a 'hidden hand' explanation is an overall pattern that cannot be explained as anyone's intention or design but shows that there are really two ideas of the 'invisible hand'. One sees an evolutionary emergence of social rationality and the other is about general equilibrium. Both ideas have become central to different forms of modern economics. R. Nozick, *Anarchy, State and Utopia*, New York: Basic Books, 1974, pp. 18–22.
21 J. N. Gray, 'F. A. Hayek on Liberty and Tradition', *Journal of Libertarian Studies*, Vol. IV, No. 2 , Spring 1980.
22 J. Habermas, *Between Facts and Norms: Contributions to a Discourse Theory of Law and Democracy,* Cambridge, MA: The MIT Press, 1999.
23 P. Berger, *Capitalist Revolution: Fifty Propositions about Prosperity, Equality, and Liberty*, New York: Basic Books, 1986.
24 A. Gorz, *Critique of Economic Reason*, New York: Verso, 1988, pp. 43ff.

2 Substantive economics and the abstractions of economism

1 Both Mike Davis (2006) and Alisdair MacIntyre (1988) find Polanyi unique, for different yet converging reasons.
2 M. Harvey, R. Ramiogan and S. Randles (eds), *Karl Polanyi: New Perspectives on the Place of the Economy in Society*, Manchester: Manchester University Press, 2007, p. 6.
3 K. Polanyi *The Great Transformation*, Boston, MA: Beacon, 2001, p. 146.
4 K. Polanyi, ibid., p. 128.
5 K. Polanyi, ibid., p. 147.
6 K. Polanyi, ibid., p. 157.
7 K. Polanyi, ibid., p. 160.
8 M. Davis, *Late Victorian Holocausts: El Nino Famines and the Making of the Third World*, London: Verso, 2001, p. 10.
9 Ibid., pp. 15–16 and 285–286.
10 Ibid., p. 127.
11 For a critique of Marx's critical theory see Trent Schroyer, *The Critique of Domination*, New York: George Braziller, 1973, pp. 75ff.
12 K. Polanyi, op. cit, p. 132.
13 K. Polanyi, op. cit, pp. 45ff.
14 N. Klein, *The Shock Doctrine: The Rise of Disaster Capitalism*, New York: Henry Holt and Company, 2007.

15 Ibid., p. 103.
16 See Bob Jessop's 'Knowledge as a Fictitious Commodity', in *Reading Karl Polanyi for the Twenty-First Century* by Ayse Bugra and Kaan Agartan (eds), New York: Palgrave Macmillan, 2007, pp. 115ff.
17 Karl Polanyi, 'The Economy as Instituted Process', in Mark Granovetter and Richard Swedberg (eds) *The Sociology of Economic Life*, Boulder, CO: Westview Press, 1992, pp. 29–52.
18 From Siddhartha, Fireflies Intercultural Center research alternative project statement (personal communication).
19 M. J. Piore and C. Sabel, *The Second Industrial Divide*, New York: Basic Books, 1984.
20 S. Marglin, 'What Do Bosses Do?' *Review of Radical Political Economics'*, No. 6, Summer 1974.
21 See Michael J.Piore and Charles F. Sabel, op. cit., Chapter 2.
22 D. F. Nobel, *Forces of Production: A Social History of Industrial Automation*, New York: Knopf, 1984.
23 K. Polanyi, *The Livelihood of Man*, New York: Academic Press, 1977, pp. 19ff. Economic Liberalism includes both classical liberalism and modern neo-liberalism.
24 P. Berger, *The Capitalist Revolution*, New York: Basic Books, 1986, and the other view is D. C. Korten, *Getting to the 21st Century*, West Hartford,CT: Kumarian Press, 1990, pp. 73ff.
25 W. Hennis, *Max Weber: Essays in Reconstruction*, Boston, MA: Allen & Unwin, 1988, pp. 50ff.
26 Hennis claims that "it is an analysis that begins from the everyday, the familiar tradition. Charisma and also 'rationalization' are in indissoluble opposition to tradition! The cost of this contradiction, the price of the dissolution of personal relations of piety . . . is the basic theme of Weber's historical studies and also his 'sociology'." Wilhelm Hennis, ibid., pp. 51ff.
27 Hennis, ibid., p. 185. Western political theory began this inquiry but the German historical school restated the inquiry in opposition to British political economics. Hennis asserts that this inquiry is continued by Max Weber's program for the critical study of economic culture.
28 H. Achterhuis, 'Scarcity and Sustainability', in Wolfgang Sachs (ed.) *Global Ecology*, London: Zed Books, 1993, p. 113.

3 Idealizations of utopian capitalism

1 J. Gray, *False Dawn*, New York: New Press, 1998, p. 21.
2 J. Habermas, *The Postnational Constellation: Political Essays*, Cambridge, MA: MIT Press, 2001, p. 94.
3 R. Weissman, '*Executive Pay and "The Market Economy"*' http://www.multinational-monitor.org/editorsblog.
4 Ironically this glorification of managerial skill goes along with maintaining great income inequalities; for example, the republicans didn't want to raise the American minimum wage to $5.85 per hour, while the democrats wanted it raised to $7 per hour. The niggardliness of this dispute, in the context of multiple millions for corporate managers, is out of proportion as the living wage movement demonstrates.
5 G. Palast, J. Oppenheim, and T. MacGregor, *Democracy and Regulation: How the Public Can Govern Essential Services*, London: Pluto Press, 2003.
6 J. Tobin, 'On the Efficiency of the Financial System,' in *Lloyd's Bank Review*, no. 153, 1984, pp. 14–15.
7 A swap is a derivative in which two counterparties agree to exchange one stream of cash flows against another stream. These streams are called the legs of the swap.

Consequently, swaps can be used to create unfunded exposures to an underlying asset, since counterparties can earn the profit or loss from movements in price without having to post the notional amount in cash or collateral.

8 N. Prins, 'Where Credit Is Due: A Timeline of the Mortgage Crisis', July/August 2008, *Mother Jones, Private Space.*

9 W. Tabb, 'Financial Appropriations', *Z Magazine*, June 2, 2008.

10 T. Tassell, 'Special Report on Hedge Funds', *Financial Times*, July 2007.

11 Bobsguide (http://www.bobsguide.com) April 17, 2007.

12 M. Bienefeld, 'Suppressing the Double Movement to Secure the Dictatorship of Finance', in *Reading Karl Polanyi for the Twenty-First Century* (ed.) Ayse Bugra and Kaan Agartan , New York: Palgrave Macmillan, 2007, pp. 25–26.

13 N. Myers and C. Raffensperger (eds), *Precautionary Tools for Reshaping Environmental Policy*, Cambridge, MA: MIT Press, 2005.

14 S. A. Marglin, 'Economics as a System of Knowledge', Discussion paper, *Harvard Institute of Economic Research.*

15 Ibid.

16 S. A. Marglin, *The Dismal Science: How Thinking Like an Economist Undermines Community* Cambridge, MA: Harvard University Press, 2008, pp. 128ff.

17 U. Beck, *Risk Society: Toward a New Modernity*, Newbury Park, CA: Sage Publications, 1992, p. 22.

18 The leading group in the U.S. is the Institute for Trade and Agriculture – consult their thinking on this future. http://iatp.typepad.com/thinkforward.

19 A major representation of this advocacy for a "third wave" in environmentalism was a series of five articles in *the New York Times* from March 21,1993 to March 26, 1993 which argued that the costs of regulation were too high, the benefits too low and that the basis of risk assessment was not sufficiently scientific. Experts should therefore be allowed to set the environmental agenda, and the public perception of risk is not relevant if the cost-benefit framework is to be basic to decision making. In response, a coalition of environmentalists, facilitated by *Rachel's Hazardous Waste News* #331 April 1, 1993, have asserted that this movement is part of the strategy to remove the major toxic laws and to defend the right to development. Their counter-charge is that the facts mobilized by the third wave advocates are totally inadequate.

20 G. Esteva, 'Development', in Wolfgang Sachs (ed.) *The Development Dictionary*, London: Zed Books, 1992, pp. 6–25.

21 M. Rahnema, 'Development', in Vinay Lal and Ashis Nandy (eds.) *The Future of Knowledge and Culture: A Dictionary for the Twenty-First Century*, New York: Penguin, 2005, pp. 70ff.

22 M. Hudson, *Global Fracture: The New International Economic Order*, London: Pluto Press, 2005, p. xx.

23 This dark history is best recorded by Susan George's *A Fate Worse than Debt*, Harmondsworth: Penguin, 1957. The entire program is put into deep question by John Perkins, *Confessions of an Economic Hit Man*, San Francisco: Berrett-Koehler Publishers, 2004.

24 W. Easterly, *The Elusive Quest for Growth*, New York: W. W. Norton & Company, 2002, p. 47; and Joseph Stiglitz, *Globalization and Its Discontents*, New York: W. W. Norton & Company, 2002.

25 N. Klein, *The Shock Doctrine*, New York: Metropolitan Books, 2007.

26 J. Perkins, *Confessions of an Economic Hit Man,* San Francisco: Berrett-Koehler Publishers, 2004.

27 M. Davis, *Planet of Slums*, New York: Verso, 2006, pp. 151ff.

28 Ibid., p. 18.

29 I. Illich, *Shadow Work*, Boston, MA: Marion Boyers,1981, p. 11.

30 Documentation can be found on the Democracy School webpage http://www.celdf.org/Default.aspx.

31 I. Illich, 'Delinking Peace and Development', in *The Mirror of the Past*, New York: Marion Boyars, 1992, pp. 15ff.
32 B. Nietschmann, 'Third World War: The Global Conflict Over the Rights of Indigenous Nations', in *Cultural Survival Quarterly* Sept. 1987; Neitschmann points out that over three-quarters of these wars are between state formations and nations trapped in these territories – which actually constitutes half the land mass of the earth!
33 N. Klein, op. cit., p. 50, and footnote reference no. 4, p. 473.
34 E. Levinas, *Totality and Infinity*, Pittsburgh, PA: Duquesne University Press, 1969, p. 21.
35 N. Geras, *The Contract of Mutual Indifference: Political Philosophy after the Holocaust*, New York: Verso, 1998.
36 S. Diamond, *In Search of the Primitive*, New Brunswick, NJ: Transaction Books,1973, pp. 176ff.

4 Illich's genealogy of modern visions

1 Apophatic means denial or negation; what God is not, how he does not exist. Explicated in Lee Hoinacke 'Why Philia?' lecture given at 'Conversations: The Legacy of Ivan Illich' at Pitzer College Claremont, California on March 26–28, 2004.
2 Illich defines "vernacular" as an old term that can be used "to denote autonomous non-market related actions through which people satisfy everyday needs . . . (in a way) that they give specific shape." Ivan Illich *Shadow Work*, Boston, MA: Marion-Boyers, 1981, p. 38. In this sense oldest forms of penance tended to be public; see Harold J. Berman *Law and Revolution: The Formation of the Western Legal Tradition*, Cambridge, MA: Harvard University Press, 1983, pp. 68ff.
3 G. B. Ladner, *The Idea of Reform: Its Impact On Christian Thought and Action in the Age of the Fathers*, Eugene, OR: Wipf and Stock Publishers, 2004.
4 I. Illich *Shadow Work* op. cit., p. 60.
5 H. J. Berman, op. cit., pp. 404ff. The Gregorian realignment of the Church in western society begins the mobilization for the crusades, which have continued till today with an ongoing demonical imaging of Islam, akin to medieval versions.
6 Illich, *Shadow Work* op. cit., p. 37.
7 Illich, *Shadow Work* op. cit., pp. 63, 73. In a similar way the Nazi state tried to formalize its language in an effort to solidify its elite control.
8 Illich tries to show that Aquinas ultimately held a radical contingency view, despite his theology also reinforcing that of the Franciscans – Bonaventure, Duns Scotus, and Francis – whose views stressed God's freedom and more directly created the dualism. Illich cites Theodor Litt *Les corps celestes dans L'universe de salnt Thomas d'Aguin*, Lowen, Paris, 1963, to document the elimination of angels as the '*instrumentalis*' for dealing with heavenly bodies. He comments that Jacques Maritain and Etienne Gilson also do this.
9 I. Illich, *In the Vineyard of the Text: A Commentary to Hugh's Disdascalicon*, Chicago: University of Chicago Press, 1993.
10 Here Illich continues to assume Aquinas' idea of revelation as a "special illumination of the intellect in which the imaginative interpretation of external signs, the recognition of these signs as revelatory, and the inner transformations of the soul were all one single indivisible occurrence". See J. Milbank, C. Pickstock and Graham Ward (eds) *Radical Orthodoxy*, London: Routledge,1999, p. 5.
11 See Ivan Illich, *Shadow Work* op. cit. especially chapter 3, 'The War Against Subsistence' and a later Illich inspired collection edited by Wolfgang Sachs, *The Development Dictionary*, London: Zed Books, 1992, that contains the beginnings of this "history of scarcity" project. Or, *The Subsistence Perspective'*, Zed Books, 1999 by Veronika Bennholdt-Thomsen and Maria Mies also picks up the same subsistence perspective logic and cites Illich.
12 Behind this perspective is an incredible amount of research into ocular phenomenon and

Church history of discourse about icons. See Ivan Illich 'The Scopic Past and the Ethics of the Gaze: A plea for the historical study of ocular perception' http://www.pudel.uni-bremen.de/100en_startseite.htm.
13 To me this is done by Illich in a way that goes beyond the Christian community and images the conditions under which human life can be affirmed in any context. It seems to be extremely relevant for post-secular and inter-religious discourse of every faith.
14 T. Schroyer and T. Golodik (eds) *Creating a Sustainable World*, New York: Apex Press, 2006, p. 91.
15 I. Illich, *Shadow Work*, op. cit., p. 11.
16 I. Illich, *Shadow Work*, op. cit., p.105.
17 I. Illich, *Gender*, New York: Pantheon Books, 1982, p. 33.
18 I. Illich *Gender*, ibid., pp. 12–13.

5 Gandhi's truth testing and India today

1 J. Kamp and H. de Puy, 'The Forgotten Thinker You Need to Know', *Ode Magazine* June 2007.
2 Can be found at http://www.gandhimuseum.org/sarvodaya/index.htm.
3 See T. Schroyer and T. Golodik (eds), *Creating a Sustainable World: Past Experiences, Future Struggles*, New York: Apex Press, 2006, for a survey of these issues in parts three and four, especially pp. 133ff. consistent with these views.
4 A. Nandy, *The Intimate Enemy: Loss and Recovery of Self under Colonialism*, Oxford: Oxford University Press, 1983.
5 Ironically American Christian fundamentalists also stress 'the cult of masculinity' as essential for a turn to theocracy and the submission of women. See the very provocative analysis by C. Hedges *American Fascists: the Christian Right and the War on American*, New York: Free Press, 2006, Chapter 4.
6 A view shared by P. Chatterjee, G. N. Devy and A. Nandy. See Robert J. C. Young *Postcolonialism: A Historical Introduction*, Malden, MA: Blackwell Publishing, 2001, p. 320.
7 L. C. Jain, 'How Nazir Saab Fought his Majesty's Collector', *Asian Age*, April 16, 2005.
8 L. C. Jain, ibid.
9 The MPLAD and MLA's programs in L. C. Jain, 2006, pp. 22, 35.
10 L. C. Jain, ibid., p. 17.
11 V. Shiva, *The Violence of the Green Revolution: Third World Agriculture, Ecology and Politics*, London: Zed Books, 1991, and *Biopiracy: The Plunder of Nature and Knowledge*, Boston, MA: South End Press, 1997; *Monocultures of the Mind: Perspectives on Biodiversity and Biotechnology*, London: Zed Books, 1993.
12 See J. McKnight, *The Careless Society: Community and its Counterfeits*, New York: Basic Books,1995, and V.Shiva, *Monocultures* of the Mind op. cit.
13 V. S. Naipaul, *India: A Wounded Civilization*, New York: Vintage, 1977, p. 154.
14 Ibid., p. 153.
15 The term 'critical traditionalist' comes from A. Nandy's classic essay 'Cultural Frames for Social Transformation: A Credo', 1987.
16 See W. Wink, *Engaging the Powers*, Minneapolis: Fortress Press, 1992; or J. Wallis, *God's Politics*, San Francisco: Harpers, 2005.
17 A. J. Parel, *Gandhi's Philosophy and the Quest for Harmony*, New Delhi: Cambridge University Press, 2006, p. 45.
18 P. K. Varma, *Being Indian: The Truth about Why the 21st Century will be India's*, New York: Penguin books, 2004, p. 46.
19 Ibid., p. 187.
20 For example, M. Nanda, 'Secularism without Secularization: Reflections on God and Politics in US and India', *Economic and Political Weekly*, Jan. 6–12, 2007.
21 S. Kakar, *The Indian Psyche*, New Delhi: Oxford University Press, 1996.

22 S. Khilnani, *The Idea of India*, New York: Penguin Books, 1998, p. 20.
23 A. J. Parel, *Gandhi's Philosophy and the Quest for Harmony*, op. cit. is a new comprehensive re-interpretation of Gandhi.
24 Siddhartha 'Open Source Hinduism', in Richard Kearney (ed) *Religion and the Arts Journal: Special issue: The Inter-religious Imagination*, Leiden: Martinus Nijhoff, 2008.
25 A. J. Parel op. cit.
26 A. J. Parel op. cit., p. 96.
27 J. Chittister, *The Rule of Benedict*, New York: Crossroads Publishing, 2004.
28 *Collected Works of Mahatma Gandhi*, New Dehli, Publications Division, Ministry of Information and Broadcasting, Government of India, 1958–1994, Vol. 63, p.320.
29 L. I. Rudolph and S. H. Rudolph, *Post Modern Gandhi and Other Essays*, Chicago: University of Chicago Press, 2006, p. 158.
30 Ibid., pp. 152ff.
31 M. L. King *Stride Toward Freedom*, New York: Harper, 1958, pp. 78–9.
32 B. Chakrabarty, 'The Idea of Swaraj in Indian Political Thought from Lajpat Rai to Subhash Chandra Bose', in S. Bhattacharya (ed.) *Development of Modern Indian Thought and the Social Sciences*, New Delhi: Oxford University Press, 2007, pp. 331ff.
33 Ibid., p. 340.
34 R. Gandhi, *Mohandas: A True Story of a Man, His People and an Empire*, London: Penguin, 2006, p. 154.
35 M. Gandhi, 'The Quest for Simplicity', in M. Rahnema and V. Bawtree (eds) *The Post-Development Reader*, Atlantic Highlands, NJ: Zed Books, 1997.
36 S. Chandra, *Continuing Dilemmas: Understanding Social Consciousness*, New Delhi: Tulika Books, 2002, pp. 274ff.
37 L. C. Jain, 'Fate of Gandhi's Economic Thinking', in S.Bhattacharya op. cit.
38 R. Swann, 'Land Trusts as Part of a Threefold Economic Strategy for Regional Integration' from E. F. Schumacher Society www.smallisbeautiful.org.
39 J. Brooke, 'Land Trusts Multiplying, Study Shows', *New York Times*, April 27, 2008.
40 L. C. Jain, 'Fate of Gandhi's Economic Thinking', in S.Bhattacharya op. cit., p. 38.
41 L. C. Jain, ibid., p. 66.
42 S. Palharya 'Decentralized Governance Hampered by Financial Constraints', *Economic and Political Weekly*, March 15–21, 2003, p. 1024.
43 J. Dreze and A. Sen, *India: Development and Participation*, New York: Oxford University Press, 2002, p. 349.
44 S. Palharya op. cit, p.1024.
45 L. C. Jain, 'Local Self-Government – Still Far Away', paper prepared for the Seminar on Local Self-Government – A Frontier of Resistance, Organized by Equations and Network Partners at ASF, Hyderabd, Jan. 5, 2003.
46 J. Dreze and A. Sen, op. cit., p. 359.
47 http://www.Swamiagnivesh.com.
48 http://www.narmada.org/gig/gig.html.
49 L. C. Jain, *Development Initiatives: of the People and By the People*, Vol. II, New Delhi: Action Aid, 2006, p. 48.
50 A. R. Vasavi, 'Agrarian Distress in Bihar: Market, State and Suicides', *Economic and Political Weekly*, August 7, 1977 and talk given at Fireflies ashram on Feb. 12, 2008.

6 Foundations of economic cultures

1 K. Ohmae, *Borderless World: Power and Strategy in the Interlinked Economy*, p. 22.
2 Quoted in Fred Dallmayr, *Dialogue among Civilizations*, New York: Palgrave Macmillan, 2002, p. 105.

3 In the current debates they use critical hermeneutics and their interpretations can be justified or refuted. This is a simplification of Jürgen Habermas' *Between Facts and Norms*, Cambridge, MA: MIT Press, 1998, not in the context of law and political will formation but in the sphere of economic cultures.
4 J.G.A. Pocock, The *Machiavellian Moment: Florentian Political Thought and the Atlantic Republican Tradition*, Princeton, NJ: Princeton University Press, 1975.
5 H. Gadamer, *Truth and Method*, New York: The Seabury Press, 1975, p. 21.
6 Ibid., p. 27.
7 R. Nisbet, *The Quest for Community: A Study in the Ethics of Order and Freedom*, Oxford: Oxford University Press, 1953, pp. 246–47.
8 A. A. Butcher, *Radical Culture Shock: The Desire for Community and the Need for Private Space*, Denver, 2008. http://www.culturemagic.org/EgalitarianCommonwealth.html
9 B. D. Zablocki, *The Joyful Community: An Account of the Bruderhof, a Communal Movement Now in its Third Generation*, 1980. The community founder is honored in Peter Mommsen's *Homage to a Broken Man: The Life of J. Heinrich Arnold*, Rifton, NY: The Plough Publishing House, 2004.
10 C. McLaughlin and G. Davidson who were at times part of both of these communities formed *The Center for Visionary Leadership* in Washington, DC.
11 O. Barfield, *Saving the Appearances: A Study in Idolatry*, Wesleyan University Press, 1988. Distributed by University Press of New England.
12 M. Hardt and A. Negri, *Multitude*, New York: Penguin Books, 2005, pp. 264–7.
13 A. Gouldner, 'The Norm of Reciprocity: A Preliminary Statement'. *American Sociological Review* 25 (2), 1960, pp. 161–78.
14 M. Mauss, *The Gift: Forms and Reason for Exchange in Archaic Societies*, London: Routledge, 1990.
15 Theorists have indeed been given a gift by debating about "gifting" and it culminates in Derrida's claim that the gift is impossible – in that it presupposes an intention to create a debt.
16 M. Osteen (ed.) *The Question of the Gift: Essays Across Disciplines*, New York: Routledge, 2002.
17 M. Godelier, *The Enigma of the Gift*, Chicago: University of Chicago Press, 1999, p. 174.
18 M. Osteen, op. cit., pp. 9–10.
19 L. Dumont, *Essays on Individualism: Modern Ideology in Anthropological Perspective*, Chicago: University of Chicago Press,1986, pp. 257ff.
20 N. H. Smith, 'Levinas, Habermas and Modernity', *Philosophy & Social Criticism*, Vol. 34, No. 6, July 2008, p. 661.
21 Rene Girard, *Violence and The Sacred*, Baltimore, MD: Johns Hopkins Press, 1977.
22 http://www.allspecies.org/ideas/greenteach.htm.
23 "Social Sculpture refers to a conception of art, framed in the 1970s by Joseph Beuys, as an interdisciplinary and participatory process in which thought, speech and discussion are core 'materials'. With this perception, all human beings are seen as 'artists', responsible for the shaping of a democratic, sustainable social order." http://www.brookes.ac.uk/schools/apm/social_sculpture/.
24 http://jace.livejournal.com/415162.html.
25 R. Wuthnow, *Learning to Care: Elementary Kindness in an Age of Indifference*, New York and Oxford: Oxford University Press, 1995, and Stanley Diamond, *In Search of the Primitive*, New Brunswick, NJ: Transaction Books, 1973, pp. 176ff.
26 See Hans-Georg Gadamer, *Truth and Method*, New York: Seabury Press,1975, pp. 86ff.
27 H. Berking, *The Sociology of Giving*, London: Sage Publications, 1999, p. 20.
28 Wuthnow, *Acts of Compassion: Caring for Others and Helping Ourselves*, Princeton, NJ: Princeton University Press, 1991.
29 D. Korten, *The Great Turning: From Empire to Earth Community*, San Francisco: Berrett-Koehler Publishers, 2006.
30 D. Bulley, 'Welcoming the Other: Negotiating Ethics as Hospitality in EU Foreign

Policy' Paper presented at the annual meeting of the ISA's 49th Annual Convention, *Bridging Multiple Divides*, Hilton San Francisco, Ca. USA, Mar 26, 2008. Online <PDF>. 2008–09–03 <http://www.allacademic.com/meta/p254219_index.html>.

31 Service learning organizations are emerging in many urban centers – see http://www.csl.umd.edu/Handouts/issues/hunger&homelessness.htm or http://www.dccentralkitchen.org.

32 R. Belk, 'Why Not Share Rather than Own?' Power Point shared on the internet.

33 Y. Benkler, *The Wealth of Networks: How Social Production Transforms Markets and Freedom,* New Haven, CT: Yale University Press, 2006.

34 Ibid., p. 58.

35 Ibid., p. 72.

36 J. Jacobs, *Cities and the Wealth of Nations*, New York: Vintage, 1985.

37 R. Putnam, *Making Democracy Work: Civic Traditions in Modern Italy*, Princeton, NJ: Princeton University Press, 1994.

38 J. Restakiks, 'The Lessons of Emilia Romagna in Commerce', Monde.com 2005–04–30.

39 Quoted in Frances Moore Lappe, 'A Market without Capitalists', *Alter-Net*, June 23, 2006.

40 B. Bowman and Bob Stone, 'Cooperativization As Alternative to Globalizing Capitalism', GEO Collective online.

41 K. Yokota, *I Among Others: An Introspective Look at the Theory and Practice of the Seikatsu Cub Movement,* Kanagawa: Seikatsu Club, 1991.

42 http://www.ncba.coop/pubs_pkit_whatare.cfm

43 H. D. Wuelker, *'The Social Economy and Co-ops- A German Perspective*', available at www.wisc.edu/uwcc/icic/orgs/ica/pubs/review/vol 88–2/21.

44 K. Polanyi, *The Great Transformation*, pp. 128ff.

45 S. A. Marglin, 'Sustainable Development: A System of Knowledge Approach', in Schroyer and Golodik, op. cit., p. 143.

46 Apffel-Marglin and Marglin, 'Dominating Knowledge: Development, Culture, and Resistance', *W I D E R Studies in Development Economics*, p. 237.

7 Substantive economic cultures

1 P. Dasgupta, 'Economic Growth Often Accompanies a Decline in a Poor Country's Wealth', *New Statesman*, Nov. 3, 2003, p. 29.

2 D. D'Monte, 'Economics vs Ecology: Progress within Limits', Record of a Meeting in Tuscany in *Green Accord* 15 March, 2005.

3 D'Monte, ibid.

4 P. Hawken, Amory Lovins and Hunter Lovins, *Natural Capitalism: Creating the Next Industrial Revolution,* Boston, MA: Little Brown, 1999.

5 Described by B. McGibben who visited them. See *Deep Economy* , New York: Times Books, 2007, pp. 200–202.

6 J. M. Benyus, *Biomimicry*, 1997.

7 The Ecologist, *Whose Common Future: Reclaiming the Commons,* Philadelphia: New Society Publishers, 1993, pp. 8ff.

8 V. Shiva, *Monocultures of the Mind*, 1993, Chapter 1.

9 G. Esteva, 'Development', in Wolfgang Sachs (ed.) *The Development Dictionary*, London: Zed Books, 1992, p. 18.

10 E. P. Thompson, *Customs in Common: Studies in Traditional Popular Culture*, New York: New Press, 1993.

11 M. Hardt and A. Negri, *Multitude: War and Democracy in the Age of Empire,* New York: Penguin Books, 2005, Part Two.

12 V. Bennholdt-Thomsen and M. Mies, *The Subsistence Perspective: Beyond the*

Globalized Economy, London: Zed Books, 1999, p. 95. They deal very critically with the Marxist perspectives and arrive at a unique economic culture conception.

13 "Enoughness" has become a theme of the sustainable consumer movement and books have been written to advance it. But its origin is in Aristotle's sixth book of *The Politics* where he distinguishes between two meanings of wealth as money making versus wealth as sufficiency or enoughness.

14 V. Bennholdt-Thomsen and M. Mies, op. cit.

15 The Montreal Intercultural Institute, in co-operation with other NGOs, has sponsored major gathering of grassroots leaders from around the world: the first in Quebec and the second in Bangalore, India. I attended both and remain indebted to these events in many ways. These views are important and need to be more fully considered by critical modernists, that is radical liberals or democratic socialists who affirm a normative ideal of reflexive modernity.

16 S. Latouche, 'The Aternative Utopia: A Realistic Agenda for NGO'S', sent to the Second INCA(D) Conference in March 2000 in Bangalore.

17 J. Mander and V. Tauli-Corpuz (eds) *Paradigm Wars: Indigenous People's Resistance to Globalization*. See http://www.treatycouncil.org/section.

18 This story is continued in a follow-up book edited by F. Apffel-Marglin and the PRATEC entitled *The Spirit of Regeneration: Andean Culture Confronting Western Notions of Development*, New York: Zed Books, 1998.

19 Paper presented to the Science, Technology and Society Conference in Arlington Virginia in 1988 entitled 'Big New Ideas –Where Are They Today?' When Bob Rodale was killed in an accident in Moscow, while helping organic farming to get going in Russia, the world lost an innovative leader. http://www.rodaleinstitute.org.

20 S.V. Chayanov, *The Theory of Peasant Economy* with an Introduction by Theodor Shanin, Madison: The University of Wisconsin Press, 1966.

21 E. Özveren, 'Polanyi, Chayanov, and Lessons for the Study of the Informal Sector', *Journal of Economic Issues*', Sept. 2005.

22 W. Berry 'The Agrarian Standard', in N. Wirzba (ed.) *The Essential Agrarian Reader*, Washington, DC: Shoemaker and Hoard, 2003, p. 24.

23 Go to http://www.foodroutes.org/ for information about food safety and to see the Local Harvest Community map that makes it easy to find sustainable farmers, farmers markets and Community Supported Agriculture projects (CSAs) in your area. Foodroutes.org is a project of Network (FRN), a non-profit organization dedicated to providing strategic communications and evaluation tools and information to on-the-ground advocates who are working to build awareness of, and support for, sustainable farming and local food systems.

24 Enabled by the Community Environmental Defense Fund www.celdf.org/Home/tabid/36/Default.aspx.

25 Greater D.C. Care organization can be accessed at http://www.dc-cares.org/aboutus.htm.

26 The Tap Root Foundation in San Francisco enables business professionals to donate their skills to help nonprofits with their marketing, human resources and information, http://www.taprootfoundation.org.

27 E. S. Cahn, *No More Throw-Away People: The Co-Production Imperative*, 2nd edition, Washington, DC: Essential Books, 2004.

28 D. Schwartz, *Crossing the River: Creating a Conceptual Revolution in Community and Disability*, Brookline, MA: Brookline Books, 1992.

8 Social learning for people's economies

1 This distinction was made at a Club of Rome Conference in Salzburg and published as *No Limits to Learning: A Report to the Club of Rome* by J. W. Botkin, M. Elmandjra and M. Malitza, Oxford: Pergamon Press,1979. The distinction converges with J. Habermas'

distinction between instrumental and communicative learning, but it is worked out in ways that more directly describe concrete social learning processes.

2 M. Yunus, *Banker to the Poor: Micro-Lending and the Battle against World Poverty*, New York: Public Affairs, 2007, p. 210.
3 Ibid., p. 145.
4 US – http://www.microenterpriseworks.org.
5 H. de Soto, *The Mystery of Capital: Why Capitalism Triumphs in the West and Fails Everywhere Else*, New York: Basic Books, 2000.
6 M. Davis, 2006, p. 180.
7 R. J. Samuelson, 'The Spirit of Capitalism', *Foreign Affairs*, January/February 2001.
8 J. Jacobs, *Cities and the Wealth of Nations*, New York: Vintage Books, 1985, p. 56.
9 J. Jacobs, ibid.
10 See T. Schroyer, 'Third Ways', in Lal and Nandy (eds) *The Future of Knowledge and Culture: A Dictionary for the Twenty-First Century*, New York: Penguin, 2005, p. 322.
11 M. Shuman, *Going Local: Creating Self-Reliant Communities in a Global Age*, New York: Free Press, 1998.
12 M. Shuman, *The Small-Mart Revolution: How Local Businesses Are Beating The Global Competition*, San Francisco: Berrett-Koehler, 2006.
13 J. Allard, C. Davidson, J. Matthaei (eds), *Solidarity Economy: Building Alternatives for People and Planet*, Papers and Reports for the 2007 Social Forum, Chicago, ChangeMaker Publications, 2008, pp. 102ff.
14 See http://www.postbank.bg.
15 See the 2007 Report on Socially Responsible Investing Trends in the United States.
16 http://thinkchangeindia.wordpress.com/2008.
17 G. Alperovitz's, *America Beyond Capitalism: Reclaiming Our Wealth, Our Liberty and Our Democracy*, Hoboken, NJ: John Wiley, 2005.
18 See S. Bruyn's 'Self Regulation, Government and the Social Market', *The Social Report*, Fall 1990.
19 T. Frank, *The Wrecking Crew: How Conservatives Rule*, New York: Henry Holt and Company, 2008.
20 G. Alperovitz, op. cit., p. 40.
21 See L. Krimerman's review of Alperovitz's *America Beyond Capitalism* in *Grassroots Economic Organizing Newsletter*, http://www.geo.coop.
22 *State of the World 2007*, New York: W. W. Norton & Company, 2007, pp. 180–81.
23 M. Arruda, 'Solidarity Economy and the Rebirth of a Matristic Human Society,' *World Social Forum*, Mumbai, India, January 2004.
24 J. Allard, C. Davidson, J. Matthaei (eds) *Solidarity Economy: Building Alternatives for People and Planet,* Chicago: ChangeMaker Publications, 2008.
25 M. Lewis and D. Swinney, 'Social Economy and Solidarity Economy' in ibid., pp. 36–40.
26 D. Schweickart, *After Capitalism*, Lanham, MD: Rowman and Littlefield Publishers, 2002, p. 47.
27 Ibid., p. 48.
28 See D. Maheshvarananda's *After Capitalism: Prout's Vision for a New World*, with Preface by M. Arruda, Washington, DC: Proutist Universal Publications, 2002, and N. Khader, 'Introduction to the Economics of Liberation, An Overview of PROUT', in Allard, Davidson and Matthaei, *Solidarity Economy*, op. cit., pp. 83ff.
29 http://www.progress.org/geonomy; www.geonomics.org.
30 http://www.earthrights.net/about/hartzok.html, and Alanna Hartzok, 'Land Ethics and Public Finance: Policy as if People and Planet Mattered' in Schroyer and Golodik (eds) *Creating a Sustainable World*, New York: Apex Press, 2006, pp. 213ff.

Appendix 1

1 Hans von Blumenberg, *Legitimacy of Modern Age*, Cambridge, MA: MIT Press, 1983.

Bibliography

Achterhuis, H. (1993) 'Scarcity and Sustainability' in W. Sachs (1993).

AFL-CIO web page (2007) *Trends in CEO Pay*. http://www.aflcio.org/corporatewatch/paywatch.

Allard, Jenna, Davidson, Carl and Matthaei, Julie (eds) (2008) *Solidarity Economy: Building Alternatives for People and Planet*, Papers and Reports from the 2007 US Social Forum, Chicago: ChangeMaker Publications.

Alperovitz, Gar (2005) *America Beyond Capitalism: Reclaiming Our Wealth, Our Liberty and Our Democracy*, Hoboken, NJ: John Wiley.

Apffel-Marglin, Frederique (ed.) (1998) *The Spirit of Regeneration: Andean Culture Confronting Western Notions of Development*, New York: Zed Books.

Apffel-Marglin, Frederique and Marglin, Stephen A. (eds) (1991) *Dominating Knowledge*, New York: Oxford Clarendon Press.

Arruda, Marcos (January 2004) 'Solidarity Economy and the Rebirth of a Matristic Human Society', *World Social Forum*, Mumbai, India: Transnationallnstitute. http://www.tni.org/detail_page.phtml?page=archives_aruda_.

Bacevich, Andrew J. (2008) *The Limits of Power: The End of American Exceptionalism*, New York: Metropolitan Books.

Baker, Raymond W. (2005) *Capitalism's Achilles Heel: Dirty Money and How to Renew the Free-Market System*, Hoboken, NJ: John Wiley & Son Inc.

Barfield, O. (1988) *Saving the Appearances: A Study in Idolatry*, Middletown, CT: Wesleyan University Press, Distributed by University Press of New England.

Beck, Ulrich (1992) *Risk Society: Toward a New Modernity*, Newbury Park, CA: Sage Publications.

Beck, Ulrich and Beck-Gernsheim, Elizabeth (2002) *Individualization: Institutional Individualism and its Social and Political Consequences*, London: Sage Publications.

Belk, Russell, 'Why Not Share Rather than Own?' Power Point shared on the internet, http://www.journalism.wisc.edu/cccp/powerpoint/Belk.ppt.

Benkler, Yochai (2006) *The Wealth of Networks: How Social Production Transforms Markets and Freedom*, New Haven, CT: Yale University Press.

Bennholdt-Thomsen, Veronika, and Mies, Maria (1999) *The Subsistence Perspective: Beyond the Globalized Economy*, London: Zed Books.

Benyus, Janine M. (1997) *Biomimicry: Innovation Inspired by Nature*, New York: William Morrow & Co.

Berger, Peter (1986) *The Capitalist Revolution: Fifty Propositions about Prosperity, Equality and Liberty*, New York: Basic Books.

Berking, Helmut (1999) *The Sociology of Giving*, London: Sage Publications.

Berman, Harold J. (1983) *Law and Revolution: The Formation of the Western Legal Tradition*, Cambridge, MA: Harvard University Press.

Berry, Thomas (1988) *Dream of the Earth*, San Francisco: Sierra Club with The University of California Press.

Berry, Wendell (1977) *Unsettling of America*, San Francisco: Sierra Club.

Bhattacharya, Sabyasachi (ed.) (2007) *Development of Modern Indian Thought and the Social Sciences*, New Delhi: Oxford University Press.

Bienefeld, M. (2007) 'Suppressing the Double Movement to Secure the Dictatorship of Finance' in A. Bugra and K. Agartan (2007).

Blaug, Mark (1986) *Economic History and the History of Economics*, New York: New York University Press.

Blumenberg, Hans von (1983) *Legitimacy of Modern Age*, Cambridge, MA: MIT Press.

Bogle, John (2005) *The Battle for the Soul of Capitalism*, New Haven, CT: Yale University Press.

Botkin, James W., Elmandjra, Mahdi and Malitza, Mircea (1979) *No Limits to Learning: A Report to the Club of Rome*, Oxford: Pergamon Press.

Bowman, Betsy and Stone, Bob, 'Cooperativization as Alternative to Globalizing Capitalism', *Grassroots Economic Organizing Collective*. http://www.geo.coop.

Brooks, David (2008) 'Missing Dean Acheson', Op-ed page in *New York Times* August 1.

Brooke, James (2008) 'Land Trusts Multiplying, Study Shows', *New York Times* April 27.

Bruyn, Severyn (1990) 'Self Regulation, Government and the Social Market', *The Social Report*, Fall issue.

Bugra, Ayse and Agartan, Kaan (eds) (2007) *Reading Karl Polanyi for the Twenty-First Century*, New York: Palgrave Macmillan.

Bulley, D. (2008) 'Welcoming the Other: Negotiating Ethics as Hospitality in EU Foreign Policy', Paper presented at the annual meeting of the ISA's 49th Annual Convention, *Bridging Multiple Divides*, Hilton San Francisco, Ca. USA, March 26. Online <PDF><http://www.allacademic.com/meta/p254219_index.html>.

Butcher, A. Allen (2008) *Radical Culture Shock: The Desire for Community and the Need for Private Space*, Denver. http://www.culturemagic.org/ EgalitarianCommonwealth. html August, 2008.

Cahn, Edgar S. (2004) *No More Throw-Away People: The Co-Production Imperative*, 2nd edn, Washington, DC: Essential Books.

Cayley, David (2005) *The Rivers North of the Future: The Testament of Ivan Illich*, Toronto: House of Anansi Press.

Chakrabarty, B. (2007) 'The Idea of Swaraj in Indian Political Thought from Lajpat Rai to Subhash Chandra Bose', in S. Bhattacharya (2007).

Chandra, Sudhir (2002) *Continuing Dilemmas: Understanding Social Consciousness*, New Delhi: Tulika books.

Chayanov. S.V. (1966) *The Theory of Peasant Economy*, with an Introduction by Theodor Shanin, Madison: The University of Wisconsin Press.

Chen, S. and Ravallion, M. (2008) 'The Developing World is Poorer than We Thought, But No Less Successful in the Fight Against Poverty', *Policy Research Working Paper* 4703, August 26.

Chittister, Joan (2004) *The Rule of Benedict*, New York: Crossroads Publishing.

D'Monte, Darryl (2005) 'Economics vs Ecology: Progress within Limits', Record of a meeting in Tuscany in the Green Accord March 15.

Dallmayr, Fred (2002) *Dialogue Among Civilizations*, New York: Palgrave Macmillan.

Daly, Herman E. (1996) *Beyond Growth: The Economics of Sustainable Environment*, Boston, MA: Beacon Press.

Dasgupta, Partha (2003) 'Economic Growth Often Accompanies a Decline in a Poor Country's Wealth', *New Statesman*, November 3.

Davis, Mike (2001) *Late Victorian Holocausts: El Nino Famines and the Making of the Third World*, London: Verso.

—— (2006) *Planet of Slums*, New York: Verso.

de Soto, Hernando (2000) *The Mystery of Capital: Why Capitalism Triumphs in the West and Fails Everywhere Else*, New York: Basic Books.

Diamond, Stanley (1973) *In Search of the Primitive*, New Brunswick, NJ: Transaction Books.

Dreze, Jean and Sen, Amartya (2002) *India: Development and Participation*, New York: Oxford University Press.

Dumont, Louis (1986) *Essays on Individualism: Modern Ideology in Anthropological Perspective*, Chicago: University of Chicago Press.

Dumont, Louis and Smith, Nicholas H. (2008) 'Levinas, Habermas and Modernity', *Philosophy & Social Criticism*, Vol. 34, 6 July.

Easterly, William (2002) *The Elusive Quest for Growth*, New York: W.W. Norton & Company.

The Ecologist (1993) *Whose Common Future: Reclaiming the Commons*, Philadelphia: New Society Publishers.

Esteva, G. 'Development', in W. Sachs (1992).

Ewart, David (2007) 'Synopsis of Charles Taylor's *A Secular Age*'. http://www.davide-wart.ca/2007.

'Executive Summary', *Index of Economic Freedom*, 2008–01–15. Retrieved on April 2, 2008.

Fallow, R. (1989) 'What is Republicanism and Is It Worth Reviving?', *Harvard Law Review*, Vol. 102.

Faux, Jeff (2006) *The Global Class War*, Hoboken, NJ: John Wiley & Sons Inc.

Frank, Thomas (2000) *One Market Under God: Extreme Capitalism, Market Populism, and the End of Economic Democracy*, New York: Anchor Books.

——(2003) 'The Agrarian Standard', in N. Wirzba (2003).

—— (2008) *The Wreaking Crew: How Conservatives Rule*, New York: Henry Holt and Company.

Gadamer, Hans-Georg (1975) *Truth and Method*, New York: The Seabury Press.

Galbraith, James K. (2008) *The Predator State: How Conservatives Abandoned the Free Market and Why Liberals Should Too*, New York: Free Press.

Gandhi, Mahatma (1958–1994) *Collected Works of Mahatma Gandhi*, Vol. 63, New Delhi: Publications Division, Ministry of Information and Broadcasting, Government of India.

—— (1997) 'The Quest for Simplicity', in M. Rahnema & V. Bawtree (1997).

Gandhi, Rajmohan (2006) *Mohandas: A True Story of a Man, His People and an Empire*, London: Penguin.

George, Susan (1957) *A Fate Worse than Debt*, Harmondsworth: Penguin.

Geras, Norman (1998) *The Contract of Mutual Indifference: Political Philosophy After the Holocaust*, New York: Verso.

Ghosh, J. (2008) 'Why We Can Not Feed Our People', *Macroscan*, February 5. http://www.macroscan.com/cur/feb08/cur050208People.htm.

Girard, Rene (1977) *Violence and The Sacred*, Baltimore, MD: Johns Hopkins Press.

Godelier, Maurice (1999) *The Enigma of the Gift*, Chicago: University of Chicago Press.

Gorz, André (1988) *Critique of Economic Reason*, New York: Verso.

Gouldner, Alvin (1960) 'The Norm of Reciprocity: A Preliminary Statement', *American Sociological Review*, Vol. 25 (2).

Granovetter, Mark and Swedberg, Richard (eds) (1992) *The Sociology of Economic Life*, Boulder, CO: Westview Press.

Gray, John (1980) 'F.A. Hayek on Liberty and Tradition', *Journal of Libertarian Studies*, Vol. IV (2) spring.

——(1996) 'From Rio to the Capitals'. http://www.joe.org/joe/1996february/comm1.html.

—— (1998) *False Dawn*, New York: New Press.

Gwartney, James and Lawson, Robert, with Sobell, Russel S. and Leeson, Peter T. (2007) *Economic Freedom of the World 2007* from the Cato Store. Data from *Economic Freedom of the World* is available for download free-of-charge at Freetheworld.com.

Habermas, Jurgen (1976) *Communication and the Evolution of Society*, Cambridge, MA: MIT Press.

—— (1999) *Between Facts and Norms: Contributions to a Discourse Theory of Law and Democracy*, Cambridge, MA: MIT Press.

—— (2001) *The Postnational Constellation: Political Essays*, Cambridge, MA: MIT Press.

——(2005) 'Religion in the Public Sphere', lecture presented at the Holberg Seminar 2005.

Habermas, Jurgen and Ratzinger, Joseph (2005) *The Dialectics of Secularization: On Reason and Religion*, San Francisco: Ignatius Press.

Hamowy, Ronald (1987) *The Scottish Enlightenment and the Theory of Spontaneous Order*, Carbondale: Southern Illinois University Press.

Hardt, Michael and Negri, Antonio (2005) *Multitude: War and Democracy in the Age of Empire*, Part Two, New York: Penguin Books.

Harriss, J. (2007) 'Institutions, Politics and Culture: A Polanyian Perspective on Economic Change', in M. Harvey, R. Ramiogan and S. Randles (2007).

Hartzok, Alanna (2006) 'Land Ethics and Public Finance: Policy as if People and Planet Mattered' in Schroyer and Golodik (2006).

Harvey, Mark, Ramiogan, Ronnie and Randles, Sally (eds) (2007) *Karl Polanyi: New Perspectives on the Place of the Economy in Society*, Manchester: Manchester University Press.

Hawken P., Amory Lovins and Hunter Lovins (1999) *Natural Capitalism: Creating the Next Industrial Revolution*, Boston, MA: Little Brown.

Hayek. F. A. (1960) *The Constitution of Liberty*, London: Routledge and Kegan Paul.

Hedges, Chris (2006) *American Fascists: The Christian Right and the War on American*, New York: Free Press.

—— (2008) *I Don't Believe in Atheists*, New York: Free Press.

Hennis, Wilhelm (1988) *Max Weber: Essays in Reconstruction*, Boston, MA: Allen & Unwin.

Hirschman, Albert O. (1986) *Rival Views of Market Society*, New York: Viking.

Hoinacke, Lee (2004) 'Why Philia?', lecture given at 'Conversations: The Legacy of Ivan Illich' at Pitzer College Claremont, California, March 26–28.

Hudson, Michael (2005) *Global Fracture: The New International Economic Order*, London: Pluto Press.

Illich, Ivan (1971) *Deschooling Society*, New York: Harper & Row.

——(1973) *Tools for Conviviality*, Berkeley, CA: Heyday Books.

—— (1981) *Shadow Work*, Boston, MA: Marion Boyers.

—— (1982) *Gender*, New York: Pantheon Books.

—— (1992) *In the Mirror of the Past*, New York: Marion Boyars.

—— (1993) *In the Vineyard of the Text: A Commentary to Hugh's Disdascalicon*, Chicago: The University of Chicago Press.

—— (1998) 'The Scopic Past and the Ethics of the Gaze: A Plea for the Historical Study of Ocular Perception'. http://www.pudel.uni-bremen.de/pdf/Illich_en_SCOPICPU.pdf.

Jacobs, Jane (1985) *Cities and the Wealth of Nations*, New York: Vintage.

Jain. L. C. (2003) 'Local Self-Government –Still Far Away', paper prepared for the Seminar on Local Self-Government – A Frontier of Resistance, organized by Equations and Network Partners at ASF, Hyderabad, January 5.

—— (2005) 'How Nazir Saab fought his majesty's collector', *Asian Age*, April 16.

— (2006) *Development Initiatives: Of the People and By the People*, Vol. II, New Delhi: Action Aid.

—— (2007) 'Fate of Gandhi's Economic Thinking', in S. Bhattacharya (2007).

Jessop, Bob (2007) 'Knowledge as a Fictitious Commodity', in A. Bugra and K. Agartan (2007).

Kakar, Sudhir (1996) *The Indian Psyche*, New Delhi: Oxford University Press.

Kamp, Jarriaan and Puy, Helene de (2007) 'The Forgotten Thinker You Need to Know', *Ode Magazine*, June issue.

Khader, Nada (2008) 'Introduction to the Economics of Liberation: An Overview of PROUT' in Allard, Davidson and Matthaei (2007).

Khilnani, Sunil (1998) *The Idea of India*, New York: Penguin Books.

King, Martin Luther (1958) *Stride Toward Freedom*, New York: Harper.

Klein, Naomi (2007) *The Shock Doctrine: The Rise of Disaster Capitalism*, New York: Metropolitan Books.

Kohr, Martin, article in *The Star* (Malaysia) on the collapse of the *WTO* talks on the Third World network webpage. http://www.twnside.org.sg/title2/wto.info/ twninfo20080805. Research. http://www.celf.org/Default.aspx.

Korten, David C. (1990) *Getting to the 21st Century*, West Hartford, CT: Kumarian Press.

—— (1995) *When Corporations Rule the World*, West Hartford, CT: Kumarain Press and San Francisco: Berrett-Koehler Publishers.

—— (2006) *The Great Turning: From Empire to Earth Community*, San Francisco: Berrett-Koehler Publishers.

Krimerman, Len (2007) 'Dreaming of America Beyond Capitalism', Review of Alperovitz's *America Beyond Capitalism* in *Grassroots Economic Organizing Newsletter*, http:// www.geo.coop/archive, Is. 72–73.

Ladner, Gerhart, B. (2004) *The Idea of Reform: Its Impact On Christian Thought and Action in the Age of the Fathers,* Eugene, OR: Wipf and Stock Publishers.

Lal, Vinay and Nandy, Ashis (eds) (2005) *The Future of Knowledge and Culture: A Dictionary for the 21st Century*, New York: Penguin.

Land, Robert Swann, *Trusts as Part of a Threefold Economic Strategy for Regional Integration,* from E. F. Schumacher Society. http://www.smallisbeautiful.org.

Lappe, Frances M. (2006) 'A Market without Capitalists', *Alter-Net*, June 23.

Latouche, Serge (March 2000) 'The Alternative Utopia: A Realistic Agenda for NGOs', letter sent to the Second INCAD Conference in Bangalore.

Levinas, Emmanuel (1969) *Totality and Infinity,* Pittsburgh: Duquesne University Press.

Litt, Theodor (1963) *Les corps celestes dans L'universe de saint Thomas d'Aguin*, Paris: Lowen.

McGibben, Bill (2007) *Deep Economy: The Wealth of Communities and the Durable Future*, New York: Henry Holt and Company.
MacIntyre, Alasdair (1988) *Whose Justice? Which Rationality?* Notre Dame, Indiana: University of Notre Dame Press.
McKnight, John (1995) *The Careless Society: Community and its Counterfeits,* New York: Basic Books.
Maheshvarananda, Dada (2002) *After Capitalism: Prout's Vision for a New World*, with Preface by Marcos Arruda, Washington, DC: Proutist Universal Publications.
Mander, Jerry and Tauli-Corpuz Victoria (eds), *Paradigm Wars: Indigenous People's Resistance to Globalization,* San Francisco: Sierra Club.
Marglin, Stephen A. (1974) 'What Do Bosses Do?', *Review of Radical Political Economics,* Summer issue no. 6.
—— (1992) 'Economics as a System of Knowledge', Discussion paper/ Harvard Institute of Economic Research. http://www.celdf.org/Default.aspx.
—— (2008) *The Dismal Science: How Thinking like an Economist Undermines Community,* Cambridge, MA: Harvard University Press.
Mauss, Marcel (1990), *The Gift: Forms and Reason for Exchange in Archaic Societies*, London: Routledge.
Mendez, Luis Lopezllera (1997) 'The Indigenous Rebellion in Chiapas', in Trent Schroyer (1997) (ed.) *A World that Works: Building Blocks for a Just and Sustainable Society*, New York: The Bootstrap Press.
Micklethwait, John and Wooldridge, Adrian (2004) *The Right Nation: Conservative Power in America*, New York: The Penguin Press.
Milbank, John, Pickstock, Catherine and Ward, Graham (eds) (1999) *Radical Orthodoxy,* London: Routledge.
Mirowski, Philip (2007) 'Naturalizing the Market on the Road to Revisionism', *Journal of International Economics*, Vol. 3 October.
Mommsen, Peter (2004) *Homage to a Broken Man: The Life of J. Heinrich Arnold,* Rifton, NY: The Plough Publishing House.
Myers, Nancy and Raffensperger, Carolyn (eds) (2005) *Precautionary Tools for Reshaping Environmental Policy,* Cambridge, MA: MIT Press.
Nagaraj, K. (2008) 'Farmers Suicides in India: Magnitudes, Trends, and Spatial Patterns', *Madras Institute of Development Studies,* March.
Naipaul. V. S. (1977) *India: A Wounded Civilization*, New York: Vintage.
Nanda, Meera (2007) 'Secularism without Secularization: Reflections on God and Politics in US and India', *Economic and Political Weekly*, January 6–12.
Nandy, Ashis (1983) *The Intimate Enemy: Loss and Recovery of Self under Colonialism*, Oxford: Oxford University Press.
—— (1987) 'Cultural Frames for Social Transformation: A Credo', *Alternatives*, January 1.
—— (2002) *Time Warps: Silent and Evasive Pasts in Indian Politics and Religion,* New Brunswick, NJ: Rutgers University Press.
—— (2006) *Talking India: Ashis Nandy in Conversation with Ramin Jahanbegloo,* New York: Oxford University Press.
Nietschmann, Bernard (1987) 'Third World War: The Global Conflict Over the Rights of Indigenous Nations', *Cultural Survival Quartely*, September.
Nisbet, Robert (1953) *The Quest for Community: A Study in the Ethics of Order and Freedom*, Oxford: Oxford University Press.
Nobel, David F. (1984) *Forces of Production: A Social History of Industrial Automation*, New York: Knopf.

Norberg-Hodge, Helena (1992) *Ancient Futures; Learning from Ladakh*, San Francisco: Sierra Club.

Nozick, Robert (1974) *Anarchy, State and Utopia*, New York: Basic Books.

—— (1995) *The End of the Nation State: The Rise of Regional Economies*, New York: The Free Press.

Osteen, Mark (ed.) (2002) *The Question of the Gift: Essays Across Disciplines,* New York: Routledge.

Özveren, Eyüp (2005) 'Polanyi, Chayanov, and Lessons for the Study of the Informal Sector', *Journal of Economic Issues*, September.

Palast, Greg, Oppenheim, Jerrold and MacGregor, Theo (2003) *Democracy and Regulation: How the Public can Govern Essential Services*, London: Pluto Press.

Palharya, Shakun (2003) 'Decentralized Governance Hampered by Financial Constraints', *Economic and Political Weekly*, 15–21 March.

Parel, Anthony J. (2006) *Gandhi's Philosophy and the Quest for Harmony*, New Delhi: Cambidge University Press.

Patel, Raj C. (2007) *Stuffed and Starved: the Hidden Battle of the World Food System*, Brooklyn: Melville House.

Perkins, John (2004) *Confessions of an Economic Hit Man,* San Francisco: Berrett-Koehler Publishers.

Pickstock, Catherine (1998) Toward a Liturgical Critique of Modernity, *Telos*, Fall issue (113).

Piore, Michael J. and Sabel, Charles (1984) *The Second Industrial Divide*, New York: Basic Books.

Pocock, J. G. A. (1975) *The Machiavellian Moment: Florentian Political Thought and the Atlantic Republican Tradition,* Princeton, NJ: Princeton University Press.

—— (1985) *Virtue, Commerce and History,* New York: Cambridge University Press.

Polanyi, Karl (1977) *The Livelihood of Man*, New York: Academic Press.

—— (1992) 'The Economy as Instituted Process', in M. Granovetter and R. Swedberg (1992), pp. 29–52.

—— (2001) *The Great Transformation,* Boston, MA: Beacon Press.

Pörksen, Uwe (1984) *Plastikwörter: Die Sprache einer internationalen Diktatur*, Stuttgart: Klett-Cotta.

Prins, Naomi (2008) 'Where Credit is Due: A Timeline of the Mortgage Crisis', *Mother Jones, Private Space,* July/August.http://www.culturemagic.org/ EgalitarianCommonwealth.html.

Putnam, R. (1994) *Making Democracy Work: Civic Traditions in Modern Italy*, Princeton: Princeton University Press.

Rahnema, M. (2005) 'Development', in Lal and Nandy (2005).

Rahnema, Majid & Bawtree, Victoria (eds) (1997) *The Post-Development Reader,* Atlantic Highlands, NJ: Zed Books.

Reddy, Sanjay G. (forthcoming) 'How Not to Count the Poor' in J. Stiglitz, S. Anand and P.Segal (eds) *Debates on the Measurement of Global Poverty,* Oxford: Oxford University Press.

Restakiks, J. (2005) 'The Lessons of Emilia Romagna in Commerce', Monde.com, April 30.

Rodale, Bob (1988) 'Big New Ideas – Where Are They Today?', Paper presented to the Science, Technology and Society Conference in Arlington Virginia. http://www.rodale-institute.org.

Rosenstock-Huessy, Eugen (1938) *Out of Revolution: Autobiography of Western Man,* New York: William Morrow.

Rothkopf, David (2008) *Superclass: The Global Power Elite and the World they are Making*, New York: Farrar, Straus and Giroux.

Rothschild, Emma (2001) *Economic Sentiments: Adam Smith, Cordorcet and the Enlightenment,* Cambridge, MA: Harvard University Press.

Rudolph, Llyod. I. and Hoeber, Susanne (2006) *Post Modern Gandhi and Other Essays,* Chicago: University of Chicago Press.

Sachs, Jeffrey (2005) *The End of Poverty: How We Can Make It Happen In Our Lifetime*, New York: Penguin Books.

Sachs, Wolfgang (ed.) (1993) *Global Ecology*, London: Zed Boks.

—— (ed.) (1992) *The Development Dictionary*, London: Zed Books.

Samuelson, Robert J. (2001) 'The Spirit of Capitalism', *Foreign Affairs*, January/February.

Schroyer, Trent (1973) *The Critique of Domination*, New York: George Braziller.

— (2005) 'Third Ways' in Lal and Nandy (2005).

Schroyer, Trent and Golodik, Tom (eds) (2006) *Creating a Sustainable World Past Experiences/Future struggles*, New York: Apex Press.

Schwartz, D. (1992) *Crossing the River: Creating a Conceptual Revolution in Community and Disability*, Brookline, MA: Brookline Books.

Schweickart, David (2002) *After Capitalism* (New Critical Theory), Lanham, MD: Rowman & Littlefield Publishers.

Shiva, Vandana (1991) *The Violence of the Green Revolution: Third World Agriculture, Ecology and Politics,* London: Zed Books.

—— (1993) *Monocultures of the Mind: Perspectives on Biodiversity and Biotechnology*, London: Zed Books.

—— (1997) *Biopiracy: The Plunder of Nature and Knowledge,* Boston: South End Press.

Shuman, Michael (1998) *Going Local: Creating Self-Reliant Communities in a Global Age,* New York: Free Press.

—— (2006) *The Small-Mart Revolution: How Local Businesses are Beating the Global Competition,* San Francisco: Berrett-Koehler Publishers.

Siddhartha (2008) 'Open Source Hinduism', in Richard Kearney (ed) *Religion and the Arts Journal from Boston College; Special issue: The Inter-religious Imagination*, Leiden: Martinus Nijhoff.

Smith, Adam (1976) *Wealth of Nations*, Vol. II, bk 4, Chicago: University of Chicago Press.

Smith, N. H. (2008) 'Levinas, Habermas and Modernity', *Philosophy & Social Criticism*, Vol. 34 (6), July.

Soros, George (2008) *The New Paradigm for Financial Markets: The Credit Crash of 2008 and What It Means,* New York: PublicAffairs.

Stanley, Diamond (1973) *In Search of the Primitive,* New Brunswick, New Jersey: Transaction Books.

Stiglitz, Joseph (2002) *Globalization and Its Discontents,* New York: W.W. Norton & Company.

Suskind, Ron (2008) *The Way Of The World: A Story of Truth and Hope in an Age of Extremism,* New York: Harper.

Tabb, William (2004) *Economic Governance in the Age of Globalization,* New York: Columbia University Press.

Tabb, William (2008) 'Financial Appropriations', *Z Magazine* June 2.

Tassell, Tony, (2007), 'Special Report on Hedge Funds', *Financial Times*, July.

Taylor, Charles (2007) *A Secular Age,* Cambridge, MA: The Belknap Press of Harvard University Press.

Teichgraeber III, Richard F. (1986) *Free Trade and Moral Philosophy: Rethinking the Sources of Adam Smith's Wealth of Nations*, Durham, NC: Duke University Press.

Theodor, Litt (1963) *Les Corps Celestes dans L'universe de Saint Thomas d'Aguin*, Paris, Lowen.

Thompson, E. P. (1993) *Customs in Common: Studies in Traditional Popular Culture*, New York: New Press.

Tobin, James (1984) 'On the Efficiency of the Financial System', *Lloyd's Bank Review, no. 153,* US-http://www.microenterpriseworks.org.

Varma, Pavan. K (2004) *Being Indian: The Truth About Why the Twenty-First Century will be India's*, New York: Penguin Books.

Vasavi, A. R. (1977) 'Agrarian Distress in Bihar: Market, State and Suicides', *Economic and Political Weekly*, August 7.

—— (forthcoming) *Suicides, and the Making of India's Agrarian Crisis*, National Institute of Advanced Studies.

Wallis, Jim (2005) *God's Politics: A New Vision For Faith and Politics in America,* San Francisco: Harper Collins Publishers.

Weissman, R. (2008) 'Reclaiming Economic Freedom', *The Huffington Post*, January 24.

Wink, Walter (1989) *Engaging the Powers: Discernment and Resistance in a World of Domination,* Minneapolis: Fortress Press.

Wirzba, Norman (ed.) (2003) *The Essential Agrarian Reader*, Washington, DC: Shoemaker and Hoard. www.wisc.edu/uwcc/icic/orgs/ica/pubs/review/vol 88-2/21.

World Watch Institute (2007) *State of the World*, New York: W.W. Norton & Company.

Wuelker, Hans Detlef, (1995) *The Social Economy and Co-ops – A German Perspective*, http://www. wisc.edu/uwcc/icic/orgs/ica/pubs/review/vol 88-2/21.

Wuthnow, Robert (1991) Acts of Compassion: Caring for Others and Helping Ourselves, Princeton, NJ: Princeton University Press.

—— (1995) Learning to Care: Elementary Kindness in an Age of Indifference, New York and Oxford: Oxford University Press.

Yokota, Katsumi (1991) *I Among Others: An Introspective Look at the Theory and Practice of the Seikatsu Cub Movement,* Kanagawa: Seikatsu Club.

Young, Robert J.C. (2001) *Postcolonialism: A Historical Introduction,* Malden, MA: Blackwell Publishing.

Yunus, Muhammad (2007) *Banker to the Poor: Micro-Lending and the Battle against World Poverty,* New York: Public Affairs.

Zablocki, Benjamin David (1980) *The Joyful Community: An Account of the Bruderhof, A Communal Movement Now in its Third Generation*, Chicago: University of Chicago Press.

Internet resources

http://www.adats.com
http://www.allspecies.org/ideas/greenteach.htm
http://www.bobsguide.com
http://www.brookes.ac.uk/schools/apm/social_sculpture/!
www.celdf.org/Home/tabid/36/Default.aspx
http://www.csl.umd.edu/Handouts/issues/hunger&homelessness.htm or
http://www.dccentralkitchen.org
http://www.dc-cares.org/aboutus.html
http://www.earthrights.net/about/hartzok.html
http://en.wikipedia.org/wiki/Ayn_Rand
http://www.foodroutes.org
http://www.gandhimuseum.org/sarvodaya/index.htm
http://www.gandhimuseum.org/sarvodaya/index.htm
http://www.geo.coop
http://iatp.typepad.com/thinkforward
http://jace.livejournal.com/415162.html
http://www.microenterpriseworks.org/
http://www.narmada.org/gcg/gcg.html
http://www.ncba.coop/pubs_pkit_whatare.cfm
http://www.postbank.bg
http://www.progress.org/geonomy/ : www.geonomics.org
http://www.pudel.uni-bremen.de/100en_startseite.htm
http://www.rodaleinstitute.org
http://www.swamiagnivesh.com
http://www.taprootfoundation.org
http://thinkchangeindia.wordpress.com/2008
http://www.treatycouncil.org/section

Index

For Product Safety Concerns and Information please contact our EU representative GPSR@taylorandfrancis.com
Taylor & Francis Verlag GmbH, Kaufingerstraße 24, 80331 München, Germany

www.ingramcontent.com/pod-product-compliance
Lightning Source LLC
LaVergne TN
LVHW021108300926
849160LV00009B/650
9780415776974